CIVIL WAR PLACES

CIVIL WAR

Seeing the Conflict through the Eyes of Its Leading Historians

PLACES

Edited by Gary W. Gallagher and J. Matthew Gallman

Photographs by Will Gallagher

THE UNIVERSITY OF NORTH CAROLINA PRESS Chapel Hill

This book was published with the assistance of the Fred W. Morrison Fund of the University of North Carolina Press.

Photographs © 2019 Will Gallagher

Designed by Richard Hendel
Set in Miller, Sentinel, and Smokler types
by Tseng Information Systems, Inc.
Manufactured in the United States of America

The University of North Carolina Press
has been a member of the Green Press
Initiative since 2003.

Front cover: Burnside's Bridge, Antietam National Battlefield, Sharpsburg, Md.; photograph by Will Gallagher. Back cover: Emancipation Oak, Hampton, Va., and McLean House, Appomattox Court House, Va.; photographs by Will Gallagher.

Library of Congress Cataloging-in-Publication Data
Names: Gallagher, Gary W., editor. | Gallman, J. Matthew (James Matthew), editor. | Gallagher, Will, 1968– illustrator.
Title: Civil War places : seeing the conflict through the eyes of its leading historians / edited by Gary W. Gallagher and J. Matthew Gallman ; photographs by Will Gallagher.
Description: Chapel Hill : The University of North Carolina Press, [2019] | Includes bibliographical references and index.
Identifiers: LCCN 2018038928| ISBN 9781469649535 (cloth : alk. paper) | ISBN 9781469649542 (ebook)
Subjects: LCSH: United States—History—Civil War, 1861–1865—Battlefields. | United States—History—Civil War, 1861–1865—Monuments. | United States—History—Civil War, 1861–1865—Museums. | United States—History—Civil War, 1861–1865—Hospitals.
Classification: LCC E641 .C585 2019 | DDC 973.7—dc23
LC record available at https://lccn.loc.gov/2018038928

To Robert E. Gallman (1926–1998),
always ready to explore a historic place.

To Tim and Marsha Gallagher,
who share my ties to a place in Colorado.

CONTENTS

III. MEMORIALS: PLACES OF MEMORY

IV. BUILDINGS: ENDURING PLACES

FIGURES

CIVIL WAR PLACES

INTRODUCTION

This is a book of essays about places. Few words are as deceptively simple and yet potentially complex as the word "place." Ask a dozen friends to select their favorite place and explain their choice, and two things will likely happen. First, they all will probably know precisely what you are asking. And second, they will answer the question in very different ways. Some will select places that somehow fit into their own personal narrative: the home where they grew up, the place they got engaged, that sort of thing. Others will immediately turn to a place visited at some point in the past, selected for its beauty or wonderful memories. Favorite places can mean all sorts of things to people.

We asked the question of two dozen friends—people who devote their careers and often their leisure hours to the Civil War—but we added a crucial constraint: select a single place related to the conflict and explain why they chose it. We gave them no other guidelines, beyond insisting that they write about a fairly precise spot and not an entire battlefield or community. (We reserved the right to veto duplications, but we did not need to use that editorial power.) Once our authors had picked their locations, we set professional photographer Will Gallagher to work capturing each place in a photograph. These illustrations are central to the project. The authors worked closely with Gallagher in determining the composition of the photos and in selecting the eventual images for inclusion. We intentionally did not opt for historic images but rather for illustrations that would help the reader see what each author is describing today.

The authors set about their tasks independently, but readers might wish to think more broadly about this notion of "place"—and more precisely, what it might

1

mean to think about "Civil War places." For the student of the Civil War, the consideration of a powerful place could begin with an understanding of what happened there, whether it is a boulder-strewn hill, or a bridge over a small creek, or a large structure created to honor citizens-soldiers. We seek out the spot where historic events occurred, perhaps to better understand what happened there, or perhaps as some sort of homage to what was lost. We visit Culp's Hill at Gettysburg to understand part of a great battle, and we climb the stairs of the Petersen House to view the room where Abraham Lincoln died. But, as many essays attest, in these historic places memories of the Civil War are intertwined with memories of our own histories. Each new visit to a Civil War site adds a layer to our own relationships to the conflict and introduces new meanings about the place.

Scholars of political culture often speak of the significance of conversations—in both word and symbol—that occur in "public spaces." The notion is that in all sorts of places where people gather, there are opportunities for citizens to declare values and beliefs, to dissent from the opinions of others, or to witness expressions of ideas created by others. Sometimes these public squares become the sites of patriotic parades or political rallies or other events, whose meanings in the original moment can evolve in ways that create sharp disagreement concerning monuments that remain in place for generations. Thus, a memorial to fallen soldiers might have had one intended meaning when installed and later be understood very differently by others in that public space. In this sense, public spaces are subject to continual debate about political meaning. Statues and other monuments tell us about the past, even while their continuing presence prompts ongoing conversations.

Several of our essays illuminate the power of historic places to inspire controversy. For example, Ari Kelman details heated exchanges over where the Sand Creek massacre actually occurred and then further describes conflicts over how those days in 1864 should be commemorated and remembered. Similarly, Gary Gallagher takes us on a tour of monuments in Charlottesville whose essential meanings remain in dispute.

In the essays that follow, our authors have shared the personal, the historical, and the political. Some opted for particular spots on Civil War battlefields, selecting locations either iconic or obscure. Several turned to gravesites, contemplating the meanings they derive from visiting cemeteries. Others wrote about locations of Civil War memory, focusing on monuments or buildings created as memorials to the war or its fallen. Finally, quite a few immediately thought of buildings where momentous things occurred during the Civil War era.

But if the places selected by our contributors fall generally into these four broad categories, they speak to the many ways a group of gifted historians can address a seemingly simple assignment. Several authors anchored their essays in historical memories tied to their own childhood experiences. For Stephen Engle, the choice was hardly a choice at all: he grew up visiting his grandfather in Charles Town, West Virginia, where—when it was still part of Virginia—John Brown stood trial in the county courthouse. Carol Reardon recalls how a childhood visit to Pittsburgh's Soldiers and Sailors Memorial Hall helped shape her eventual career path. Stephen Cushman, who is from Connecticut, tells us about childhood pilgrimages to Augustus Saint Gaudens's statue of William Tecumseh Sherman at the Grand Army Plaza in Central Park. Brenda Stevenson shares childhood memories of a very different site of commemoration: the majestic Emancipation Oak on the grounds of Virginia's Hampton University. Catherine Clinton, a leading scholar of Mary Lincoln, recalls her youthful indifference to all things Lincoln, including the Petersen House where the sixteenth president died. The essays by Caroline Janney and Matthew Gallman turn on photographs from their youth. Gallman recalls a photograph that turned out to be not quite as it seemed. Janney organizes her essay around a childhood photograph of Burnside's Bridge, a landmark beautifully reproduced by Will Gallagher.

Teachers who focus their work on the Civil War commonly use physical places as classrooms. Several authors explore how they unravel the meaning of places with their students. In his essay on Arlington National Cemetery, William Blair explains how he challenges tour groups to wrestle with the meaning of headstones marking the graves of enslaved men and women. Gary Gallagher describes a walking tour of Charlottesville's Confederate monuments, uncovering how these works of art have very different histories and meanings and challenging us to understand Confederate monuments as far from monolithic sources of memory. On the other side of the country, Joan Waugh leads students on a walking tour of the Los Angeles National Cemetery, which includes the gravesite of her own great-grandfather. Waugh recounts how she selects multiple sites in the cemetery to uncover and discuss the complex meaning of commemoration and memory.

For many of our authors, the invitation to contribute to this volume became an opportunity to reevaluate sites of their own scholarship and professional life, contemplated from new perspectives. In working on her book *War Stories*, Frances Clarke devoted long hours to the papers of Nathaniel Bowditch and his family,

housed in the Massachusetts Historical Society. For her essay she takes the reader to Cambridge's Mount Auburn Cemetery to consider what Bowditch's grave tells us about his short life. In 1998 Lesley Gordon used the life of Confederate general George E. Pickett as the focus of an innovative study of history and memory. For this essay, Gordon revisits George and LaSalle Pickett and the fascinating, ongoing history of their commemoration at Richmond's Hollywood Cemetery. David Blight has written eloquently about aspects of Frederick Douglass's life and is now completing a full biography. For his essay Blight uses Douglass's home at Cedar Hill, in the southeast part of the District of Columbia, as a window into the great orator's later life. In 2008 Jacqueline Jones wrote a history of Savannah, Georgia, during the Civil War era; five years later Elizabeth Varon published an innovative study of Appomattox and the end of the war. Jones devotes her essay to Savannah's Green-Meldrim House, where local African American leaders met with William Tecumseh Sherman in January 1865. Varon focuses on the McLean House, where Robert E. Lee surrendered to Ulysses S. Grant three months later. The two essays are very different, but both share the historian's eye for the historic place and for the nature of historic memory in commemorating—or failing to properly commemorate—that place. Ari Kelman's 2013 study of the Sand Creek massacre in history and memory won widespread acclaim and four major book awards. Here he returns to Colorado to reconsider this powerful place.

Other contributors give us a different glimpse into how the personal and professional intertwine. Drew Gilpin Faust, the former president of Harvard University, writes eloquently about Harvard's Memorial Hall, a place fraught with meaning for both the Civil

War historian and the university president. And Edward Ayers, one-time president of the University of Richmond and the inaugural chair of the board of the American Civil War Museum at the Tredegar Iron Works, offers a superb analysis of the history of the ironworks as an underexamined bulwark of the Confederate economy and Richmond's broader history. As president of Pamplin Historical Park and Virginia's National Museum of the Civil War Soldier, A. Wilson Greene brings tremendous knowledge of military history to the project. But rather than turning to one of Virginia's more familiar military sites, Greene takes us on a tour of Camp Allegheny, which calls on the reader to think about altitude and weather and the true complexities of the Civil War battlefield. James Marten is one of the leading scholars on the history of Civil War veterans. His essay on Milwaukee's Soldiers' Home is not drawn from his scholarship, but it sings out his passion for veterans and for his town. Peter Carmichael's contribution brings the personal, the professional, and the pedagogical together in a careful discussion of a Culp's Hill burial pit. Carmichael, the Robert C. Fluhrer Professor of Civil War Studies and director of the Civil War Institute at Gettysburg College, unravels the complexities in understanding— and attempting to explain—a remote spot on a famed battlefield.

The essays that follow are in very different voices, but each author has managed to combine the scholarly with the personal, revealing something about how she or he thinks about places and about the past. The people are all our friends, and when we read their essays we can hear their voices. Judith Giesberg—who edits the *Journal of the Civil War Era*—describes her ongoing personal relationship with the Lincoln Memorial, a place she jogs to whenever she visits the nation's capital,

and with the nature of Civil War memory. For Stephen Berry, the humble chapel on the Shiloh battlefield in southwestern Tennessee—so marvelously captured by Will Gallagher's photograph—becomes the occasion for a contemplation of how we ought to think about the horrors of war. Aaron Sheehan-Dean cleverly destabilizes our sense of the meaning of history and hindsight by looking at Vicksburg as a site of optimism as opposed to the place frozen in time as the site of a great Confederate defeat. Sarah Gardner, who writes about reading and writing and history, uses Vicksburg for a very different sort of essay. She shares her story about reading a Vicksburg woman's wartime journal while she lay confined in a hospital room and how the personal and the historical became intertwined.

To close the volume, we asked Will Gallagher to put down his camera and take up his pen to discuss several things. First, the professional photographer provides the enthusiastic amateur a wealth of insights about his tools and his craft. Second, the nonspecialist adds a valuable perspective on the places he visited. And, finally, Will offers some thoughts about taking on a project with his father.

We believe this book lends itself to sampling rather than to reading from the first essay through the last. Whatever order readers might employ, their traversing the pages will underscore the rich spectrum of meanings, impressions, and memories that cluster around Civil War sites. The black-and-white photographs that precede each essay provide evocative points of departure that set up the ruminations that follow. We hope, finally, that these essays will trigger contemplation of historic places among our readers— perhaps inspiring new visits to old favorites or to some of those our contributors have found so captivating.

I BATTLEFIELDS
PLACES OF FIGHTING

1 THE CHURCH IN THE MAELSTROM

STEPHEN BERRY

But go ye now unto my place which [was] in Shiloh,
where I set my name at the first, and see what I did to it
for the wickedness of my people.
—Jeremiah 7:12

(previous page)
Interior of Shiloh Church, Tennessee
(Photograph by Will Gallagher)

Before it named a battle and a battlefield, Shiloh Church was the center of a community. Erected in 1851, the humble church sat at a small crossroads in heavily wooded tableland three miles west of the bend in the Tennessee River where waters that have run all the way from the Appalachians cease their westward track across the top of Alabama and plunge due north, back into Tennessee and all the way to the Ohio River. The congregants of Shiloh Church were mostly Methodist, but their meetinghouse was more than a place of worship; it was their school and their muster grounds, the place where they went to picnic and play, gossip and talk politics. What they couldn't get at the church, they got at the only other public facility within walking distance: Pitts Thacker's grog shop located just up the road at Pittsburg Landing on the Tennessee. Prior to its demolition, then, Shiloh may not have been a town, but it did possess the minimal qualifications of an American community: a church and a bar.

Growing up around Shiloh Church, Elsie Duncan remembered her community as an idyll in the woods. The forest was beautiful, she said, "with every kind of oak, maple and birch, [with] fruit trees and berry bushes and a spring-fed pond with water lilies blooming white." As the nine-year-old daughter of Shiloh's circuit-riding minister, Elsie knew the woods well. On the morning of the battle, she remembered that "the sun was shining, birds were singing, and the air was soft and sweet. I sat down under a holly-hock bush which was full of pink blossoms and watched the bees gathering honey."[1]

Disembarking at Pittsburg Landing, many of Ulysses S. Grant's soldiers saw not an idyll but a muddy, squalid waste, which, in fairness, Shiloh also was. (Even one local historian damningly noted that "a more unprofitable spot of land, perhaps, could not have been selected … for a battleground … with less loss to the country.") "Pittsburg Landing … excited nothing but disgust and ridicule," said one Federal. "A small, dilapidated storehouse was the only building there." The surrounding area was "an uninteresting tract of country, cut up by rough ravines and ridges, [where] here and there an irregular field and rude cabin indicated a puny effort at agriculture."[2]

The Federals were equally unimpressed with Shiloh Church—a "rude structure in which … the voices of the 'poor white trash' of Tennessee mingle in praise to God." "It is not such a church as you see in your own village," one New Englander explained: "It has no tall steeple or tapering spire, no deep-toned bell, no organ, no singing-seats or gallery, no pews or carpeted aisles. It is built of logs … chinked with clay years ago, but the rains have washed it out. You can thrust your hand between the cracks [making it] the 'best-ventilated' church you ever saw." Such estimations drip with class bias. They also drip with judgment.[3]

The Federals knew that Shiloh Church was proslavery, pro-Confederate. It was formed after the great schism in the Methodist Church in 1844, when, ironically, the local proslavery congregants fled a church called "Union" to form their own church west of the river. To many of the invading Federals, Shiloh Church was a perversion—"a little log building in the woods," said one, "where the people of the vicinage were wont to meet on the Sabbath and listen to sermons about the beauties of African Slavery." Reading their Bibles, such Yankees had decided that God demanded a rough equality—no man should be a master; no man should

be a slave. Reading the same Bible, the Duncans and their neighbors had concluded that God had fitted an entire race for slavery—whites had been chosen, blacks had not.[4]

I have often wondered whether, in naming their church Shiloh, the parishioners knew what they were letting themselves in for biblically. Certainly they knew their Bible better than I. Then again, they didn't have Google. "Shiloh" is typically translated as "Place of Peace"—which is, let's face it, the kind of irony Civil War historians and the public find irresistible. But as anyone who has lived long enough knows, there are richer complications (and deeper sadnesses) than irony. Before Shiloh was a "town" in Elsie Duncan's west Tennessee, it was a city in ancient Samaria. As the book of Jeremiah tells us, the ark of the covenant resided there for untold years before the locals, somewhat typically, ran afoul of the Almighty. Ancient Shiloh's inhabitants were guilty of the usual crimes: they had oppressed "the stranger," "shed innocent blood," and otherwise profaned the name of God. And so did God smite Shiloh in a biblical bloodletting intended to serve as an example to the Israelites of how lucky they were to be merely enduring the Babylonian captivity: "Therefore thus saith the Lord GOD; Behold, mine anger and my fury shall be poured out upon this place, upon man, and upon beast, and upon the trees of the field, and upon the fruit of the ground; and it shall burn, and shall not be quenched."[5] "Shiloh" is probably correctly translated as "Place of Peace," but it could also be translated as "Place of Desolation."

In his memoir, Grant said that Shiloh "has been perhaps less understood, or, to state the case more accurately, more persistently misunderstood, than any other engagement between National and Confederate troops during the entire rebellion." Grant had a vested interest in saying so: most observers at the time believed that he had made grave mistakes there. To his everlasting credit and occasional shame, Grant was doggedly offense-minded, and by his own admission, prior to Shiloh, he had never quite considered the possibility that he might be attacked. "Contrary to all my experience … we were on the defensive," he said of the opening action on April 6, "without intrenchments or defensive advantages of any sort." This might seem to implicate him as a commander, but he said he had decided that his men were so green they needed drill more than trenches. Probably they needed both. Certainly I agree with a Confederate officer's assessment that Grant's position "simply invited attack."[6]

Leading the Confederates, Grant's antagonist Albert Sidney Johnston had a bad first day too—not least because he got killed. Most historians regard Johnston as more or less complicit in his own undoing, for having sent off his surgeon and for generally leading from the front. The truth, however, is that Grant and William Tecumseh Sherman had close calls at Shiloh also. It was that kind of fight. As one soldier remembered, the bullets seemed to come "from too many points of the compass." "A man who was hit on the shin by a glancing ball … [was] hurt … awfully," the soldier continued, "and he screamed out. His captain said, 'Go to the rear.' As the line broke and began to drift through the brush, this soldier came limping back and said, 'Cap, give me a gun. This blamed fight *ain't got any rear*.'"[7]

The sense of chaos at Shiloh was undoubtedly amplified by the terrain. "I had always supposed, from pictures I had seen, that armies were drawn upon each side of a big field," noted one Federal. "I didn't understand how we could fight in those woods."[8]

Certainly many of them did not fight very well. Grant admitted that most of his men were "entirely raw … hardly able to load their muskets according to the manual." "In two cases, as I now remember," he later said, "colonels led their regiments from the field on first hearing the whistle of the enemy's bullets."[9]

Where some of the soldiers had trouble shooting, others had trouble *not* shooting. "As many of the guns had been wet by the rain," remembered Lieutenant Edwin Rennolds,

> it was thought best to fire off all of them, clean them out and reload. Major Swor rode rapidly along the line, saying: "When I give the command, 'ready, aim, fire,' aim about ten paces in front and fire into the ground." Before he reached the end of the line some of the men, catching the word "fire," thought the enemy were advancing and began to fire, and soon most of the guns were emptied. Several men who were standing in front were in great danger and some were wounded. Much confusion prevailed for a little while, many believing that the battle had opened.[10]

At Shiloh, many officers were so green they didn't even know what their generals looked like. Colonel H. T. Reid was approached by a stranger who said gruffly, "After the men have had their coffee and received their ammunition, … move [them] to the top of the bluff and stop all stragglers and await further orders." Reid stared at the man blankly for a moment before the stranger satisfied his curiosity: "I am General Grant." Another officer requested ammunition from a stranger "with stars on his shoulders" who sat on his horse as a king might a throne. "I [do not] believe you want ammunition, sir," the latter said furiously. "I looked at him in astonishment, doubting his sanity," the officer noted, "but made no further reply than to ask his name." "It makes no difference, sir," came the reply, "but I am General Buell."[11]

Such mix-ups are amusing. They could also be deadly. After his heroic holdout at the Hornet's Nest, Union general Benjamin Prentiss tried repeatedly to surrender, but every time he successfully did so new rebels would emerge from the woods and fire on his men even after being ordered to stand down. As one survivor remembered, "The firing did not cease until General Prentice [*sic*] told the rebel officers that if they did not stop, he would order his men to take their guns and sell their lives as dearly as possible."[12]

Where their greenness most showed was immediately after the battle, when they got their first look at the carnage. "They were mangled in every conceivable form," said one soldier. They were "mangled in every conceivable way," said another. They were "torn all to pieces," said a third, "leaving nothing but their heads or their boots." "They were mingled together in inextricable confusion," said a fourth, "headless, trunkless, and disemboweled."[13]

There is a problem in Civil War history that I will dub the "problem of gore." Those of us who have written a lot of Civil War history inevitably face a conundrum: when it comes to the material realities of the battlefield, how much is "enough"? Do I really tell my audience that, at the end of day one, Shiloh's spring dogwoods, in full bloom, are festooned with arms, legs, and entrails? Is that *gratuitous*? Or is it *necessary*?

Generally, Civil War writers have determined that it is gratuitous. Stalking the battleground at Seven Pines, General George B. McClellan famously ruminated, "I am tired of the sickening sight of the battlefield with its mangled corpses & poor suffering wounded. Victory has no charms for me when purchased at such cost." McClellan lacked what Civil War historians

unreflectively call "moral courage"; he was unwilling to "face the arithmetic," in Lincoln's actuarial phrasing. We are generally prouder of Grant because he could pay the "butcher's bill."[14]

There are few bills I would not pay for my country to have ended slavery even a year sooner. There are, after all, greater sadnesses than festooned dogwoods. There were generations of black children who never went to school, a vast industry of commodified human beings, endemic rape, and leveraged sex, all of which is humiliating and painful to look upon as an American. Surely ending all of this—surely emancipation— "redeemed" this conflict.

And yet there are images of Shiloh I can't get out of my head: the wounded Federal who lay strewn across a log, legs on one side, body on the other, conscious but immobile as fire crept across the leaf litter to ignite the log, burning his legs from his body but leaving his smoking feet on one side and his still-breathing torso on the other.[15]

Or the Confederate, bayoneted through the temple, eye distended, lying in a state of madness, pulling on his eye stalk: "He seems unconscious, and yet he has not lost sensation. He evidently received a bayonet thrust in his temple which caused the eye on that side to bulge out of its socket, and he has pulled at it till the optic nerve is out at full length. How it pops when the eyeball slips out of his hand. He has pulled at it till the optic nerve is real dirty; and from the delicate structure of the eye and its connection with the brain, we know he must suffer fearfully."[16]

Am I really supposed to elide *this*? Am I supposed to edit this out because I am told that it is gratuitous, sophomoric, gauche, or unpleasant? Perhaps I am. But who exactly decided that reading about war should be pleasant? When Oliver Wendell Holmes said of the Civil

War generation, "In our youth our hearts were touched with fire," I think what he really meant was that "In our youth our retinas were burned with images that would never let us go."[17]

On his second day at Shiloh, Mississippian Augustus Mecklin was awakened at midnight by orders to fall in. The rain was coming in torrents and the darkness was so intense he could barely see the officer leading him into position. Every so often, however, "vivid peals of … lightning" would ignite the landscape, searing Mecklin's mind with one appalling image after another: first a "dead man, his clothes ghastly, bloody face turned up to the pattering raindrops," then his friend slipping upon a corpse that lay dismembered in the road, then a Golgotha of "dead, heaped & piled upon each other." How, Mecklin wondered, had men so quickly taken a beautiful "Sabboth morn" and rendered it an infernal hellscape where "monster death" held "high carnival"?[18]

Edmund Wilson was not a Civil War historian when he produced *Patriotic Gore* in 1961. He was, if anything, a renderer of literary judgment, having presided over earlier literary trials of French symbolism and Russian revolutionary thought. When he came to the Civil War during its celebratory centennial, then, he came to it with every bias of his age, sex, political persuasion, and quixotic temper *except* that of a Civil War historian. And when he finished reading more of what the war had produced than anybody before, he said flatly, "The Period … was not one in which belles lettres flourished." But what did move him—and indeed moved him to the point of missing the point and condemning the war's whole enterprise—was the articulate way these people wrote about horror. Walt Whitman embodied the same conclusion. Traveling to Fredericksburg to nurse his wounded brother, he discovered that his brother was fine. But Whitman was never the same:

"These thousands, and tens and twenties of thousands of American young men, badly wounded, all sorts of wounds, operated on, pallid with diarrhea, languishing, dying with fever, pneumonia, &c. open a new world somehow to me, giving closer insights, new things, exploring deeper mines than any yet, showing our humanity … tried by terrible, fearfulest tests, probed deepest, the living soul's, the body's tragedies, bursting the petty bounds of art."[19]

With all due reverence for Whitman's ejaculatory style, I think what he is saying is that the real war will never get into the books until we figure out how to grapple deeply with the violence. I entirely grant that the men and women of the Civil War era had an extraordinary tolerance for other people's pain. Some of them could make fun of a dying man, wave at people with a dismembered arm, or boil a dead man's bones to make jewelry. But it is cavalier to think that the national bloodletting didn't affect them deeply or that behind their occasionally feeble metaphors—"corpses stacked like cordwood" and "hails of gunfire"—there wasn't an ocean of feeling being poured out in a puddle of blood. "As if the soul's fullness didn't sometimes overflow into the emptiest metaphors," Flaubert once explained, "for no one, ever, can give the exact measure of his needs, his apprehensions, or his sorrows; and human speech is like a cracked cauldron on which we bang out tunes to make bears dance, when we want to move the stars to pity."[20]

Of all the battles fought in the Civil War, I have always thought that tragicomic Shiloh had the best chance of moving the stars to pity. Rightly and wrongly, the Civil War stands as an American *Iliad*; each of its battles has been translated into a mythic character and asked to play a specific part in a national morality play. Gettysburg stands as the great test of democracy, the darkest hour in a national struggle to determine whether "any nation so conceived, and so dedicated, can long endure." (In the South, Gettysburg also long stood as a "high-water mark" and fabled land of "what if." "For every Southern boy fourteen years old, not once but whenever he wants it, there is the instant when it's still not yet two o'clock on that July afternoon in 1863 ...")[21]

Shiloh may be equally fabled and fabulous, but the moral is different. Shiloh represents the death of national innocence. On an idyllic spring Sunday in America, War took an Edenic field of dogwoods and peach blossoms and painted it with gore.

The fact that "War" did nothing of the kind—the fact that we inflicted it all ineptly upon ourselves—is something the national morality play is designed to elide. Lincoln employed the same elision: "And the war came."

Wars may be fought outside, but they are made inside—in the halls of Congress and the White House, in parlors, kitchens, and churches. Elsie Duncan's father may have been a preacher, but he was also the community's drillmaster. "He would prepare our young men to go into the army to fight other men that they did not even know, nor have anything against," Elsie Duncan later marveled. "I use to sit and watch them go marching by and I wondered how many of them would be killed." Duncan's final time inside Shiloh Church was when she performed in a community concert. She enacted a skit in which the South was the goose that laid the golden egg, but Lincoln squeezed it too hard and it ran away. The girls waved Confederate flags and sang "Dixie." The men threw "their hats up yelling, 'hurrah for Jefferson Davis and the Southern Confederacy.' How that old Shiloh Church did ring."[22]

Shiloh Church was everywhere in the battle. At different times it served variously as headquarters for both armies, a hospital, a prison, and a morgue. Albert Sidney Johnston's body was carried to the church for a time. At the church, P. G. T. Beauregard, Johnston's successor, decided not to follow up on the gains of April 6, giving Grant a chance to rally and recapture the church the next day. And while the church was not killed on the field, it was certainly a casualty. In the days and weeks after it gave its name to the battle it was torn down for firewood, bridges, and especially souvenirs. "No one who visits Pittsburg Landing has a thought of returning without first making a pilgrimage to Shiloh Church," noted one newspaper, "and few have returned without bearing home with them 'a piece of the church as a trophy.' Shiloh Church is now in ruins."[23]

Shiloh Church got what it deserved, I suppose. But I am glad it has been reconstructed as part of the effort to restore and preserve the battlefield. I like to think that people will sit there, contemplating hubris and confronting the fact that we are a sometimes hardheaded, hard-hearted, misguided people.

We are tenderhearted, too, and capable of redemption. "When I came to," wrote one wounded soldier at Shiloh,

I found my gun gone and the fellows around me saying it was no use taking [me] off the field. [I had] gone up at the spout.... I had not the courage to open my eyes. My first movement was to feel if I still lived.... Every action of my life seemed written before me. When I opened my eyes the battle was still going on, and many had bit the dust like myself. I put my hand to my head where I remember having been struck, for I felt no pain, and my hand, when I looked at it, told a fearful story, and [I] felt the warm blood running down my back in a perfect stream....

While drooping in this way, my head leaning against the tree, I noticed a little violet looking up to me from under the trampled grass, and a thought of past scenes of a different nature passed through my mind as I plucked it and put it in my sketchbook next to my bosom.... The little flower I carefully kept and pressed in my journal was the only trophy I took from the fire of battle.[24]

In the photograph that leads this essay, Will Gallagher captures the soul of Shiloh. Morning light slants in on empty pews and an unoccupied pulpit. The scene is quiet but shrouded in ambivalent shadow, and we are unsure what to make of it: Is this a place of peace or a place of desolation? Are the congregants dead, their church abandoned? Or maybe this church is about to flood with life? Perhaps the preacher will enter and pronounce a new sermon full of deep decency, deeper humility, and deepest truth. I hope so. Because what God does to indecent nations is fearful to behold.

NOTES

1. *The Diary of Elsie Caroline Duncan Hurt*, online at https://shilohdiary.files.wordpress.com/2015/09/elsie-diary-text-part-1.pdf (accessed October 14, 2017).

2. B. G. Brazelton, *A History of Hardin County, Tennessee* (Nashville, Tenn.: Cumberland Presbyterian Publishing House, 1885), 67; *The Story of the Fifty-Fifth Regiment Illinois Volunteer Infantry in the Civil War, 1861–1865* (Clinton, Mass.: W. J. Coulter, 1887), 67. In fairness, some Northern authors did see beauty in the primitive landscape: "The Tennessee woods were fast putting on the garb of spring, and the peach trees thus early showing their pink flowers [came as] a sort of tropical revelation" (*Story of the Fifty-Fifth Regiment*, 68).

3. "The Fall of Shiloh Church," *Cincinnati Daily Times*, June 13, 1862; Charles Carleton Coffin, *My Days and Nights on the Battle-field* (Boston: Estes and Lauriat, 1887), 159.

4. *Story of the Fifty-Fifth Regiment*, 69.

5. Quotes are from the King James Version. See Jer. 7:6, 20.

6. Ulysses S. Grant, *Memoirs and Selected Letters: Personal Memoirs of U.S. Grant, Selected Letters 1839–1865*, ed. William S. McFeely (New York: Library of America, 1990), 247, 239; F. A. Shoup, *Confederate Veteran* (Nashville, Tenn., 1894), 2:137.

7. Ephraim C. Dawes, "My First Day under Fire at Shiloh," in Ohio Commandery of the Military Order of the Loyal Legion of the United States, *Sketches of War History, 1861–1865*, vol. 4 (Cincinnati: Robert Clarke Company, 1896), 13–14.

8. D. Lloyd Jones, "The Battle of Shiloh," in Military Order of the Loyal Legion of the United States, *War Papers: Being Papers Read before the Commandery of the State of Wisconsin*, vol. 4 (Milwaukee: MOLLUS, 1914), 54.

9. Grant, *Memoirs and Selected Letters*, 228, 231.

10. Lieutenant Edwin H. Rennolds, *A History of the Henry County Commands Which Served in the Confederate States Army* (Jacksonville, Fla.: Sun Publishing Company, 1904), 35.

11. William W. Belknap, *History of the Fifteenth Regiment, Iowa Veteran Infantry, from October 1861 to August 1865* (Keokuk, Iowa: R. B. Ogden and Son, 1887), 189; John H. Rerick, *The Forty-Fourth Indiana Volunteer Infantry, History of Its Services in the War of the Rebellion and a Personal Record of Its Members* (LaGrange, Ind.: published by the author, 1880), 241–42.

12. Abraham Van Meter quoted in *Unionville (Mo.) Republican*, June 30, 1894.

13. Hugh C. Bailey, ed., "An Alabamian at Shiloh: The Diary of Liberty Independence Nixon," *Alabama Review* 11 (April 1958): 144–55; Andrew Hickenlooper, "The Battle of Shiloh (in Two Parts)," in Ohio Commandery of the Military Order of the Loyal Legion of the United States, *Sketches of War History, 1861–1865*, vol. 5 (Cincinnati: Robert Clarke Company, 1903), 434.

14. George B. McClellan, *The Civil War Papers of George C. McClellan: Selected Correspondence, 1860–1865*, ed. Stephen W. Sears (New York: Ticknor and Fields, 1989), 288.

15. Chaplain John M. Garner quoted in David R. Logsdon, ed., *Eyewitnesses at the Battle of Shiloh* (Nashville, Tenn.: Kettle Mills Press, 1994), 93. (Original publication of Garner's

account was in serial form in the *Unionville (Mo.) Republican*, October 5, 1892, to December 26, 1894.)

16. Garner quoted in Logsdon, ed., *Eyewitnesses at the Battle of Shiloh*, 93.

17. Oliver Wendell Holmes Jr., "Memorial Day Address, May 30, 1884" (delivered at Keene, N.H.), reprinted in *The Fundamental Holmes: A Free Speech Chronicle and Reader*, ed. Ronald K. L. Collins (New York: Cambridge University Press, 2010), 25.

18. Augustus Mecklin diary, April 6, 1862, Augustus Henry Mecklin Papers, Mississippi Department of Archives and History, Jackson.

19. Edmund Wilson, *Patriotic Gore: Studies in the Literature of the American Civil War* (New York: Oxford University Press, 1962), ix; Walt Whitman, *Selected Letters of Walt Whitman*, ed. Edwin Haviland Miller (Iowa City: University of Iowa Press, 1990), 52. See also David Blight, *"Patriotic Gore* is Not Really Much Like Any Other Book by Anyone," *Slate*, March 22, 2012, online at http://www.slate.com/articles/life/history/2012/03/edmund_wilson_s_patriotic_gore_one_of_the_most_important_and_confounding_books_ever_written_about_the_civil_war_.html (accessed October 14, 2017).

20. Gustave Flaubert, *Madame Bovary: Patterns of a Provincial Life* (1856; repr., New York: Modern Library, 1957), 160.

21. William Faulkner, *Intruder in the Dust* (1948; repr., New York: Doubleday, 2011), 194–95.

22. *Diary of Elsie Caroline Duncan Hurt* (accessed October 14, 2017).

23. *Daily Evansville (Ind.) Journal*, June 3, 1862, 2.

24. Conrad Wise Chapman, *Ten Months in the "Orphan Brigade": Conrad Wise Chapman's Civil War Memoir*, ed. Ben Bassham (Kent, Ohio: Kent State University Press, 1999), 70.

2 MY CAVE LIFE IN HOSPITAL

SARAH E. GARDNER

n the mid-1990s, I was hard at work on my dissertation, an examination of white Southern women's Civil War narratives. Among other things, I was interested in the ways these women carved out space for their stories in an increasingly crowded literary marketplace that catered to an ever more urbanized and industrialized reading audience hungry for tales about America's defining event. As part of my work I read Mary Webster Loughborough's 1864 memoir, *My Cave Life in Vicksburg: With Letters of Trial and Travel.*

My brief discussion of Loughborough's account bears traces of the historian I have become, one who is interested in print culture, the literary marketplace, book history, and the Civil War era. I noted, for example, the different ways in which the 1864 and the 1881 editions of the memoir were pitched to different reading audiences. The postwar edition, I wrote, framed *Cave Life* as a paean to heroic Confederate soldiers who had courageously defended Vicksburg against all odds. "Words cannot express the wonder and admiration excited in [Loughborough's] mind by the conduct of those brave men at Vicksburg," the preface ran, "how they endured with unflinching courage the shower of ball and shell, how they confronted the foe with undaunted resolution … how they endured with steadfast perseverance, the hunger, the wet, the privation."[1] This was standard stuff for the 1880s, penned by Southern writers, published by Northern presses, and eagerly consumed by much of the nation's readers. Capitalizing on the popularity of Loughborough's account at the time of its initial publication, D. Appleton had successfully repackaged *Cave Life* to fit the needs of a Jim Crow reading audience.

The 1864 edition carried no such tribute. Wartime

Entrance to cave surrounded by kudzu, Vicksburg battlefield, Mississippi (Photograph by Will Gallagher) readers (and those who perhaps picked up the book in the early years of Reconstruction, before the contours of the myth of the Lost Cause had yet to be defined) encountered instead an unmediated account of Loughborough's ersatz defenders. The scene of the fleeing Confederate soldiers across the Big Black River on May 17, 1863, thus reads quite differently in the 1864 edition. No words of ultimate admiration, simply those of recrimination, uttered by angry and frightened women who accused their protectors of desertion: "We are disappointed in you.... Who shall we look to now for protection?" As if to mock the fleeing men, Loughborough recorded her escape through enemy fire from her cave to the house where her husband was stationed. The Confederate soldiers, camped nearby, "stood curiously watching the effect of the sudden fall of metal around me. I would not for the world have shown fear, so braced by my pride I walked with a firm and steady pace, notwithstanding the treacherous suggestions of my heart that beat a loud 'Run, Run.'" Certainly, in this section, Loughborough seems much more interested with detailing the hardships and privations of noncombatants in a town under siege than with glorifying the Confederate soldiers.[2]

Though instinctually attuned to many of the priorities that animate the study of book history— a subfield that, at the time, I did not know even existed—I still missed a lot. But then again, I had other, more pressing concerns. As I was writing my dissertation and reading Loughborough's account of her cave life, I was diagnosed with cancer that had already metastasized to my lymph nodes and surrounding tissue. It had not spread to my lungs or bones, so the prognosis wasn't utterly dire, but neither was it particularly rosy. Part of the treatment included stints in isolation. Loughborough's account suddenly took on a new kind of relevance—one that was not welcomed.

My reading of Loughborough's account of her cave life—and of the siege of Vicksburg more generally— was profoundly influenced by my time in the hospital. I imagined a kind of affinity with civilians forced to hole up in these earthen bunkers, in part because I imagined they suffered from the same sorts of constraints under which I labored. Largely cut off from human contact (except for a disembodied voice that came over the intercom every two hours reminding me to drink an absurd amount of water and brief visits from my medical personnel dressed in hazmat gear), I was left to my own imagination. Loughborough at least had the occasional visitor and could, should conditions be propitious, leave the cave. "I am told by my friends," she wrote, "that I am looking worn and pale, and frequently asked if I am not weary of this cave life." She deflected when she could, but truth be told, she confessed, "I *am* tired and weary—ah! so weary! I was never made to live underground," she exclaimed. "What wonder that I vegetate, like other unfortunate plants, grow wan, spindling, and white."[3] I understood those words. I was never meant to live in isolation.

I felt increasingly claustrophobic as the days ticked by. So too did Dora Richards Miller, another Vicksburg cave dweller. Her cave was larger than most, Mark Smith notes, and yet, as she entered, she anticipated "a premature death": "'The earthy, suffocating feeling, as of a living tomb, was dreadful to me. I fear I shall risk death outside rather than melt in that dark furnace.'"[4] My room was spacious, at least compared with typical hospital rooms. Still, it is stunning how small a room can become when one is not allowed to leave it. I, like Loughborough, was wan, if not spindly, and if the room didn't quite take on a tomb-like quality, it certainly became a bunker and I had adopted a siege mentality.

I had little to distract me except physical pain and the acute fear about my own mortality. It is hard to know what to wish for in such circumstances, a sentiment Loughborough captured as rumors circulated that Vicksburg could not hold out for long. "The ladies all cried, 'Oh, never surrender!'" she explained. But the constant shelling and dwindling provisions forced her to admit, "I really could not tell what I wanted, or what my options were."[5] Later in the text, but earlier in the chronology—she had appended letters that she had penned before her time in Vicksburg's caves—Loughborough reflected on the Confederate soldiers headed off to Corinth. How many, she wondered, would dream of victory only to be silenced "forever in death! Or, worse, perhaps, lamed and maimed for life."[6] That ambivalence, that uncertainty, sounds about right. Living this way was hardly sustainable, yet the alternative was scary as hell.

When a friend suggested that we celebrate my release by taking a driving tour of the South, I added only one location to the itinerary: Vicksburg. This represented something of a departure for me. I am confident I had never been to a national park before. I had certainly never visited a Civil War monument. My family simply did not go in for that sort of thing. My Italian mother, whose idea of a proper vacation fixated on stories of seemingly endless nights in Havana's nightclubs and casinos, never quite forgave Fidel Castro for cutting off Cuba from American tourist dollars. (To be clear, only one person was to blame for this dismal state of affairs.) Our family vacations were spent in Miami, an ersatz Havana populated by expats, all in a desperate attempt to replicate the experiences of my great-aunts and uncles in 1950s Cuba. But when it came time for me to travel, post-op, post-treatment (at least for this go around), I chose to enter the belly of the beast.

I'm not sure I had much of a plan. I do know that I thought (and frankly, still do) that staving off physical death depends, at least in part, on staving off professional death. I didn't want my career to end before it even began. Best to keep moving. So off to Vicksburg we went, all in the name of "research." But I also needed to know what this place looked like—this besieged place that I had been reading about while my body was under siege; this place, choked by Union soldiers, that I had been reading about while physicians worked to save my trachea; this isolated, blockaded place that I had been reading about during the time I was quarantined. This place. I needed to see this place.

I was unprepared for much of what I saw. I was too focused on published material about Vicksburg during the Civil War to know of the postwar monuments and memorials. "The Art Park of the World." Who knew? Similarly, I was surprised by the park's expansiveness. My family didn't really do nature. We did cities. Turn left on 42nd, then a hang a right on 9th. I get that. Cities I understood. I don't know what to do with trees and hills. And a river that doubles back on itself? What is that? Vicksburg was massive in ways that I did not anticipate and had a landscape that I could not comprehend.

The national park certainly didn't look like the illustration that accompanied the 1864 edition of *Cave Life*, my only visual cue to what I might encounter. The most striking feature of the illustration is the figure of a solitary individual, presumably Loughborough, sitting in a cave's threshold. She is small. The surrounding trees dwarf her, and she is engulfed by the cave's framed entrance. The Union soldier, who is placed in the foreground, appears to be three times her size. What possible chance of survival does she have?, the illustration seems to asks. But her placement also suggests a kind of agency. It is unclear whether she is entering the cave or exiting it. Presumably, she could do either. (A freedom I did not have while in treatment.) And although the surrounding landscape poses danger—steep slopes and tangled brush—the Union soldier appears to be the greatest threat, but even that interpretation is mitigated by his diverted attention. His focus is fixed on a nearby cave that, at least from his point of view, seems to be vacant. The figure sitting in the cave's entrance is out of his line of sight. Maybe, then, Loughborough will make it.

The 1864 publication date lets readers know that Loughborough does, in fact, survive the siege of Vicksburg. Whatever doubts she harbored—at one point she wondered whether the ignominy of Confederate defeat would be preferable to another night in the cave; at other times, she was convinced she'd be buried alive—her readers could rest easy knowing that Loughborough escaped to tell her tale.[7] (This is a kind of luxury for Loughborough's readers. They knew the end of the story—at least on this one critical point—before cracking the book's binding.) The summer I read *Cave Life*, I craved that kind of luxury. I knew Loughborough would survive. I doubted whether I would.

The photo that accompanies this essay bears little resemblance to the book's illustration. It is far more menacing and certainly evokes what I felt that summer and at every recurrence afterward. The caves at Vicksburg have long since collapsed. We should hardly be surprised. Cave dwellers feared being buried alive, and with good reason. The "constant trembling of the earth and the jolting of the soil," Mark Smith

Cover of Mary Ann Loughborough's My Cave Life in Vicksburg: With Letters of Trial and Travel *(New York: D. Appleton and Co., 1864)*

has written, and "the cracks appearing in the ceilings, courtesy of shells," served as "haunting reminders of their precarious, fragile situation."[8] What was designed as temporary shelter built out of soft sediment could hardly survive the onslaught of time.

As the photograph demonstrates, what remains of the terraced landscape is covered in kudzu, an invasive, noxious plant that spreads rapidly, takes root, and kills all surrounding shrubs and trees by blocking out the light. Kudzu was first imported to the United States in 1876 for the Centennial Fair; some sixty years later it came south, when Southern farmers were encouraged to plant the vine to stem soil erosion. There is some kind of irony at work here. To mark the seventy-fifth anniversary of Union victory, kudzu takes over the South.

Kudzu. A near perfect analogue to cancer; near perfect because kudzu is an import. Cancer is organic to its host, a rogue cell that attacks its own. The body is at war with itself, and the odds are not often in favor of the good guy. Leonard Cohen's song "Anthem," which had come out a few years before I was diagnosed, offers a modicum of hope to its listeners: "There is a crack in everything / That's how the light gets in." Not so with kudzu. The hole at the center of the cave is not a remnant from the siege; it was dug out by the photographer in a failed attempt to get an interior shot. The kudzu had undoubtedly covered the temporary hole by the following morning. That is how fast kudzu grows. There is no light.

Loughborough had wondered about light. She had marked her first night in a small cave by recording the strike of a shell fragment in the cave's ceiling. "I shall never forget my extreme fear during the night, and my utter hopelessness of ever seeing morning light," she wrote. As the shelling continued, Loughborough

prepared "for the sudden death" that surely awaited her.[9] But one learns to live with the fear, and that might be the scariest part of all. What had once been extraordinary becomes normalized. Ways of living that seemed unthinkable become habitual.

Mark Smith has written that "Vicksburg revealed what those on the home front would have to do to survive."[10] I get it. But survival is not without its costs. The gnawing anxiety and the anticipatory dread abates but never quite leaves. And though Loughborough ends the account of her time in Vicksburg with her leaving town, the view of the Mississippi River behind her, she closes her memoir with a series of letters purportedly written in the months leading up to her cave life. This seems odd. Quite odd. Why end at the beginning? Why leave her audience with the author poised to enter a cave that had amplified her fears and dulled her sensibilities? Why include the letters at all?

Although the memoir betrayed no sense of lasting trauma, no sense that Loughborough's reentry to life above ground was hard or difficult, perhaps the author did not want to convey any degree of certainty or offer any sense of an easy resolution to her wartime readers. In 1863, she had entered a cave. For a short while, she had become acclimated to a life that would have been unimaginable months before. And then she had left a cave. In 1864 that's about all she could say. After that, who knows? Best to leave it at that.

In 1994, I had entered a hospital room. For a short while, I had become acclimated to a life that was unimaginable months before. And then I had left a hospital room. After that, who knew? Best to head to Vicksburg.

NOTES

1. Mary Webster Loughborough, *My Cave Life in Vicksburg: With Letters of Trial and Travel* (New York: D. Appleton, 1881), 8.

2. Mary Loughborough, *My Cave Life in Vicksburg: With Letters of Trial and Travel* (New York: D. Appleton and Co., 1864), 43–44, 95; Sarah E. Gardner, *Blood and Irony: Southern White Women's Narratives of the Civil War, 1861–1937* (Chapel Hill: University of North Carolina Press, 2004), 24–25.

3. Loughborough, *Cave Life* (1864), 114.

4. Mark M. Smith, *The Smell of Battle, the Taste of the Siege: A Sensory History of the Civil War* (New York: Oxford University Press, 2015), 98 (Miller quoted in Smith).

5. Loughborough, *Cave Life* (1864), 46.

6. Loughborough, *Cave Life* (1864), 157–58.

7. Loughborough, *Cave Life* (1864), 58, 63.

8. Smith, *Smell of Battle*, 98.

9. Loughborough, *Cave Life* (1864), 56.

10. Smith, *Smell of Battle*, 101.

3 THE TRIANGULAR FIELD AND DEVIL'S DEN

J. MATTHEW GALLMAN

grew up in North Carolina, a great distance from the Civil War's iconic battlefields. My first boyhood experience visiting a battlefield was a trip to Gettysburg. My vivid memory is standing before piled rocks in Devil's Den, gazing at a reproduction of Alexander Gardner's photograph *Home of a Rebel Sharpshooter* on display there. It was, and is, a remarkable scene to contemplate. In the photograph, the fallen Confederate soldier lies with his head against the boulder to the viewer's right. Another boulder to the left creates the other half of a perfect V-shaped hiding place. The sharpshooter's rifle leans on a pile of rocks between the two boulders. Those rocks had clearly been stacked up there, presumably by the soldier intent on perfecting his nest of stone.[1]

Behind the display with the photograph were the rocks themselves. The markings in the large boulders matched those in Gardner's image, testifying to the realness and immediacy of this picture. (Much later I would learn that Gettysburg residents speak of "witness trees" that stood when the battle was fought. These were, without question, witness rocks.) If you stand in front of the piled stones, precisely where the corpse lay in the photograph, you can look up to Little Round Top, the end of the famed fishhook that defined the Union's lines on July 2, 1863. A child gazing to the east from there could easily see why a sharpshooter would choose such a spot. Gouverneur K. Warren's statue stands on Little Round Top, several dozen yards to the left of the castle commemorating the New Yorkers who fought there. I did not know who he was, but I could see that he would have made an inviting target from this perch.[2]

Historians devote much of their time to contemplating what we know, how we know it, and what it means. This essay is a small example of the meaning of places, both in history and in memory. It is

(previous page)
Devil's Den from the Confederate perspective, Gettysburg battlefield, Pennsylvania (Photograph by Will Gallagher)

also an essay about how the details of the place matter, and where you are standing when you look at that place might matter too. For me this story starts standing before those boulders, but—as is so often the case—it will not end up precisely where it began.

For years I recalled that pile of rocks amid the boulders of Devil's Den, although I could tell you nothing else about that early trip to Gettysburg. That recollection was so powerful that many years later, when I was in graduate school, I returned to that very spot. I was on a long road trip with a friend, and our route took us close enough to Gettysburg that I insisted that we make a very short detour. Daylight was fading when we finally reached the battlefield, but all I really wanted to do was see this one place. Devil's Den is a boulder-strewn ridge at the southern end of the battlefield. Although those boulders witnessed many devilish horrors in July 1863, it is instructive to know that the locals had named the spot long before. By the time we found the general location, darkness was falling, giving it an appropriately eerie feeling. Alone on that end of the battlefield, we scrambled among the boulders until we found the "Home of a Rebel Sharpshooter" of my memories.

Here is a complication. Between my first visit to Devil's Den and this second brief pilgrimage, the historian of photography William A. Frassanito had uncovered an unsettling truth. The "sharpshooter" in that famous photograph had not really died where we had been told. Thanks to Frassanito's research, we now know that Gardner and his team had photographed this poor rebel soldier multiple times in at least two places. They had moved the unfortunate man to this final resting place because it made a compelling photograph. Once I found myself in the classroom, that photograph became a wonderful teaching tool, opening up conversations about the meaning of evidence and also the ultimate meaning of photographs to the people who first saw them.[3]

There is another set of facts that was impressed in my mind, although perhaps not entirely accurately. Standing in Devil's Den—and particularly at that nest of rocks—one could not miss Little Round Top, not much more than a half mile away.[4] The very casual student of Gettysburg as a military event can intone the words of John Buford, as penned by Michael Shaara in his novel *The Killer Angels* and performed by the wondrous Sam Elliot in the film *Gettysburg*: the wise old soldier seeks "good ground." And that only-sort-of military historian, whose knowledge of Gettysburg pretty much stopped with Shaara, knows that not far from this spot on the battlefield the 20th Maine held off Alabamians at the far end of the Union line on day two, while farther up the line intrepid New Yorkers held that good ground on the other side of Little Round Top, roughly where the castle monument honoring New York's regiments now stands.[5] All things being equal, higher ground is to be preferred. And I had figured out that the folks on Little Round Top had that advantage.

Long after that twilight romp around Devil's Den, I found myself on the faculty at Gettysburg College, teaching courses on the Civil War and joining students on battlefield tours both at Gettysburg and on a dozen other Eastern battlefields. I never became a military historian, but I did come to know many of the leading scholars and guides. Each year my students and I would take one daylong tour of the entire battlefield and two half-day micro-tours of specific Gettysburg locations, learning to walk the ground and think about the significance of that terrain in shaping decisions and events. On my own, I spent hundreds of hours walking portions of the battlefield. Sometimes it was just a great place for a long walk, but many afternoons I went with a text and a map in hand, trying to figure out the mysteries of the Wheatfield, or Culp's Hill, or Barlow's Knoll. I do not recall returning often to the rebel sharpshooter's home on these hikes. Like other folks who have spent many hours on that battlefield, I came to spurn those spots on the auto tour that attracted the crowds of visitors.

But I did learn about what had happened at that southern end of the battlefield, especially on July 2. Although Pickett's Charge on the final day looms large in popular memory, the events on the Confederate right on the second day at Gettysburg are thick with stories large and small, with hugely consequential results. At the level of high command decisions, this was the day when Robert E. Lee ordered General James Longstreet to send his men up the Emmitsburg Road and to attack the far left of the Union line, hopefully flanking General George Gordon Meade's men arrayed along Cemetery Ridge. That grand plan went awry in multiple ways. Longstreet's attack unfolded far too slowly, and by the time the rebels were prepared to move on their foes, the Yankees had extended their line as far as Little Round Top, and their center had moved well forward of where Longstreet expected to find them. The result was a disjointed attack that failed to meet Lee's objectives. The Union lines held. But before the fighting on day two had come to a close, Longstreet's attack had produced a host of bloody engagements stretching from the Peach Orchard, through the Wheatfield, across Devil's Den, and ending on the back side of Little Round Top to the south.

When one makes the transition from broad descriptive accounts to detailed maps and micro-histories, the stories shift. Lovers of military maps can hardly do better than Gettysburg. The maps tell tales as complicated as we wish to make them. Here are some observations that this neophyte quickly learned. In the early afternoon of July 2, 1863, before Longstreet's assault was really underway, the Union Third Corps, under the impetuous Daniel E. Sickles, had moved forward 500 yards to higher ground near the Peach Orchard and stretched its line southward into those boulders on Devil's Den, on the south side of Houck's Ridge. (In short, Devil's Den, the enticing spot with all the boulders, is at one end of a ridge. At midday Union troops occupied this key location.) When the advancing 1st Texas—one of the lead regiments from Jerome B. Robertson's brigade of General John Bell Hood's division—arrived on Houck's Ridge, it faced Union infantry occupying the higher ground. The 124th New York—known as the Orange Blossoms—charged the 1st Texas on the western slope of Houck's Ridge, slowing the Confederate advance while absorbing heavy casualties.[6] The fighting for Devil's Den was fierce. The Union troops finally fell back off the ridge into the valley between Devil's Den and Little Round Top, as fighting raged in the Wheatfield just to the north and their comrades above them to the east fought to control Little Round Top.

An expert eye can look at a map, and especially a good topographical map, and immediately imagine the terrain in three dimensions. I can train myself to look at those squiggly lines as clues to the true terrain, but my eye for the complexities of slopes and valleys on the printed page is weak. For me, there is much more to learn about the place by walking the ground. By the time I left Gettysburg I had a good sense of the events atop Little Round Top and of the hard fighting both in Devil's Den and in the "valley of death" between the two, but my understanding of the surrounding terrain in that section of the battlefield was still pretty limited.

After I left Gettysburg College, the Gettysburg National Military Park completed an ambitious plan to return the battlefield to a closer approximation of its 1863 appearance. Park employees removed huge numbers of trees, installed fences where they had divided farm properties during those days in July, and generally sought to reproduce the ground—as much as was possible—that Civil War soldiers and their commanders saw during those three days. In June 2008 I was back in the borough for a Civil War event and joined five other historians for a hike on this reconstructed battlefield, led by Gary Gallagher. That day transformed my understanding of Devil's Den and the surrounding dramas.

Our happy band set off from the Confederate lines near the Emmitsburg Road, following the July 2 march of the 1st Texas Infantry, part of Robertson's brigade in Hood's division. With the trees gone, we were able to get a much clearer sense of how Hood had planned his assault on the Union left and what his men would have seen as they marched. By the time the Texans reached the point where our walk began, they had already been a part of Longstreet's long and complex march and countermarch.[7] They were no doubt tired from their lengthy maneuvers, but the worst part of their day was ahead.

In their march toward Houck's Ridge, the men of the 1st Texas covered some pretty uneven ground, first moving down into a depression and then moving up—and east—through the "triangular field" toward the mouths of Union artillery pieces up on the ridge. The photograph preceding this essay captures some semblance of the terrain that Robertson's brigade faced on July 2. Time changes the details, but those boulders in the foreground are surely more witness rocks. Our route in 2008 took us through that oddly shaped field, up onto the ridge. The path we followed is to the left in the picture.

The picture also offers a good sense of another crucial fact that we hikers, and no doubt those weary Texans, quickly discovered: the Triangular Field rises substantially from the west up to the east. Taken from the foot of the Triangular Field, the photograph captures that fact that the men of the 1st Texas faced quite an uphill climb. The viewer can see two Union monuments, barely visible on the horizon. Those monuments provide a useful frame of reference. The one on the left is to the 124th New York Infantry. The Orange Blossoms' monument features a seven-foot statue of Colonel Augustus Van Horne Ellis, who was killed leading the downhill charge against the 1st Texas Regiment. Ellis's statue stands atop a granite shaft that is of similar height. That monument, so small on the horizon, stands about fifteen feet high on the western slope of Houck's Ridge. That is where the Texans were headed on that hot July afternoon.

The Confederate sharpshooter's stone nest is up and to the right, not too far out of sight over the ridge in the picture. The unknown rebel—almost certainly not a sharpshooter at all—in Gardner's picture was probably from Benning's brigade of Georgians who followed the Texans, slightly to the south (to the right of the photograph). From this position, well below Devil's Den, the landscape feels very different than it does when one is standing among those boulders and looking in the other direction, up at Little Round Top. Devil's Den was not merely an appealing place to deploy before threatening those Union regiments on the hill. Devil's Den—and the entire ridge—was formidable high ground in its own right, far above where Hood's men had launched their afternoon assault. When the 1st Texas faced the 124th New York under Colonel Ellis, the oncoming Confederates had the advantage of numbers, with more men following behind them, but the New Yorkers who fought to stall that advance certainly had the "good ground." At least for a moment.

From the perspective of a young boy, or even an enthusiastic graduate student, Devil's Den seemed to be a place to fight *from*. It was a spot where rebel sharpshooters could fire up at the Union troops on Little Round Top. But walking the ground taught me that Devil's Den was the high ground those charging Confederates fought *for* as evening fell on July 2. Being on the ground can still produce a distorted perspective. If one stands at the base of the monument to the 124th New York and walks the few paces to the top of the Triangular Field, the incline does not seem all that dramatic (at least to me). It was not until we walked up from below—following the path of the Texans—that the magnitude of the slope became clear.

On a beautiful day in July 2017, nine years after tromping the field with my five friends—all authors in this book—I returned to that corner of the battlefield with photographer Will Gallagher. I got there a bit early and watched the children climbing on the boulders. A group of Boy Scouts were on tour, and before long they had all gathered around the "Home of the Rebel Sharpshooter." When Will arrived he suggested that we could identify good shooting locations and he would return early in the morning and get images with no tourists in the frame. But when we walked down the Triangular Field, we found that there would be no need to return at dawn. Although there were dozens of tourists on the ridge, and many more on Little Round Top, nobody else was down there to see what things

might have looked like to the Texans as they headed up that treacherous slope, well below Devil's Den.[8]

NOTES

1. Fitting with the larger theme that things are never precisely as they seem to us, although Alexander Gardner is generally credited with this photograph, the earliest production of the image was attributed to Timothy O'Sullivan, Gardner's assistant. The Library of Congress website shows the original Alexander Gardner photograph and includes some analysis of the picture based on William Frassanito's work; see https://www.loc.gov/resource/cwpb.04337/.

2. The *Gettysburg Daily* website includes a modern photograph of the *Home of a Rebel Sharpshooter* with the Gardner photograph displayed in front: http://www.gettysburgdaily.com/devils-den-and-wheatfield-waysides/.

3. William A. Frassanito, *Gettysburg: A Journey in Time*, 2nd ed. (Gettysburg, Pa.: Thomas Publications, 1996), 187–92.

4. This is how the crow flies. The walk would be considerably longer.

5. Readers who have stumbled upon this essay with no knowledge of the battle of Gettysburg should not despair. The preceding text refers to Michael Shaara's Pulitzer Prize–winning *The Killer Angels* (1974) and the Ron Maxwell movie *Gettysburg* (1993), based on the novel.

6. Both the regiment's colonel and major were shot in the head and killed in this engagement.

7. The details of Longstreet's countermarch on July 2 are pretty interesting. But all you really need to know here is that by midafternoon, these men had already marched a considerable distance.

8. When we finished our serious work, Will took a picture of his son posing in the "Home of the Rebel Sharpshooter." Somewhere in my digital files I have a 2008 photograph of five friends in precisely the same spot.

4 CAMP ALLEGHENY

A. WILSON GREENE

What an unusually delightful March day in the Valley of Virginia! I was planning a bus tour covering Stonewall Jackson's 1862 Valley campaign, and when I left McDowell battlefield the temperature was pushing seventy. Although it was growing late, I thought I'd drive through Monterey and up Allegheny Mountain to visit my favorite Civil War site. With my now superfluous warm coat and sweater tossed haphazardly aside, I headed west on U.S. 250, which mimics the historic Staunton-Parkersburg Turnpike, in many places borrowing the old road's original right of way.

Camp Allegheny sits astride that venerable highway, which is now a gravel-and-rock one-lane track that departs from 250 at the West Virginia state line. I arrived at the turnoff about 4 P.M. with at least ninety minutes of daylight remaining to negotiate the two and a half miles to the battlefield, commune with the landscape, and make it back to the main road before dark.

When I rolled down the window at the top of the grade, I quickly realized that the early spring I had experienced in the valley had not ventured uphill. The temperature was at least thirty degrees colder, with a healthy breeze making it more bracing still. I reached for my coat and started down the old turnpike, dodging the ubiquitous mud holes and keeping the wheels on the higher surface. It was obvious that the annual grading was overdue as the road seemed more challenging than I remembered.

The first two miles to the battlefield are shaded by a forest canopy so thick that some puddles of rainwater never evaporate. The sun—especially in mid-March— is no match for this arboreal gloom, and as I bumped farther along the road I noticed that the puddles began to take on a certain solid consistency. Several hundred yards farther, a stretch of road had been completely inundated so that even the crown retained moisture—and that moisture was now an unbroken sheet of ice. My little truck began to fishtail—even at five miles per hour—and it became obvious that my excursion had taken a turn for the worse.

By this time the setting sun no longer penetrated the laurel thickets and the oak, hickory, and pine forest that surrounded me. Reluctantly, I stopped and decided to cancel the trip and return to the highway. Putting my overmatched Toyota in reverse, I started to back up, hoping to reach the wide spot about 500 yards to the east where I might be able to turn around. Wheels spun. The truck lurched sideways toward the eminently perilous drop-off on my right. I stopped, pulled forward, and then tried again. Same result. After about twenty minutes, during which I managed to progress seventy-five feet on the ice, it began to occur to me that I might be in a spot of trouble. But being a midwesterner with years of experience driving on frozen precipitation, I eventually reached thawed ground well after dark, straining to see with my feeble back-up lights, until I lurched all the way out to U.S. 250. Welcome to Camp Allegheny.

The battlefield sits atop its namesake mountain at an elevation of 4,400 feet. Local residents, including Hunter Lesser, who first introduced me to Camp Allegheny, confirm that these ridges exist in a micro-climate that—as my experience that March afternoon attests—bears little relation to the weather in the surrounding lowlands. The first snow in the region in 1861 fell on August 13. A Confederate soldier camped atop the mountain that November reported, "It is snowing; the wind is blowing a hurricane; it is as cold as the North Pole; and of all the dreary and desolate places on earth, this is entitled to the palm." Eight inches of powder fell on November 16, signaling the beginning of a season that would not relent until April.[1]

What in the world was an army doing in a place like this?

The war came to what was then northwestern Virginia (Pocahontas County is now in West Virginia) in the autumn of 1861. Union forces had won small but important victories a few dozen miles to the west during the summer—victories that eventually launched George B. McClellan to command of all Union armies. Now Federal forces sought to push east across the mountains and into the Shenandoah Valley. A small Confederate detachment stood in their way, intent on preventing further Union encroachment into the Old Dominion. "If the Northern Secretary of War, or any other moon-struck Yankee expects that Virginia will surrender one acre, one foot, or one inch of her soil to any other power on the face of the earth," avowed a Richmond newspaper editor, "they labor under a delusion to which that of the most raving maniac of the lunatic asylums is the height of reason and moderation."[2] The rebels, who had known little but defeat in the western Virginia mountains in 1861, had drawn a line in the sand—or more accurately on the rocks—and that line lay across Allegheny Mountain.

Their commander was Colonel Edward Johnson, a forty-five-year-old West Pointer and commander of the 12th Georgia Infantry. The ranking officer in the region had recently transferred, leaving Johnson to assume responsibility. His "army" consisted of three small infantry regiments and two battalions—his own Georgians and the rest Virginia units—supplemented by a tiny contingent of cavalry and two artillery batteries boasting eight guns, numbering in all about 1,200 soldiers.[3] In mid-November, these Confederates abandoned their defensive positions in the valley west of the mountain, called Camp Bartow, and adopted a new fortified cantonment some Southerners named Camp Baldwin. "The mud was ankle-deep and cold and we could scarcely find our quarters, which were generally tents, but occasionally unfinished log-huts," complained one Confederate. "A bleak and disagreeable winter will we have here, after a hard and unfortunate campaign."[4] The boys from the 12th Georgia objected strenuously to their new abode. "It seemed unjust to place us," groused one man, "some of whom are from a climate, almost tropical, upon these bleak, snow-clad mountains, and send Virginia troops, whose homes are here ... into other portions of the service."[5] Such protests fell on deaf ears, however, and along with their comrades the Georgians completed snug log quarters with stone chimneys in the pastures on both sides of the turnpike, the south side of which was called Buffalo Ridge.

Their opponents occupied the next range, twenty road miles to the west, called Cheat Mountain. There, Federals commanded by Brigadier General Robert H. Milroy—"Gray Eagle," as he was known to his men— experienced similarly unpleasant conditions in their windswept camps. Ohio and Indiana troops composed Milroy's Cheat Mountain garrison. "It was a strange country," admitted the Hoosier soldier and future writer Ambrose Bierce. "Nine in ten of us had never seen a mountain, nor a hill as high as a church spire, until we had crossed the Ohio River.... To a member of a plains-tribe, born and reared on the flats of Ohio or Indiana, a mountain region was a perpetual miracle."[6]

Both the Federals and Confederates expected that the early advent of winter meant that they would be fighting a war against the elements rather than the enemy, at least until the spring. But when five

Confederate deserters entered Milroy's camp and reported that their comrades were demoralized, weak, and vulnerable, Gray Eagle saw his chance. He summoned some 1,900 soldiers to the crest of Cheat Mountain on December 11, 1861, to launch a surprise attack against Camp Allegheny. The force reached old Camp Bartow the next night, scattering a Confederate picket post, and Milroy issued his orders for the pending assault. He split his force into equal portions, sending the 9th Indiana and 2nd (West) Virginia under Colonel Gideon Moody to ascend the mountain to the right along the Greenbank Road, while he personally led the 25th Ohio, 32nd Ohio, and 13th Indiana via the turnpike. He hoped to attack both flanks of Johnson's position simultaneously, bringing to bear the elements of surprise and superior strength to overwhelm his opponents. He was so confident of success that seventy-five Indiana artillerists accompanied the expedition without their guns, expecting to capture the Confederate ordnance.[7]

The Federals began their ascent of some eight or nine miles near midnight. Both columns struggled against the steep and rocky terrain, and Moody's contingent encountered a sea of fallen timber that slowed progress in the dark to a crawl. When Milroy's portion of the army reached a point about one mile below the Confederate camp, the men left the turnpike and hiked up and across the mountain to gain the enemy's right and rear. Shortly after daylight a Confederate picket fired at the approaching figures, and the battle of Camp Allegheny was on.

Both Milroy's and Johnson's after-action reports described the ebb and flow of the battle north of the turnpike in great detail and in essential agreement.[8] The element of surprise vanished with the sound of that picket's musket, so the Federals quickly deployed into line of battle and advanced toward the Southern huts, scattering the small group of Virginians sent to meet them. The Confederates rallied, and when reinforced they counterattacked, driving the Yankees back into the sheltering forest on the outskirts of the camp. For three hours this pattern persisted, each side dashing against the other only to be repulsed and rallied. Colonel Johnson played a conspicuous role in the fighting. Dressed in a teamster's overcoat and brandishing "a stout bludgeon"—apparently a large oak branch or root—Johnson dashed among his troops and personally led them to the fray. Newspaper accounts reported that the colonel shouted "words of encouragement" or gave his commands "in the most emphatic manner," but an eyewitness quoted Johnson as advising his men to "Give 'em hell boys, give 'em hell!"[9]

While many of the Federals displayed the "steady coolness of veterans, and … bravery worthy of their glorious cause," Milroy lamented the numerous soldiers who left the field in panic and fear. "Too much execration cannot be poured upon the many base cowards who deserted the battle-field and left their brave companions, in violation of orders," he raged: "They should be remembered in eternal infamy." Probably more to the point, Milroy's men had run low on ammunition, and, despairing of any word from Moody, they gathered up most of their wounded and dead and retreated down the mountain.[10]

Just then the sound of gunfire erupted south of the turnpike on the Confederate left. Moody's Hoosiers and western Virginians—"a traitor regiment," in the opinion of one Confederate—arrived after their grueling march and an unscheduled stop at a cider mill. They managed to kill Captain Pierce B. Anderson, one of Johnson's battery commanders, who mistook the Federals for Confederate pickets and, standing on the parapet of

the works, fell while inviting the misidentified enemies to come in. The action here lacked the hand-to-hand drama of the earlier combat. Federals took cover in the thick woods and shot over the ramparts of the Confederate defenders, who returned their fire with spirit. Eventually Southern artillery made the Unionists' position exceedingly uncomfortable, and about 2 P.M. the bluecoats withdrew, ending the battle.[11]

Both sides greatly exaggerated the enemy's strength and casualties. Johnson estimated that he had bested 5,000 Federals, inflicting hundreds of casualties. Milroy numbered the Confederates at 2,500 and reported that he had killed 300 of them, including Colonel Johnson. Modern scholarship suggests that the Confederates lost 162 out of 1,200 engaged, while the Federals suffered 143 casualties out of about 1,800 on the field.[12] Johnson, quite alive, emerged as the hero of the battle. "We cannot be mistaken in saying that with one accord it is agreed that Col. Johnson bore himself throughout with distinguished gallantry," gushed a Virginia editor, "leading on his men in the thick of the fight, with a disregard of personal danger, which warmed the hearts and nerved the arms of all of his men." The Confederate Congress agreed, promoting Johnson to brigadier general to date from December 13, 1861. The press began to call him "Allegheny" Johnson, a moniker still familiar to modern students of the war.[13]

I have visited just about every Civil War battlefield between Picacho Peak, Arizona, and St. Albans, Vermont, and I believe none exceeds Camp Allegheny in what historic site managers call "integrity." With the exception of one empty stone dwelling on the fringe of the battlefield, Camp Allegheny is entirely devoid of twenty-first-century intrusions. The aforementioned Staunton-Parkersburg Turnpike still bisects the field of combat, no wider and arguably no more passable than it was in 1861. The fields where Milroy attacked, now owned by the U.S. Forest Service, remain fringed by the woods that sheltered the retreating Federals. Johnson's fortifications south of the turnpike, on property privately owned and accessible only by permission, are readily visible, including four distinct artillery lunettes that likely were not fully developed at the time of the battle.

Perhaps the most remarkable feature of this pristine site rests in neatly aligned piles of rocks—the remains of the stone chimneys used by the frozen Confederates in their log huts to ward off the elements that awful winter. The arrangement of these dwellings—the company streets—is easily discernible. Some of the hut sites retain their well-defined fireboxes that accommodated a comforting blaze. The footprints of the huts require no archaeologist's trowel—with just a little imagination it is quite easy to visualize this military village perched atop one of the most isolated landscapes of the Civil War.

Imagination. Everyone who visits a Civil War battle-field employs it with varying degrees of success. Guides paint word pictures, using the original language of the participants whenever possible. Sometimes photographs help erase the vicissitudes of time, although no images of wartime Camp Allegheny have been found. But the best witness to the war is always the landscape itself. This is the essence of our motivation to preserve Civil War sites—to let the ground tell its story to modern generations. The photograph preceding this essay captures the isolation of the camp juxtaposed against a background of ridges and valleys and shows the surviving groupings of rocks that define the company streets. It helps convey why contemporary terrain at no other place speaks more eloquently, at least to me, than at Camp Allegheny.

Visit there at any time of the year—even in the late spring or early fall it can be shockingly reminiscent of the brutal conditions endured by the soldiers in 1861 and 1862. Chances are almost certain that you will be alone. Listen to the incessant wind. Stand next to the preserved remains of a soldier's hut or along the earthworks where Captain Anderson fell, or on the crest of the mountain where Allegheny Johnson swung his war club. You may not see ghosts, but you will feel their presence.

NOTES

1. Hunter Lesser's *Rebels at the Gates* (Naperville, Ill.: Sourcebooks, 2004) is by far the best source on the 1861 campaigns in western Virginia, including the battle of Camp Allegheny, which is summarized on pp. 249–60. Confederate soldier quoted in the *Richmond Daily Dispatch*, November 30, 1861; Martin Fleming, "The Northwestern Virginia Campaign of 1861," *Blue and Gray Magazine* 10 (August 1993): 63. Most of the participants spelled the mountain "Alleghany," although the version used in the text is now preferred.

2. *Richmond Daily Dispatch*, December 13, 1861.

3. U.S. War Department, *The War of the Rebellion: A Compilation of the Official Records of the Union and Confederate Armies*, 127 vols., index, and atlas (Washington, D.C.: Government Printing Office, 1880–1901), ser. 1, vol. 5, 460 (hereafter cited as *OR*; all references are to ser. 1); Lesser, *Rebels at the Gates*, 254. Johnson's force included the 12th Georgia, the 31st Virginia, Major Albert Reger's battalion, the 9th Virginia Battalion, Pierce Anderson's Lee Battery, John Miller's Second Rockbridge Artillery, and a small company of Lieutenant C. E. Dabney's Pittsylvania Cavalry.

4. Soldier quoted in the *Richmond Daily Dispatch*, November 30, 1861. Camp Baldwin referred to Colonel John B. Baldwin of the 52nd Virginia and a respected state politician. Lesser, *Rebels at the Gates*, 348n579.

5. Quoted in Lesser, *Rebels at the Gates*, 248.

6. Ambrose Bierce, *Ambrose Bierce's Civil War*, ed. William McCann (Washington, D.C.: Regnery Gateway, 1956), 4.

A. WILSON GREENE

34

7. Milroy's after-action report in *OR*, 51 (1): 51–54, outlines the composition of his force, his battle plan, and the march to Camp Allegheny.

8. Milroy's report is cited above. Johnson wrote several reports that may be found in *OR*, 5:460–64.

9. *Richmond Daily Dispatch*, December 17 and 23, 1861; Private John Henry Cammack, *Personal Recollections of Private John Henry Cammack: A Soldier of the Confederacy, 1861–1865* (Huntington, W.Va.: Paragon Printing and Publishing, 1920), 42.

10. *OR*, 51 (1): 54.

11. *Richmond Daily Dispatch* December 18 and 23, 1861; *OR*, 5:463; Cammack, *Personal Recollections*, 42–43.

12. *OR*, 5:457, 459–64, 51 (1): 51–54; Lesser, *Rebels at the Gates*, 350n607.

13. *Staunton (Va.) Spectator and General Advertiser*, December 17, 1861; *OR*, 5:464–65.

5 BRIDGE TO THE PAST

CAROLINE E. JANNEY

There is a Civil War photograph that has hung in a prominent place for me since I was in high school. I took it to college with me. It moved with me to the first home my husband and I shared while I attended graduate school. And now, it hangs in my office at the University of Virginia.

The photograph is not a wartime image of a military leader or a ravaged landscape. Nor is it the work of a professional photographer. Instead, it is an image I took of Burnside's Bridge at Antietam twenty-five years ago. Shot with my first, humble 35mm camera and subsequently framed (again, by me), I have carted that photograph everywhere. In doing so, Burnside's Bridge has become more than an iconic Civil War image, more than one of the great landmarks on the battlefield. For me, it has come to represent the very meaning of memory—the way it ebbs and flows, changes with the times, and is intensely attached to place.

The Rohrbach Bridge, or Lower Bridge, was one of three limestone bridges traversing Antietam Creek on what became the bloodiest one-day battlefield of the Civil War on September 17, 1862. Constructed in 1836 by John Weaver, the triple-arched structure spanned 125 feet, offering a connection between Sharpsburg to the west and Rohrersville to the east. On the morning of September 17, Major General Ambrose E. Burnside placed the Ninth Corps' four divisions, which included nearly 12,500 men and fifty artillery pieces, alongside the hills overlooking the east bank of Antietam Creek near the approach to the Rohrbach Bridge. In the fighting that followed, the meaning of the bridge, as well as its name, would be forever altered.[1]

Burnside and Brigadier General Jacob D. Cox, who had direct command of the Ninth Corps but reported to Burnside under an earlier system of wing commands,

Burnside's Bridge, Antietam battlefield, Maryland
(Photograph by Will Gallagher)

must have recognized the difficult odds they faced. Opposite them, on a steep wooded bluff overlooking the stone bridge, 400 men of the 2nd and 20th Georgia under the command of Colonel Henry L. Benning had entrenched in rifle pits behind a stone wall. Downstream, the 50th Georgia along with a company of South Carolinians, in all 120 men, covered the approach to the bridge. On the higher ground behind them, three batteries with a dozen guns offered support, as did two more batteries from the plateau near Sharpsburg known as Cemetery Hill.[2]

Though few in number, the Confederates enjoyed a tremendous advantage. Not only did they have the benefit of elevation, but the layout of the Sharpsburg-Rohrersville Road on the east side of the bridge was also in their favor: just before reaching the creek, the road dipped down before turning at a sharp angle, creating a bottleneck at the bridge crossing. Even though they vastly outnumbered their Confederate counterparts, the narrow passage severely limited the strength of the Federal forces. Yet neither Burnside nor Cox had bothered to reconnoiter the creek or make an attempt to locate the ford discovered two-thirds of a mile downstream the previous day by Major General George B. McClellan's engineers.[3]

For a good part of the morning, the Ninth Corps waited for orders as the battle raged to the north. Finally, around 10 A.M. one of McClellan's aides arrived with instructions to attack. Under heavy fire, the 11th Connecticut attempted to clear the bridge. The results were disastrous; in less than fifteen minutes the regiment lost 139 men, nearly a third of its strength. Throughout the morning and afternoon, Burnside and Cox continued to assault the bridge, the 2nd Maryland suffering casualties of 44 percent in the second charge. Finally, around 12:30, the Ninth Corps launched its breakthrough attack. Supported by artillery, New Yorkers and Pennsylvanians from Samuel D. Sturgis's division stormed straight down the hill toward the bridge under an enfilading fire.[4]

Above them, the Georgians had been fending off the repeated assaults for nearly three hours. And they were running low on ammunition. As the New Yorkers continued to shoot up at them under cover of fence rails, and the Pennsylvanians did likewise from the protection of a stone wall that ran along the creek bank, fire from the Georgians waned. In twos and threes, the Georgians began to flee their positions, heading back up the steep bluff. Soon, the Federals poured across the bridge, and Benning called for his men to withdraw. By 1 P.M. Burnside had captured the bridge, but not without the loss of 500 of his own men and 120 Confederates. Yet it would take two more hours before the Ninth Corps could organize for the final assault on the Confederate right, a delay that allowed reinforcements under Major General A. P. Hill to arrive from Harpers Ferry. Slamming into the Federal flank, Hill's men saved Lee's army.[5]

I stood on the western bank of the creek 130 years later to take my photograph from the same vantage point as that which accompanies this essay. That June, my grandparents Roby and Marion Janney offered to take me and my cousin on a spur-of-the-moment trip to Antietam—a short two-hour drive. Pops, as I called him, had always been an avid reader about the Civil War, perhaps because he grew up hearing stories about it as did so many Southern children. But more likely he was drawn to the war because he was a soldier, a veteran of World War II who served in the 4th Marine Division and saw action at Saipan, Tinian, and Iwo Jima. He never—not once—talked to me about his wartime experiences, but he did share his passion for the Civil War with me. On the shelves that lined my grandparents' home, I would admire his countless books on the war—those by Douglas Southall Freeman, Bruce Catton, Shelby Foote, and others. When I was about eight years old, he and my grandmother took me to Gettysburg for the first time. There, he walked the fields by himself while Grandma and I toured the visitor center and Cyclorama. I never quite understood as a child why he preferred the solitude of the field. What was he thinking about out there all alone? Though now, I can speculate on where his thoughts might have taken him.

Our visit to Antietam in the summer of 1992 proved a short one, with Grandma still recovering from one of the many surgeries to treat her rheumatoid arthritis. We stopped first at the visitors' center, where my ever-tight Pops (a child of the Great Depression) was delighted to learn he would have to pay nothing: he and Grandma qualified for a free senior admission, while my cousin and I were under sixteen and therefore likewise free. Having saved a pretty penny, he allowed us to purchase something from the gift shop. My selection: an interesting-looking novel titled *The Killer Angels*. (All these years later I still have that copy, yellowed, dog-eared, and just a bit tattered.) With Grandma unable to walk more than short distances, we headed back to the car and proceeded to the Bloody Lane, where we had time to walk the sunken pathway and climb the tower. Our next stop: the Lower Bridge. With summer in full bloom, I could not resist climbing down the hill and taking a picture of the stone bridge surrounded by tall purple wildflowers.

I knew relatively little about what happened at that particular spot, of who the regiments were on either side of the creek, or why the bridge proved important during the battle. But the place—the bridge—spoke

to me. I found in it something compelling enough to warrant scrambling down the hillside toward the slow-moving water to snap a picture. Once home, I had the photograph enlarged to an 8 x 10 and framed it with a violet mat to draw out the wildflowers in the foreground.

To this day, whenever I think about Antietam, my mind turns first to Burnside's Bridge. As someone who has spent a great deal of time thinking and writing about memory, I am conscious that the meanings I have attached to the bridge—and by extension to the photograph—have changed over time, that they have become piled up, one on top of another, each adding a new significance and altering the way in which I relate to the place.

I am, of course, immediately reminded of my grandfather. I can recall that entire trip. (Including our brief foray into Harpers Ferry. Pops refused to pay to park and take the shuttle into town, so when he couldn't find a parking spot, he simply drove through and said, "Well, kids, that was Harpers Ferry." Thankfully my parents took me and my brothers back for an extended visit.) But there are other memories layered on top of that trip. I recall, for example, that the fall after our visit I chose the battle of Antietam as a topic for my junior history class project. Using the Time-Life series on the war as well as other photographs I took during the visit, I drew maps of the battle's three phases and prepared a lengthy talk that must have bored my classmates to tears.

The bridge brings still other recollections. My first time on a battlefield with Gary W. Gallagher was at Antietam. It was on this class visit that I truly started to understand what had unfolded along the banks of that meandering stream and where I realized with certainty that I wanted my graduate career to focus more specifically on the war. And in the summer of 2012, as a first-time faculty member at Gettysburg College's Civil War Institute, I stood at the overlook and watched as Mark Grimsley waded shoulder-deep in the creek in an effort to demonstrate why it could not be easily forded during the battle. Now when I teach, I relate this story to my students, passing along one of my personal experiences as part of the larger narrative of what happened there— in 1862 and 2012.

As I reflect on the way in which this place has continued to change meaning for me, I can't help but consider how the same must have been true for the men who fought there. The bridge surely evoked some mixture of determination and angst from the men of the 11th Connecticut as they stormed it in 1862. But how did the survivors experience the place when they returned to dedicate their regimental monument on October 8, 1894? Some must have paused to think of those no longer with them, those who had fallen along the banks of the Antietam or on another bloody field. Equally as important, more than thirty years later, the survivors had a better grasp of what had been happening elsewhere on the field in 1862— something they could not have comprehended during the battle. But they also knew that their cause had triumphed, that in taking the bridge, they had helped ensure that the battle was not a defeat for the Army of the Potomac. Because of their valiant efforts, in the days that followed Lincoln had been able to issue the preliminary Emancipation Proclamation, forever linking the battle to this profound new addition to the Union cause. Consciously or unconsciously, many must have understood their role as part of something bigger, something unthinkable on September 17, 1862. Moreover, when they subsequently told their children and grandchildren about this place, they could add stories of the dedication, of the reunion with their former comrades.[6] Memories layered upon memories. Memories evoked by a sense of place.

Yet it is not only the memories that have evolved. Soon after the battle, the bridge shed its old name for that of "Burnside's." But it also physically changed. In 1898, it became part of the memorial landscape when veterans of the 21st and 35th Massachusetts placed their regimental markers on its corners. Even with these visible reminders of the past, the bridge retained its primary purpose: automobiles continued to travel across it until the mid-1960s, when the National Park Service embarked on a plan to remove all but tour traffic from the battlefield. With through traffic rerouted to a northern bypass, the NPS restored the bridge to its 1862 condition by stripping it of asphalt and moving the regimental markers to the eastern bank. On the south hill overlooking the bridge, the Park Service added an overlook.[7] Rather than a thoroughfare or an insurmountable obstacle to be taken during battle, the bridge would be a focal point, a memorial unto itself.

If memory and place become only more intertwined over time, then writing this piece has added another layer, another way in which the bridge has taken on new meaning for me—both professionally and personally. I could only smile when I picked up what is now my copy of Stephen W. Sears's *Landscape Turned Red* for this essay and found my grandfather's initials and date on the inside cover, the way in which he always marked the books he read (a habit I learned from him and continue to this day). He read it in August 1987. But he finished reading it for a second time on June 14, 1992, the precise day we took what I had always thought was an impromptu trip to the field. Now I know better. My interpretation of that trip has been altered, filtered through this new information. Having read the book again, he wanted to walk the field. To the see the place.

To feel it. Thank you, Pops, for passing that same yearning, that same enchantment with this place, along to me.

NOTES

1. Stephen W. Sears, *Landscape Turned Red: The Battle of Antietam* (New York: Ticknor and Fields, 1983), 169, 260; Dennis E. Frye, *Antietam Revealed: The Battle of Antietam and the Maryland Campaign as You Have Never Seen It Before* (Collingswood, N.J.: C. W. Historicals, 2004), 115; D. Scott Hartwig, *To Antietam Creek: The Maryland Campaign of September 1862* (Baltimore: Johns Hopkins University Press, 2012), 484; Helen Ashe Hays, *The Antietam and Its Bridges: The Annals of an Historic Stream* (New York: G. P. Putnam's Sons, 1910), 3, 78; Antietam Battlefield—Burnside Bridge, National Park Service website, https://www.nps.gov/places/antietam -battlefield-burnside-bridge.htm (accessed August 28, 2017). There is a fourth bridge, the Antietam Iron Works Bridge, three miles downstream from the Lower Bridge, but it did not witness any action during the battle.

2. Sears, *Landscape Turned Red*, 171, 235, 258–61; Ronald H. Bailey et al., *The Bloodiest Day: The Battle of Antietam* (Alexandria, Va.: Time-Life Books, 1984), 120–21.

3. Sears, *Landscape Turned Red*, 259–61.

4. Sears, *Landscape Turned Red*, 265.

5. Sears, *Landscape Turned Red*, 267.

6. "Monuments Erected by the Veterans of Connecticut," *New York Times*, October 7, 1894; "Antietam Monuments," *National Tribune*, October 25, 1894.

7. Antietam National Battlefield, National Park Service website, https://www.nps.gov/anti/learn/historyculture/mnt -pa-51st-inf-2.htm (accessed August 28, 2017); *Daily Mail* (Hagerstown, Md.), April 9 and October 25, 1963, May 12, 1965, October 23, 1966. The 51st Pennsylvania added a memorial to the bridge in 1906.

6 AN UNKNOWN GRAVE

PETER S. CARMICHAEL

The ground was frozen, the trees were barren, and there was not a visitor in sight on Culp's Hill. I stood behind the 2nd Maryland Confederate monument with former National Park Service historian Scott Hartwig, who knows the ground of Gettysburg as well as anyone. He asked me if I had ever seen the remains of a Confederate burial trench just behind the Maryland monument. I had no idea of its existence, as I had always assumed that the thousands of individual burial pits across the battlefield had faded away over time because of the forces of Mother Nature or the work of a farmer's plow.

Scott headed into the woods but we did not go far, stopping at the edge of the tree line where he pointed behind some boulders to the faint remains of an oval-shaped depression some ten feet long and no more than six feet wide. At that moment, while I stared into the shallow grave, Gettysburg felt like a battlefield for the first time and not a commemorative shrine. The physical isolation of the burial trench intensified the feeling of having a piece of the battlefield all to one's self. This spot was nothing like the tourist meccas at Little Round Top and the High-Water Mark, where people buzz around on Segways or speed down park roads in miniature scoot coupes. At Culp's Hill, where visitation is always light, there were no modern distractions, nor even a National Park Service marker noting the location of the burial spot. It was just the grave and nothing else. I stared at the slight depression, and it felt like a portal into the past where history is imagined and felt.

The well-known Alexander Gardner photograph of three South Carolinians readied for burial near the Rose Farm immediately came to mind. I transposed the image to fit the slight depression before me. I could

Confederate burial site on Culp's Hill, Gettysburg battlefield, Pennsylvania (Photograph by Will Gallagher)

see the three corpses perfectly aligned, all slightly tilted on their right sides, fitting together as if they were puzzle pieces—all three were striking a macabre pose, with their left arms slightly raised and locked in place by rigor mortis. Their bloated bodies were nearly bursting through their sack coats and trousers, which days before had been baggy and loose-fitting. Under the makeshift headboards were the initials of the fallen, etched by survivors who in the midst of a battle tried to give their comrades a decent burial. Despite their best efforts, as Gardner's photograph reveals, the living could not perform the respected rituals of death. There was no coffin or makeshift box, army blankets were turned into shrouds, and there was no minister to offer a final prayer over the grave.

The pit before me, like Gardner's photograph, conveyed the anonymous nature of death in the Civil War. Whether the Confederates buried in the slight depression before me were ever identified is impossible to say, but for nine years following the battle they remained in this shallow grave, neglected and nearly forgotten as were the thousands of other slain Confederates resting in scattered trenches across the battlefield. In 1871, the Southern women of the Ladies Memorial Association contracted Dr. Rufus Weaver to begin the process of disinterring the dead, which was an overwhelming operation given that local farmers understandably did not tend to the graves that had, as a result, largely fallen into disrepair. Few markers likely stood when Weaver began his grisly work, but his father, Samuel, had taken copious notes on the location of the graves when he had moved the Union dead to the National Cemetery during the spring months of 1864. The records were invaluable to Rufus, who also used his connections in the Gettysburg community to identify the burial pits of Southern soldiers. I wondered what Rufus and the team of African American laborers had discovered at Culp's Hill. Did they find partial skeletons protruding from the ground, or were the bones scattered and in disarray from the plow of an indifferent farmer eager to clear his fields? Maybe they found some personal effects like a Bible or a diary or a button, possibly a buckle or the leathery remnants of some brogans.

The detritus of death was long gone, but my wonderment about the macabre proved irresistible, even though I had long criticized tourists for their morbid curiosity. I expected my tour groups to ask questions about why soldiers fought or thought that they might consider the impact of the battle on the survivors. Instead, people seemed to care only if there were still bodies or relics under the sod of Gettysburg. I am sure I did not always do a very good job of hiding my frustration, even though I knew that the impulse to find relics had a long history that hearkened back to the first wave of Gettysburg visitors who scoured the battlefield for knapsacks, canteens, letters, cartes de visite, broken bayonets, bullets, shell fragments, musket parts, pieces of clothing, and cartridges. These things of war, made sacred by the shedding of blood, were not only treasured as mementos for relic hunters but also hawked for profit. The first battlefield visitors did not give much thought to whether pillaging the battlefield and scavenging from the dead were morally questionable, and the passage of time has not dulled the desire of Americans wanting a physical link to the past. But any temptation to bring a piece of the battlefield home runs up against the National Park Service, which vigorously prosecutes anyone who disturbs the historical landscape. Regulations, however, cannot contain the imagination of visitors who dream of what it would be like to "eyeball" a relic, to pick it up and put in it in their hands, to run their fingers along the jagged edges of a shell fragment, or to feel the smooth surface of a lead minié ball.

The year after Scott showed me the burial trench, I accepted a position at the Civil War Institute at Gettysburg College, and one of the most attractive aspects of this new position was having the battlefield as a teaching resource. I immediately thought about the burial trench as an outdoor classroom, but I would need to tame the inner pedant in me if I were to tap its potential. No one needed me to lecture that deep historical understanding comes from research and knowing historiography and that the urge to dig up stuff is puerile and contemptible from a preservationist and scholarly perspective. And yet I could not allow myself to forget how I felt when Scott took me to that inconspicuous pit on Culp's Hill. My imagination had taken over, just as it did during my first visit to Gettysburg when I was nine years old, when thinking about the past did not call for historiographical fluency or require that one make an original argument. It was a time when exploring the past possessed an element of escapism, but the idea of leading my students to this unassuming spot and encouraging them to let their imaginations roam free was unsettling to me. I have never believed that historical landscapes can speak for themselves. Battlefield visitors need public historians to help them unlock the historical significance and emotional power of any cultural landscape. I needed to find a way of preserving the evocative nature of this obscure spot while also helping my students see the importance of asking big questions about small places, even the sites that seem no larger than postage stamps hidden on a remote corner of the Gettysburg battlefield.

Turning this site into a classroom would not be easy. What kinds of questions could I possibly ask of such a small piece of the battlefield that lacked any kind of visual or written documentation? It was impossible to determine who was buried in the pit. I did not have a single clue about the disinterment and reinterment of the bodies. Because of the heavy fighting in that area on July 2 and 3, I could not even speculate about which regiments the fallen might have belonged to. With so little site-specific evidence, I worried that there was little I could say about this obscure place until I read George Lipsitz's analysis of Willa Cather's *My Antonia*, in which he explains how a cultural landscape, even when only a vestige remains, offers a pinhole through which we can see larger historical processes at work. Lipsitz focuses on the novel's narrator, Jim Burden, who returned to Nebraska after years of being in New York City. The countryside seemed almost foreign to him upon his arrival. As he was surveying it, he struggled to find the old wagon road that had carried him and his childhood friend Antonia from the train depot into the vastness of the Plains. Wherever he looked, all Burden could see was a carpet of tall grass until he walked into a swale between two ridgelines. There the old road trace suddenly appeared before him. Over time, the rain had deepened the wheel cuts left by teams of muscular workhorses pulling wagons up the steep incline. Burden could not imagine that a stranger would have even noticed these gashes in the landscape, but to him the ruts unleashed a torrent of childhood memories that transported him back in time. He could still hear the rumbling sounds of the wagons and feel the physical presence of Antonia when they were children, lying together on a bed of hay, looking at an expansive sky, and wondering what the future might hold. That road would ultimately take Burden away from Antonia, but its physical remnants made history reachable to him as an adult. When he looked at that small fragment of a road trace, he not only reconnected with his own personal history but also discovered how his life had been enveloped by larger historical forces that had forever changed the world that he had left behind for New York City.[1]

After putting down Lipsitz's article, I realized that this slight depression in the ground possessed a range of stories I could recreate for my students. In fact, the anonymity of death that hung over the shallow pit at Culp's Hill was not a constraint as I had imagined. Instead, the site told many stories, even though I could not determine what exactly had happened on that ground with any degree of certitude. I was straying from what I had learned throughout my National Park Service career, which had spanned a little more than a decade, from the mid-1980s to the late 1990s. I had never left a training session without receiving a lecture about the importance of being site-specific during battlefield tours. Referencing anything that the visitors could not see right before their eyes violated the cardinal rule of interpretation. But adherence to this principle over the years had become the defensive posture of some historians to argue that the battlefields were made only for traditional tactical history. Some interpreters even insisted that any story that did not connect the troops to the immediate surroundings violated the memory and sacrifices of the men who had fallen there.

Such spurious logic has lost its hold on most interpreters, who see battlefields as places to explore the lives of citizen-soldiers who were deeply ideological and politically engaged and whose lives were inextricably linked to the civilian households that sent them off to war. The trace of the burial pit, I realized, offered a diverse range of stories that I could tell that enhanced the military narrative of the battle by showing the reverberations of organized killing. I needed a story that could be centered on the burial pit but could also go beyond the site without cutting off my audiences from the battle itself. The experiences at Culp's Hill of John and Charlie Futch, two brothers serving in the 3rd North Carolina Infantry, opened up important inquiries that possessed incredible interpretive power. Not far from the pit, the Futch brothers found themselves loading and firing their weapons during the late afternoon attack of July 2. A Union bullet sliced the top of Charlie's head but did not penetrate it, and when John looked at his brother, Charlie's mouth was moving, as he was desperate to speak, but no words came out. John must have known that the wound was fatal. He left the ranks, carrying his brother to the rear, and for the rest of the night he never left his sibling's side until Charlie died early the next morning. A distraught John dug a grave for his brother, knowing that he would never see him again. As I tell my students this story, I have them look at the burial pit before us, asking them to imagine the intense emotional suffering that the survivors must have felt when they laid their comrades to rest while the shedding of blood had made sacred the political cause for which they fought.

The loss of his brother left John Futch convulsed in despair, and his letters after Gettysburg are truly exceptional, especially given that Futch was illiterate and dictated his thoughts to comrades who themselves could barely read or write. While we are standing around the gravesite, I have my students read transcriptions of his letters, including a July 19 letter written from Virginia in which John expressed himself with astonishing openness to his comrade:

Charly got kild and he suffered graideal from his wound he lived a night and a day after he was

PETER S. CARMICHAEL

wounded we sead hard times thare but we got a nugh to eat ther but we dont now as to my self I get a nugh for I dont want nothing to eat hardly for I am all must sick all the time and half crazy I never wanted to come home so bad in my life. but it is so that I cant come at this time but if we come down south I will try to come any how for I want to come home so bad that I am home sick I want you to kep Charlys pistol and if I ever git it back I will keep it.[2]

When reading this passage, students enter the private world of a soldier who was trapped in the throes of a deep depression, and the emotional openness of John's words, written down by a comrade as they were spoken, help students appreciate how the experience of combat could forge emotionally intense bonds among comrades. Students typically conclude that John was reeling from his brother's death and that he suffered from extreme homesickness. I ask them if this letter should be seen as a political document. Almost always they say no, that Futch was weary and traumatized and nothing more. I then relate to them that at the end of August, Futch and at least ten other men deserted their camps near James Madison's Montpelier, carrying their muskets and loading up with ammunition before heading off into the woods with the intent of reaching North Carolina. Less than three days after fleeing, a Confederate patrol intercepted Futch and his fellow runaways near the James River, where a gun battle erupted and the arresting officer was killed before Futch and his comrades were captured. The following week, they were tried and convicted of desertion and killing a Confederate officer, and if the verdict was read out loud, it is hard to imagine that anyone was shocked when Futch and his comrades were condemned to execution by musketry.

Students have an opportunity to rethink how the private sides of historical actors can nurture political thought and even radical action, as in the case of Futch. I also remind them to look around the burial pit, to take in the area around Culp's Hill, and to recreate in their minds a scene of unrelenting terror that lasted for more than five hours. No other part of the Gettysburg battlefield witnessed such sustained fighting, and the men who survived this ordeal were the same soldiers who stood in a hollow square two months later and witnessed Futch and his fellow deserters shot down by firing squads that totaled more than 100 soldiers. I ask my students again to look at the pit, to think about the violence that engulfed this hillside and how its reverberations were felt beyond Lee's army. What about Futch's wife, an impoverished woman living with a child and having to manage a household without slaves? While she was in mourning, Confederate papers denounced her slain husband as a criminal, a man without honor who had brought eternal shame to the family because he had abandoned his army. The students read newspaper accounts of Futch's execution, and I remind them that the silences in public condemnations of deserters are as important as what is stated—that the editors never mention the suffering of Futch's family, that his brother had died in his arms at Gettysburg, that he had a solid combat record, that he was sick after the battle, and that, above all else, he had endured the hellish fight at Culp's Hill.

I ask the students to look at the pit for a final time to remind them that even though we have no idea who occupied this grave, we must use our historical imagination or we lose touch with lower-class soldiers like Futch, who were embedded in a world that was not of their making, and that the violence on Culp's Hill unleashed forces that were difficult for the survivors to communicate in the wake of the fierce fighting. One can feel the tragedy of war while standing at the pit and reading Futch's words just as he spoke them to a comrade. I want my students to feel empathy for Futch—a risky proposition, given that he was wearing the uniform of Confederate gray—but to my relief, students want to understand people in the past from a historical perspective, even though they find the Confederate cause to be reprehensible.

Asking my students to understand the perspectives of others has faced a relatively new test at the burial pit at Culp's Hill. Since 2013, as Will Gallagher's photograph indicates, some visitors have planted Confederate flags around the brim of the grave. I could barely contain my disappointment when I encountered this shrine. I considered this a violation of the battlefield as a historical space, and I resented the display of flags for infusing the politics of so-called heritage groups into a place that was untainted by the cultural wars of today. Yet if I succumbed to my outrage I would miss an opportunity for my students to consider issues of historical memory and to discuss the complicated reasons why even today some people feel compelled to pay tribute to the Confederate cause. In talking not just

to my students at this site but also to teachers and other educational groups, I have listened to an assortment of reactions and explanations as to why some people continue to venerate soldiers who died for a slaveholding regime. The conversations seek understanding rather than the reflexive answers that have become popular on the Far Right and Left during heated confrontations regarding Confederate monuments. The sight of the grave reminds everyone that even a small fragment of the historical landscape possesses the power to communicate the experiences of a diverse group of historical actors and that our attempts to understand them should be a humbling experience when there is always so much more to know and when the evidence we encounter—like the burial pit at Culp's Hill—is partial, ephemeral, and barely discernible.

NOTES

1. George Lipsitz, "Cultural Theory, Dialogue, and American Cultural History," in *A Companion to American Cultural History*, ed. Karen Halttunen (Malden, Mass.: Blackwell, 2008), 265–66.

2. John Futch to Martha Futch, July 19, 1863, Futch Family Papers, North Carolina Office of Archives and History, Raleigh.

ARI KELMAN

Help Respect Sacred Ground

Please, Stay on this Side of the Fence

Will Gallagher's haunting photograph captures some of the most salient features that I have experienced through the years while visiting the Sand Creek Massacre National Historic Site. The texture of the vegetation, sharp sedges and the occasional stunted tree, punctuates the scene. The prairie landscape, flat for miles and miles around, rises suddenly as it nears the dry creek bed; then it breaks, becoming in the middle distance a storm-tossed wave of grass and dirt. The vastness of the Western sky, clear except for a small squadron of scudding clouds, looms above, stretching to the distant horizon. But the most striking part of the composition stands in the foreground, capturing and then orienting the viewer's gaze: a rough-hewn, split-rail fence upon which the National Park Service has posted entreaties. Gallagher's visual rhetoric, his choice to frame the words "Help Respect Sacred Ground" and "Please, Stay on this Side of the Fence," alludes to some of the uncertain boundaries—between public and private spaces, between Native nations and an American empire that exploded westward in the mid-nineteenth century, between history and memory, between the past and the present, and between the Indian Wars and the United States Civil War—that have characterized my understanding of the Sand Creek story.

Before dawn on November 29, 1864, approximately 700 volunteer soldiers from the 1st and 3rd Colorado Regiments descended upon perhaps a thousand Arapaho and Cheyenne people gathered in a village along the banks of Sand Creek. Some of the Native Americans, their ponies startled by the noise of approaching soldiers, initially hoped that a herd

(previous page)
Sand Creek battlefield, Colorado
(Photograph by Will Gallagher)

of bison had thundered past. By the time they realized their mistake, troops had opened fire on the encampment. Panicked Arapahos and Cheyennes fled for their lives, and the ensuing engagement covered more than ten miles of mostly open ground. As the day wore on, some of the Native people, desperate to escape the onslaught, dug pits in the sandy soil. These makeshift trenches provided scant shelter from artillery, mountain howitzers that rained down shot from positions at the Federal rear. The assault lasted until evening; soldiers ran roughshod, firing indiscriminately. When darkness finally descended upon the killing field, some 200 Arapahos and Cheyennes lay dead, the vast majority of whom were women, children, and the elderly.[1]

In a series of dispatches dashed off after the slaughter, Colonel John M. Chivington, commander of the troops at Sand Creek, justified the violence by claiming that it had clarified a murky boundary between civilization and savagery in Colorado. In the run-up to the massacre, Chivington had whipped his troops into a righteous fury. He pointed back to depredations committed by Native people the previous spring and summer. He insisted that warriors in the Sand Creek camp were culpable in those attacks, including the murder, on June 11, 1864, of the Hungate family. Following that tragedy, neighbors hauled the Hungates' remains to Denver, where their mangled corpses waited in public, equal parts memorial and incitement to revenge. Over the course of the next few months, Colorado's governor, John Evans, redoubled efforts to persuade the War Department to fund a regiment of Indian fighters. A vast confederation made up "of several thousand warriors," Evans warned, stood poised "to sweep off our settlers." Federal authorities responded to this ostensibly existential threat by

allowing Evans to raise the 3rd Colorado. After Sand Creek, Chivington noted that his men had found the scalps of several white people in the Indian village. He boasted that his troops had imposed order on chaos, retaliating for past wrongs by effecting "almost an entire annihilation" of the Arapaho and Cheyenne people.[2]

One of the ways that Chivington painted bright lines between the decency of Western settlers, including the citizen-soldiers who served under him, and the bloodthirstiness of the indigenous people they attacked was by muddying the boundary between the Civil War and the Indian Wars. For Chivington, a Methodist elder, abolitionist, loyal Republican, regional booster, and fierce nationalist, ideological commitments combined to form a sacred duty: to fight for the Union and against Indians. Chivington also understood the rhetorical power of the context in which the conflicts between North and South and settlers and Native peoples took place. As a result, he took great care after Sand Creek to place the violence against the backdrop of the Confederate rebellion. He pointed back to the Dakota War in Minnesota and to the Cherokees' decision to fight with the Confederacy, suggesting that the Arapahos and Cheyennes were part of a pan-Indian conspiracy against the United States. Rebel agents, he claimed, had inflamed Colorado's tribal peoples, casting the Civil War as an opportunity to stem the tide of westward expansion. In this way, liberty and empire became inextricable for Chivington, and indigenous peoples became enemies not only of a settler-colonial project but also of the Union.[3]

From the first, critics questioned Chivington's version of events, suggesting that he had inflated the heroics of his men, ignored the rules governing legitimate combat, and, in the end, sundered the norms upon which a just society rested—that, in other words, rather than policing the boundaries between civilization and savagery, Chivington had erased them. Silas Soule, a captain in the 1st Colorado Regiment, refused to commit his company to the fight at Sand Creek; he chose instead to absent his men from the bloodletting. Soule later insisted that what Chivington labeled a heroic battle had actually been a "massacre [of] friendly Indians," which, because of its perfidy, had tarnished the fight to preserve the Union. Months afterward, Soule testified before federal investigators. He recalled that, in September 1864, Black Kettle had led a delegation of Arapaho and Cheyenne peace chiefs to Denver, where they met with Governor Evans and Colonel Chivington. The Native leaders hoped to defuse tensions in Colorado. But Evans said that he had no role to play in the discussion, because violence in the territory had spun so far out of control. He demurred and then turned negotiations over to military authorities, including Chivington. Soule reported that Chivington had suggested that Black Kettle should return to southeastern Colorado, where his people would be under the protection of the United States flag.[4]

From Soule's perspective, not only had Chivington dishonored his uniform by breaking the compact he had struck with Black Kettle, but the colonel had also sullied the good name of Colorado soldiers by using that agreement as a road map to the Sand Creek camp, perpetrating atrocities once he arrived there. Black Kettle and his followers, Soule explained, had complied with Chivington's directive after the Denver meeting. Confident that they had forged a truce with white officials, they rode southeast, camping on familiar ground near Sand Creek. Chivington's forces swept down upon them on November 29, 1864, visiting unspeakable cruelties on the Arapahos and Cheyennes. The Colorado volunteers engaged in the wholesale slaughter of Native American women and children and then, after the fighting concluded, took grim trophies— scalps, fingers, and genitalia—from the blood-soaked ground to commemorate their victory. Soule later wrote to one of his former commanders that "you would think it impossible for white men to butcher and mutilate human beings as they did there." That Colorado soldiers had so debased themselves left Soule struggling to make sense of racial hierarchies that no longer seemed immutable.[5]

George Bent, a Cheyenne survivor of Sand Creek, later echoed Soule's memories of the massacre. Worried that conversations about the West's past and future remained segregated, that they rarely featured Native voices, around the turn of the twentieth century Bent collaborated with a trio of scholars—James Mooney, a renowned Smithsonian ethnographer; George Bird Grinnell, a founder of the field of professional anthropology; and George Hyde, a relatively obscure historian—who promised to help him preserve Cheyenne lore. First in articles and then in a memoir, Bent recounted particulars of Chivington's double-dealing and the carnage that ensued. Chivington, in Bent's view, had crossed the border between good and evil when he betrayed the peace chiefs. On the morning of the attack, Bent wrote, Black Kettle had flown a white flag and an American flag over his lodge, signaling to the onrushing soldiers that they were attacking a peace camp. Chivington ignored both the flag of his country and the flag of surrender. His men ran unfettered among the Arapahos and Cheyennes. They killed pregnant women and elderly chiefs who had worked their whole lives for peace. Chivington thus destroyed any chance for amicable relations between Colorado's settlers and Native peoples, Bent suggested. Rivers of blood would snake across the Plains from

Sand Creek, exacerbating the problem Chivington claimed he had solved. For decades to come, violence would slow the march of westward expansion.[6]

On only one point did Bent agree with Chivington: the massacre represented a key chapter in the history of the Civil War. Early in the fighting, Bent served in the 1st Missouri Cavalry. In the summer of 1862, Union soldiers captured and then paroled him, at which point he returned to his Cheyenne family in Colorado. Although Bent later granted that he had fought with the South, he rejected Chivington's claim that he had served as a rebel agent, a fifth column among the West's Native peoples. Bent also mocked the idea that the Arapahos and Cheyennes were in league with the Confederacy, though he acknowledged that those tribes had at best attenuated loyalties to the Union, which, after all, had repeatedly broken its treaty obligations with indigenous peoples. In the end, Bent understood the Civil War as a war of empire rather than one of liberation, a conflict that initially hinged on sectional bickering over who would control the West and then ultimately resulted in the Reservation Era for Native Americans. President Lincoln's Republican Party had enacted a grand plan for conquering, colonizing, and improving the region, passing the Homestead Act, Pacific Railroad Act, and Morrill Act and creating the Bureau of Agriculture, all in the spring and summer of 1862. The Republicans envisioned a torrent of settlers washing away Western tribes. Massacres such as Sand Creek seemed like a predictable outgrowth of federal policy. For Bent, there stood no line of demarcation between the Civil War and the Indian Wars.[7]

More than 150 years later, the Sand Creek site remains a contested landscape, and, as I have argued in my work, memories of the massacre are still freighted with politics. The product of a collaboration between the National Park Service, the state of Colorado, local ranchers, and descendants of the massacre's victims—members of the Northern and Southern Arapaho and Cheyenne tribes—the memorial very nearly never opened its gates. In 1998, when Park Service officials began studying the feasibility of commemorating Sand Creek, they discovered that the mists of time had shrouded the massacre's precise location. The ensuing hunt proved contentious when methodological and epistemological disagreements over how to interpret the historical record divided the site searchers. The Sand Creek descendants, relying upon ethnographic research conducted within their communities and turn-of-the-century maps penned by George Bent, insisted that they had never lost track of the massacre site. Tribal elders shared with me that through the years they had heard women and children crying in the shadow of a rise overlooking a lazy bend in the creek, which they identified as the "traditional site." The Park Service, by contrast, looked to testimony collected from Chivington's troops and then relied upon a different map, penned by an officer named Samuel Bonsall, who took William Tecumseh Sherman on a tour of Western military sites in the wake of the Civil War. Bonsall's diagram clearly marked the location of "Chivington's Massacre" along the banks of Sand Creek just a bit less than a mile upstream from the bend that the descendants believed had hosted the violence.[8]

The descendants felt betrayed by representatives of the federal government, who, they explained to me, were recapitulating historical crimes. Connecting past and present, Otto Braided Hair, director of the Northern Cheyenne Sand Creek Office, raged, "They tried to wipe us out at Sand Creek. Now they're trying to commit cultural genocide." For Braided

Hair, it seemed the Park Service wanted to dictate the particulars of tribal history to tribal peoples, robbing them of cultural authority by insisting that they trust sources generated by the shock troops of settler colonialism and housed in imperial archives. The Park Service, in short, relied for information on Sand Creek's perpetrators rather than on its victims. The descendants, meanwhile, looked to maps produced by George Bent, a venerated member of the Cheyenne tribe and a massacre survivor. This contest over competing cartographies was resolved only when the Park Service floated a compromise: a commemorative landscape featuring a perimeter capacious enough to encompass otherwise incommensurable accounts of Sand Creek. On April 28, 2007, the Sand Creek historic site, the 391st unit in the National Park System, opened to the public. Approximately 200,000 people have made their way there in the years since. I have frequently been among them, navigating the dusty back roads of southeastern Colorado. Each time I arrive, I rediscover a memorial built atop some of the painful ironies, the open wounds, that define our national narrative.[9]

As the photograph that heads this essay depicts, the Park Service now urges visitors like me to stay on designated paths at the Sand Creek site. Were I to stray from these marked trails, I would tread upon soil sacred to Arapahos and Cheyennes, ground hallowed by their ancestors' blood during an episode that endures for Native people as an emblem of dispossession. The creek bed where Black Kettle's people camped on November 29, 1864, is now off-limits to sightseers, who instead are encouraged to look down upon that site of slaughter from the heights above. At a nearby tribal cemetery, bounded by another split-rail fence but otherwise unmarked by interpretation, the descendants have interred repatriated scalp locks and other body parts

from the Sand Creek dead. These human remains, previously housed in museums, repositories, and private collections, were taken by Chivington's men from their victims on November 29, 1864. I know the recent chronology of the site's development, but for many onlookers the cemetery apparently resembles a stockade or a paddock. Regardless, the message is clear: visitors should, as the signs in Will Gallagher's photograph make clear, confine themselves to authorized spaces; they should not transgress boundaries. But in the end, no matter how many barriers the Park Service erects, the grim events recounted at the Sand Creek site demonstrate that Native and national histories are irrevocably interwoven and that the past is too messy to stay within neat lines.

NOTES

1. Stan Hoig, *The Sand Creek Massacre* (Norman: University of Oklahoma Press, 1974), 145–62; Ari Kelman, *A Misplaced Massacre: Struggling over the Memory of Sand Creek* (Cambridge, Mass.: Harvard University Press, 2013), 2–43; Elliott West, *The Contested Plains: Indians, Goldseekers, and the Rush to Colorado* (Lawrence: University Press of Kansas, 1996), 298–312.

2. Evans quotation from Governor John Evans to Secretary of War Edwin M. Stanton, December 14, 1863, *Report of the Commissioner of Indian Affairs for the Year 1864* (Washington: Government Printing Office, 1865), 225–26. Chivington quotation from Colonel John Chivington to Messrs. Beyers and Dailey, Editors News, November 29, 1864, in U.S. War Department, *The War of the Rebellion: A Compilation of the Official Records of the Union and Confederate Armies*, 127 vols., index, and atlas (Washington, D.C.: Government Printing Office, 1880–1901), ser. 1, vol. 41., pt. 1, 951. See also Hoig, *Sand Creek Massacre*, 58–61; Kelman, *Misplaced Massacre*, 147–49; and West, *Contested Plains*, 290–91.

3. Kelman, *Misplaced Massacre*, 9–18.

4. Quotation from Gary Leland Roberts and David Fridtjof

Halaas, "Written in Blood: The Soule-Cramer Sand Creek Letters," *Colorado Heritage*, Winter 2001, 25. See also Kelman, *Misplaced Massacre*, 22–29.

5. Quotation from Roberts and Halaas, "Written in Blood," 25.

6. George Bent, "Forty Years with the Cheyennes," *Frontier: A Magazine of the West*, ed. George Hyde, 4 (October 1905): 6; George Bent to George Hyde, June 9, 1905, Letter 10, Bent Manuscripts 54, History Colorado, Denver; George Bent to George Hyde, September 26, 1905, Coe Collection, Beinecke Library, Yale University, New Haven, Conn.; George E. Hyde, *Life of George Bent: Written from His Letters*, ed. Savoie Lottinville (Norman: University of Oklahoma Press, 1968), xiv; Kelman, *Misplaced Massacre*, 33–43.

7. David F. Halaas and Andrew E. Masich, *Halfbreed: The Remarkable True Story of George Bent—Caught between the Worlds of the Indian and the White Man* (New York: De Capo Press, 2004), 47–52; Bent, "Forty Years with the Cheyennes," 4; Hyde, *Life of George Bent*, 147–51.

8. "Chivington's Massacre" from Samuel Bonsall Map, National Archives, Great Lakes Region, Chicago, Ill. "The traditional site" from Steve Brady, president, Northern Cheyenne Sand Creek Descendants (interview by author, August 29, 2004, Lame Deer, Mt.). See also George Bent Map, folder 1, Bent-Hyde Papers, Western History Collections, University of Colorado Library, Boulder; George Bent Map, Oklahoma Historical Society, Oklahoma City; Jerome A. Greene and Douglas D. Scott, *Finding Sand Creek: History, Archeology, and the 1864 Sand Creek Massacre Site* (Norman: University of Oklahoma Press, 2004), 26–97; and Kelman, *Misplaced Massacre*, 87–179.

9. Quotation from Otto Braided Hair, director, Northern Cheyenne Sand Creek Office (interview by author, May 11, 2007, Lame Deer, Mt.). See also Greene and Scott, *Finding Sand Creek*, 26–97; Kelman, *Misplaced Massacre*, 87–179; National Park Service, Intermountain Region, *Sand Creek Massacre Project, Volume 1: Site Location Study* (Denver: National Park Service, Intermountain Region, 2000), 63–119; and National Park Service, Intermountain Region, *Sand Creek Massacre Project, Volume 2: Special Resource Study and Environmental Assessment* (Denver: National Park Service, Intermountain Region, 2000), 11–46.

If you stand on the bluffs at Vicksburg and look out over the Mississippi River, you can almost see Confederate victory. The commanding view from Vicksburg convinced Confederates they could win the war—not this view alone, of course, but the perspective it offers. When white Southerners evaluated the possibility of war with the North, they looked out from a similarly commanding height. They controlled cotton and believed that the prosperity and power it had brought them in the antebellum decades would continue after they established an independent nation. This can be a hard perspective to recapture with words alone. Thanks to hindsight, too often we look beyond the river and see only the fall of the city to Union troops.

Most people believe that distance from the past improves our ability to explain it. Removed from the ideological fights that animated participants, we should see their perspectives more impartially. As time elapses, we uncover more sources and expand our base of knowledge. New techniques of historical investigation open up vistas inaccessible to participants. Balancing all these gains, however, is the iron weight of hindsight. Once we know how a particular moment or process concluded, this knowledge colors how we view what came earlier. The more often we repeat stories, the more we obscure possibilities that people saw at the time. This is especially true for now-iconic moments, like General Robert E. Lee's surrender at Appomattox or the liberation of Europe from Nazi rule in World War II. Did General Ulysses S. Grant's strategy of exhaustion make Union victory inevitable? Was the D-day invasion the right strategy for Allies to adopt against Germany? Because we know the outcomes, the historical decisions we need to explain appear manifestly foolish or wise, when at the time they looked merely uncertain. Knowing how things turned out can denude a story

View from upriver toward Vicksburg, Mississippi
(Photograph by Will Gallagher)

of both drama and the ambiguity and anxiety that shroud our decision-making in real life. Although we know much more about the Civil War than any of its individual participants did at the time, the central questions about the war—What made Confederates choose to fight? What made the war so terrible? Why did both sides continue to fight despite the toll it exacted?—are, in some ways, harder to answer today because of how much we know, not how little.

The perils of hindsight appear most striking in the context of battles. Once the smoke has cleared and historians can see the outcome, it becomes difficult not to tell the story without judging the wisdom of decisions large and small. Nowhere was the contrast between pre-battle optimism and post-battle despair starker than at Vicksburg. General John C. Pemberton surrendered the Mississippi River town to General Grant on July 4, 1863. Without control of the city the Union could never control the "Father of Waters," and for Northerners, the date manifested the divine favor they saw behind the Union war effort. The arduous months of campaigning and the 10,000 Union casualties became a necessary part of the sacrifice that enabled the great victory. Grant achieved prominence as the most successful Northern commander.

For the Confederacy, Vicksburg became an unequivocal failure. When Pemberton surrendered, Grant captured his entire army—29,000 soldiers—and enormous stocks of war matériel.[1] This was the largest capture and clearest defeat of any army in any battle in the Civil War. Confederate soldiers, now prisoners, were not the only victims. Confederate citizens, stuck in the city as Grant implemented a siege beginning May 25, had been subjected to nearly six weeks of round-the-clock artillery bombardment and the cutting of railway lines that carried supplies into the city. The

result was a legendary experience of suffering. By the end, residents and soldiers subsisted on mule meat and rats (selling at a dollar per rodent). Pantry staples were scarce and exorbitantly expensive. Citizens abandoned their homes for the safety of caves dug into the hillside. Even loyal Confederates were forced to recognize that the city had been "visited with a terrible scourge." The Louisiana soldier who made this record observed "houses dilapidated and in ruins, rent and torn by shot and shell; the streets barricaded with earth-works. . . . The avenues were almost deserted, save by hunger-pinched, starving and wounded soldiers." "The stores," he continued, "looked like the ghost of more prosperous times with their empty shelves and scant stock of goods, held at ruinous prices." Union soldiers' observations of residents after the surrender confirmed the extent of suffering: "a wretched looking set of men rag[g]ed dirty and half-starved," resulting in the "hip bones of some of them com[ing] through the skin, and their bodies a mass of sores caused by vermin." A Northern woman who traveled with the Union fleet reported home, "Just now there came a little boy who was literally a living skeleton. He says he and his mother lived in a cave for the last two weeks with nothing to eat but corn meal and peas." This was not the outcome that Confederates anticipated. Indeed, it was not an outcome they could imagine even two months before the end, so convinced were they of their superior position.[2]

Explaining why people choose to fight wars requires thinking at multiple levels. "Causes" move people like all grand processes do—invisibly and irresistibly. The political, economic, and moral struggle over slavery divided Americans with increasing acrimony in the 1850s. This conflict was the root cause of the war. "Motives" inspire people at the individual level. Some men volunteered for military duty to impress

AARON SHEEHAN-DEAN

girlfriends, and others did so from a belief that national loyalty compelled the physical defense of their country. The context within which people recognized and balanced these sometimes competing influences played yet another role. To understand if white Southerners thought secession and war were wise (as opposed to whether they were just or necessary) requires that we investigate more quotidian aspects: Did they believe they had the resources and skill to make a successful defense? Because we know the war's outcome, the wisdom of secession and war looks quite dubious for most people today. We often begin, even if only unconsciously, by admitting that the Confederates fought for a lost cause, but most white Southerners did not believe that at the time. They believed in their cause, an independent, slaveholding republic; drew succor from a diverse range of inspiring motivations; and saw in their geography, martial skill, and material resources the necessary ingredients to successfully resist the Union's military campaign. Recapturing the Confederate perspective requires suspending hindsight and inserting ourselves into participants' worlds.

Standing on the bluff above Vicksburg helps accomplish this. It gives us a chance to see the war's decision-making in something like real time, or at least real space. It puts us on the same plane as participants in the war. The river has shifted its path slightly over the last century and a half, and though modern objects dot the landscape, the bluffs remain the same height. Looking south, as the photograph preceding this essay shows, they offer the same majestic vantage of the river and the town below. This is where Confederate defenders of the "Gibraltar of the Mississippi" stood when they assessed the approach of Grant's Northern army in 1862. If we begin by knowing that Grant was successful, we will have a hard time appreciating the decision to stay and fight. Instead, we should start by standing on the bluff and looking out over the Mississippi River.

The Mississippi makes a hairpin bend before Vicksburg, shifting direction nearly 180 degrees as the Yazoo River joins its path from the east. The city sits just south of this twist. The fortifications that guarded the city sat north of the town, offering a perfect view of vessels coming down the river—as they navigated the turn—and on the city below. The fort and parts of the city occupied high bluffs, in some places as much as 200 feet above the river. The elevation difference enabled Vicksburg's defenders even greater range with their heavy guns. These geographic conditions encouraged a belief in the city's impregnability. After the war, when the Lost Cause attained its stranglehold on American memory, the North's advantages in manpower, technology, and matériel were regarded as ensuring Union victory. But none of these factors was visible in mid-1863 from Vicksburg. The physical realities suggested just the opposite—whatever resources the North might marshal, it would never be able to conquer Vicksburg.

Both Northerners and Southerners regarded the city as the key to controlling the Lower Mississippi River. Union admiral David G. Farragut had easily steamed upriver after his conquest of New Orleans in April 1862 and was just as easily rebuffed when he attacked Vicksburg in June and July of that year. Ulysses S. Grant's efforts to capture the city, which began in earnest in December 1862, produced nothing but hardship and suffering for his troops (who dug canals and battled cold and disease). Months of Union failures—widely reported in the press of both sections—reinforced Confederate confidence in the spring of 1863.

Grant solved the problem he faced at Vicksburg by

marching his troops down the west side of the river, ferrying them across, and then marching back up to attack the city from the landward (eastern) side. To do this, he still needed transport ships south of the city. When Admiral David Dixon Porter finally ran through the turn and down to meet Grant, he converted one of the presumed advantages of the Confederates against them. As his ships began receiving fire from the Confederates' shore batteries, they moved to the river's eastern bank, which, in some places, was so steep that it rendered artillery pieces unusable. The technical term is "depressing muzzles," which describes the steep angle necessary to hit targets nearby but much lower in elevation. It is a term of military art that could also apply to the condition of white Vicksburgians in coming months. The transports slipped through in April, and Grant's forces fought across the state in a wide arc, defeating Confederates at each point, and arrived back at Vicksburg by late May. After a costly failed assault, Grant initiated the siege that captured the city.

The fall of Vicksburg did not ensure Confederate defeat in the Civil War, but by gaining control of the river, the Union strengthened its hand significantly. After mid-1863, the Confederate South was cut in two, with supplies and personnel in Texas, parts of Louisiana, and Arkansas isolated on the western shore of the Union-controlled Mississippi River. This also gave the Union the ability to proceed up tributary rivers like the Red in Louisiana and the Yazoo in Mississippi. The fall of Vicksburg made the Deep South uniquely vulnerable. Defeat dispirited Confederates as profoundly as they had been buoyed by the city's preservation in previous years. The Union's unstoppable force had triumphed over their own unmovable place.

Alongside its strategic value, Vicksburg's fall possessed great symbolic value for the war's

participants. "'THE DAY OF JUBILEE HAS COME' Vicksburg Surrendered on the 4th" trumpeted the *Wisconsin Daily Patriot* in what was a typically enthusiastic rendering of the news.[3] If this Mississippi fastness was not impregnable, then perhaps neither was the Confederacy itself. After two terrible years of war, Northerners saw their labors begin to bear fruit.

Although modern historians do not usually engage in moral judgment about the phenomena we explain, readers often do. Historians might explain why something occurred and describe its consequences, but a reader can take that information and decide if the action was wise or foolish. With hindsight, the suffering of Vicksburg residents in 1863 might seem like criminal stupidity on the part of its defenders. The Union's resource advantage, which Confederates recognized but disregarded in this instance, was exactly the element that mattered most in a siege. Drawing on hindsight, historians have asserted the same thing for the Confederacy as a whole. According to this line of thought, men like Jefferson Davis and Robert E. Lee should have recognized that even a military stalemate with the North was unlikely and would necessitate massive death and suffering on the part of the people they were pledging to protect. They might have anticipated this outcome and proceeded anyway, believing that an honorable resistance was proper even if useless. More surprising is that both Davis and Lee expected victory, despite the manpower and resource imbalance between the two sides. As Davis assured listeners at his inauguration in 1861, "Obstacles may retard, but they cannot long prevent, the progress of a movement sanctified by its justice and sustained by a virtuous people."

Davis spoke with the confident vigor of a national leader hoping to will his country into existence. But he also had good reason for believing in Confederate victory. The South controlled the third-largest economy in the world in 1861. The product fueling that economy—cotton—was a most coveted object, particularly for the wealthy and expanding empires of Britain and France. Just as cotton had made the South king in the antebellum era, Davis and other Confederates expected to retain the crown as an independent nation. In addition to economic power, the South could boast of its political dexterity (its leaders had long been at the helm of American government) and martial prowess. The new Confederacy, its vice president boasted, "is an area of country more than double the territory of France or the Austrian empire.... It is greater than all France, Spain, Portugal, and Great Britain."[4] How would it not succeed?

There is no gainsaying the fact that things did not turn out as Confederates hoped they would. But interrogating their experience from the perspective they occupied helps make their decisions a little less confusing. If we stand on the Vicksburg bluff and appreciate that the strategic confidence such a view encouraged had an intellectual counterpart in Confederates' estimates of their capacities, their decision to secede and fight looks more intelligible. Standing on the high ground of Vicksburg helps us mitigate the corrupting influence of hindsight by restoring to us the view held by the war's participants.

NOTES

1. Michael Ballard, *Vicksburg: The Campaign that Opened the Mississippi* (Chapel Hill: University of North Carolina Press, 2004), 398.

2. Ballard, *Vicksburg*, 388, 399; Bradley R. Clampitt, *Occupied Vicksburg* (Baton Rouge: Louisiana State University Press, 2016), 34.

3. *Wisconsin Daily Patriot*, July 7, 1863.

4. Matthew Karp, *This Vast Southern Empire: Slaveholders at the Helm of American Foreign Policy* (Cambridge, Mass.: Harvard University Press, 2016), 241.

II CEMETERIES

PLACES OF MOURNING

The grave of my great-grandfather lies in Section 31, C-17, in the Los Angeles National Cemetery. It is flanked by Antietam Avenue to the east, Gettysburg Avenue to the west, Shiloh Drive to the north, and Appomattox Drive to the south. Until recently, I was unaware that I had an ancestor who fought in the Civil War. It just goes to show that sometimes a very special place can be hidden in plain sight. Shortly after I was asked to contribute an essay to this volume, I began making a list of sites visited and revisited throughout my career as a Civil War historian. The list was overly long at first, but I slashed it to five places, all east of the Mississippi River. At no point in those early deliberations did I consider the Los Angeles National Cemetery, which lies between Brentwood, where I live, and Westwood, where I work.

Why did I ultimately jettison frequently visited places at battlefields and cemeteries or the memorial structures that have captivated me in favor of a local landmark that few readers of this book will know? Two intertwined discoveries will frame the essay's narrative, providing answers to this animating question. The first, and more important, discovery was finding the *place* itself to be a powerful venue for interpreting memory, an example of "hallowed ground"; the second was a revelation of my previously unknown personal connection to the conflict. Here in "La La Land," so far from the famous places of the American Civil War, a fresh perspective on the meaning of the sacrifice of America's most deadly war was revealed to me.

I have taught thousands of undergraduate students about the Civil War era during my twenty-three years at UCLA, but it was the creation of a seminar in 2000 titled "The Memory of the Civil War in American Culture" that led me to the cemetery. The seminar's

(previous page)
Soldier's monument in Los Angeles National Cemetery, California (Photograph by Will Gallagher)

purpose is for students to learn about how the Civil War has been remembered and commemorated through national and local celebrations, monuments, movies, reenactments, national military parks, and cemeteries. So-called memory wars have raged in the early decades of the twenty-first century; ferocious controversies appear with startling regularity, providing lively fodder for discussion. From its inception, the seminar required a field trip. Having led a number of UCLA summer travel study classes to Gettysburg, Antietam, Harpers Ferry, Petersburg, Richmond, and other Civil War hot spots, I knew the benefits of teaching in "outdoor classrooms."

Southern California offers a surprising number of good locations for examining the war's impact. For example, one year we journeyed to the Lincoln Memorial Shrine and Museum in Redlands; another outing featured a visit to the Henry E. Huntington Library in San Marino; still other trips found us viewing area reenactments or touring the Drum Barracks Civil War Museum in Wilmington. All proved to be successful endeavors, but all had various logistical issues. More important, not one of them truly crystallized the meaning behind that resonant phrase "sacred ground," leaving me searching for a better place. In 2006, I read a brief article in a local newspaper on the Civil War–era origins of the L.A. National Cemetery. Despite proximity, I had never visited it. The current veterans' complex (both hospital system and cemetery) is bordered by some of the city's busiest thoroughfares: Wilshire Boulevard, Sepulveda Boulevard, Veteran Avenue, San Vicente Boulevard, and the 405 Freeway. How many millions of weary commuters (including myself) have driven by the southern edge of the cemetery (at the corner of Wilshire and Veteran) without even glancing at the large United

Spanish War Veterans monument thrusting upward from that congested corner or giving a thought to the sacrifice of those thousands who are buried just a few dozen yards away?

Excited by the challenge, I hastened to collect all available materials from the small visitors' center as well as from the cemetery's website. These sources revealed that the Pacific Branch of the National Home for Disabled Volunteer Soldiers was authorized by an act of Congress in 1887. The first of the federally funded branches to be constructed west of the Rocky Mountains, it served an area where thousands of veterans—Union and Confederate—had headed after 1865. Like its Midwestern and Eastern branches, the home sought to provide shelter for honorably discharged Union veterans whose documented disabilities rendered them unable to live independently. Two prominent real estate developers secured the branch for Los Angeles by donating to the government 300 acres of Santa Monica ranch land. They sweetened the deal with a long list of promised improvements, free of charge. Their generosity was leavened with the hearty strain of boosterism that characterized most of the public/private arrangements behind the building of the National Homes.

The first structure of the "Old Soldiers' Home," as the Pacific Branch facility was popularly known, opened in July 1888, and George Davis, Co. B., 14th New York Cavalry, became its first official resident. Soon the numbers swelled to a thousand, with more acreage and more buildings—including hospitals, stores, recreation and eating areas, and additional barracks—added to accommodate the growing needs of the community. In 1889, two members died and were buried on a 20-acre piece of land set aside as a cemetery about half a mile from the home (the cemetery was later expanded to 114 acres). The Los Angeles National Cemetery became one of eleven facilities operated by the Veterans Administration on lands shared with national veterans' homes or asylums for disabled soldiers. Every burial featured a military funeral presided over by a minister, with music provided by the Branch Home Band, and was followed by a procession of mourners. Eventually, 11,000 Union veterans were interred on the gently sloping grounds of the beautiful, then-rural cemetery. Today it is still beautiful, a strikingly tranquil oasis amid the urban sprawl of Westwood, Brentwood, Santa Monica, and greater West Los Angeles. The L.A. National Cemetery presently holds the remains of 89,000 veterans from a number of wars and conflicts, including the Civil War, the Spanish-American War, World Wars I and II, Vietnam, and the Gulf Wars.[1]

After receiving permission from cemetery officials to hold one of my three-hour seminar sessions on the grounds, I set to work preparing a tour that would demonstrate viscerally what students had been studying in the classroom. The first tour, in November 2006, was an experiment, and I awaited with some trepidation the arrival (by car, of course; it's Los Angeles) of twenty students. I was confident that all were intellectually aware of the vital role that the veterans' sacrifice played in shaping both the history and the memory of the Civil War. But was this going to be a place where UCLA students would *feel* the strong intersection between history and memory? The debut tour featured six stops selected to evoke both specific and general class topics with the goal of promoting wide-ranging open-air discussions. The first tour was a grand success and has been repeated each year I have offered the course. My students commonly report that the experience makes them realize the power of a particular place to induce almost a prayerful reflection and that there truly can be such a thing as "sacred ground."

A description of my field trip to the Los Angeles National Cemetery will illustrate how I use the site. Stop 1 begins just past the entrance, where we gather in front of the Bob Hope Memorial Chapel, a small white Spanish Revival structure designed in 1938 and named after the comedian in 2002. After a few opening remarks, I ask the students to read the selected stanzas of "The Bivouac of the Dead" that are carved on small tablets placed along the path leading into the main part of the cemetery. The famous poem, written by Theodore O'Hara, appears on many memorials to fallen soldiers, including the gateway of Arlington National Cemetery.[2] The poignant elegy was embraced after the war as a symbol of reconciliation; its sentiment still resonates in the twenty-first century and alerts students to the profoundly sorrowful nature of the journey they are undertaking. Stop 2 requires strolling up Constitution Avenue and pausing to view a cast-zinc statue of a Civil War soldier standing at parade rest on a boulder. The attached plaque reads, "Dedicated to the Department of California and the Nevada Grand Army of the Republic." This inexpensive monument began its life (circa 1896) inelegantly perched atop a huge drinking fountain at the home for Union veterans that stood just across Sepulveda Boulevard on the grounds of what is now called the VA Greater Los Angeles Health System. Here, we engage in a conversation about why and how these ubiquitous monuments preserve Civil War memory. Who funded them? What did they represent in the 1880s and 1890s? Do they speak to us today? Here also I address the history of the Brentwood Old Soldiers' Home and the cemetery, asking them to consider the ways L.A.'s local story dovetails with that of the generation who fought in the conflict.

A short walk up an incline brings us to the central portion of the cemetery. Stop 3 places students near a pergola, the flagpole, the rostrum, and the columbarium. As we approach the rostrum, I point out the plaque in front with Abraham Lincoln's famous address given at the dedication of the Gettysburg National Cemetery in November 1863 and subsequently placed in every national cemetery. The students are well prepared to reflect on the transformative nature of Lincoln's address and its wider impact on memorialization. The majority claim never to have visited any cemetery, much less the one consecrated by the sixteenth president, and are pleased to hear that there is a ceremony held every February in the Los Angeles cemetery to commemorate Lincoln's birthday. I seize the opportunity to educate them about Veterans Day and especially Memorial Day, both set aside to honor the men and women who served in, or who died in, service in the U.S. armed forces. Originating in the years after the Civil War, Memorial Day, always the last Monday in May, attracts several thousand to the Westwood cemetery. I ask if they know that California has the biggest veteran population in the nation. Most do not, and several pledge to attend at least one of the events before graduation. Stop 4 is beyond the flagpole where students read the plaque "A National Cemetery System." Next we go to the Spanish-style columbarium containing the ashes of veterans. The only indoor columbarium in the national cemetery system, it was built, along with the chapel mentioned above, in the late 1930s, as part of President Franklin D. Roosevelt's Work Projects Administration.

We next proceed up an incline on Gettysburg Avenue where the Union veterans are located for Stop 5. I point out one or two (or more) of the five Civil War Medal of Honor recipients who are buried in those sections. I discuss the origins of all the distinctive Union grave markers while noting the special designation on the headstones of those receiving the Medal of Honor.

The stories of these particular men provide me with an opportunity to mitigate the impersonal effect of endless rows of white graves. Kentucky-born Charles Rundle, who volunteered in the 116th Illinois Infantry, distinguished himself at the battle at Vicksburg, Mississippi, in 1863; Sergeant Luther Kaltenbach of the 12th Iowa Infantry, a boy when his family left Germany, received commendation for his heroics in the battle of Nashville in 1864. Two of the five Civil War Medal of Honor recipients buried in the L.A. National Cemetery were born in Ireland. Timothy Sullivan, a coxswain on the USS *Louisville*, displayed unusual courage at Fort Donelson and Vicksburg, while Sergeant George McGee of the 89th New York Infantry earned his medal at the 1864 assault on Fort Gregg at Petersburg. Last, James Sweeney, born in England, served as a corporal in the 1st Vermont Cavalry and during the 1864 battle of Cedar Creek exhibited undaunted courage. A good number of my students come from first- or second-generation immigrant families, and they are intrigued by the high percentage of immigrants in the Union army. In addition, as they wander around the gravesites (respectfully), they often express surprise at the variety of states represented on the headstones. Everyone seemed to have come from somewhere else, something many Californians can appreciate. Overall, Stop 5 inspires the most intense discussion as students debate the meaning of service, of sacrifice, with the importance of commemoration made visible.

My commentary at Stop 5 has changed over the years because I was able to add a personal story for one of the graves. Although I am a proud third-generation Californian, my historical interests have always lain outside the Golden State. But my discovery of the L.A. cemetery's Civil War origins was followed by another discovery that brought my lifelong immersion in nineteenth-century U.S. history full circle. In 2013 my brother, Michael Arboit, tracing our family history on Ancestry.com, found that our great-grandfather Charles S. Whitmore served in the Civil War. This led me to order his service and pension records from the National Archives. I learned that Charles Whitmore (1844–1916) volunteered for the 2nd Minnesota Infantry in St. Paul. At the time of his enlistment, Charles was seventeen and an apprentice for the *St. Paul Pioneer Press*. His underage status required written permission from his mother, which she granted. Assigned to Company D, Charles was mustered in on July 5, 1861, at Fort Snelling, receiving his honorable discharge on July 4, 1864. The 2nd Minnesota took part in actions in Kentucky, Georgia, and Tennessee and in 1863 saw heavy fighting at the battles of Chickamauga and Missionary Ridge. Charles was seriously injured in the campaigns and remained in a Chattanooga hospital until the late spring of 1864, when he was well enough to muster out. Pension files show that he moved to Kansas City, Missouri, and, making that city his base, worked across various states in the West—Washington, Utah, Nevada, Colorado, California, and Arizona. Mostly, Charles was a railroad man, but he also worked as a printer and a miner and in construction. Along the way he married Nora McLaughlin, fathered two children, and bought a house in Kansas City, where he lived for fourteen years. With hundreds of thousands of fellow veterans, he joined the Grand Army of the Republic and eventually applied for a pension due to his war-related injuries and illnesses. At his pension hearing in 1895, he testified, "My business is that of a Watch man during the day time for the Atchison, Topeka and Santa Fe Rail Road, at the yards in Kansas City, Missouri."[3] After making their final move, Charles and Nora appeared in the 1900 census records as Los Angeles residents, and he entered the L.A. soldiers' home in 1905, with his death and burial recorded in 1917. Although I am still searching, I have not located any letters, diaries, or photographs that might shed more light on his wartime or peacetime existence.

Charles S. Whitmore did not distinguish himself as either a soldier or a citizen. I confess to feeling at first a slight twinge of disappointment that my ancestor was one of the "common soldiers" who have occupied so much of the recent literature of the field. Yet like the low-cost zinc statue featured at Stop 2, my great-grandfather's story stands for something very important, and I am disappointed no more. Indeed, as I tell my students, his life resembles a great number of those who served in the Civil War for the Union. They were working-class youth whose motivations for volunteering were less patriotic than practical; less thrilled by mastering the martial life than by a monthly paycheck; less interested in securing the fruits of emancipation than in securing employment and establishing families. Charles did his duty and proceeded to make a decent life. The simple and inexpensive common soldier monuments honor the collective sacrifice made by individual men such as my great-grandfather. Like many other veterans, he experienced serious health problems directly attributable to his wartime service. Charles Whitmore applied for and received a pension, a place to live, medical care, and, when the time came, a respectful burial in a special place—all from a federal government that had pledged to assist the men who fought to "Save the Union." I conclude my presentation at Stop 5 with a quotation from the architect of Arlington National Cemetery, Quartermaster General Montgomery C. Meigs, who said, "All care for the dead, is for the sake of the living." It is how the survivors found solace and bestowed meaning on the wholesale death and destruction wrought by the American Civil War and provides good food for thought as we conclude our tour.

Stop 6 takes us to the highest point of the cemetery, along the street named "San Juan Hill." At the top is an impressive granite obelisk commemorating the sacrifice of all soldiers in the area where many Spanish-American War veterans are buried. It was erected in "Memory of the Men Who Offered Their Lives in Defense of Their Country." After taking the by-now traditional class picture posed in front of the obelisk, we adjourn to the lovely grassy park behind the monument; the students arrange themselves in a seated semicircle, and I ask for reflections. We ruminate on the notion of "sacred" or "hallowed" ground and apply it to the past and present. Each time, students seem genuinely affected by the experience. Overall, they come away with a much deeper appreciation of the meaning of sacrifice and loss, respect for commemorative features, and a heightened awareness of the profound impact of the Civil War on places near and far. Many of them have been deeply moved by the experience and inspired to begin exploring historical sites on their own. A few tell me that they took their parents on the same tour. It just goes to show that sometimes a very special place can be hidden in plain sight.

NOTES

1. Cheryl Lynn Wilkinson, "The Veterans in Our Midst: Disabled Union Veterans in West Los Angeles, 1888–1914" (M.A. thesis in history, California State University at Northridge, 2013). This fine thesis represents the only substantial researched work existing on the home and the cemetery.

2. John E. Kleber, "Theodore O'Hara," in *The Kentucky Encyclopedia*, ed. John E. Kleber (Lexington: University Press of Kentucky, 2015), 687. Kentucky lawyer, journalist, and soldier Theodore O'Hara originally wrote his poem in 1847 to honor Kentuckians who died in the Mexican War. After the war, O'Hara's poem became widely popular in both the North and the South.

3. Quotation from "Declaration for an Original Invalid Pension," Certificate Number 516,393, taken on September 3, 1895, Charles S. Whitmore Federal Pension Application, SC 576–393, National Archives, Washington, D.C.

10 A "RIGHTFUL PLACE" THE GRAVES OF GEORGE AND LASALLE PICKETT, HOLLYWOOD CEMETERY, RICHMOND, VIRGINIA

LESLEY J. GORDON

first set out to understand Confederate major general George E. Pickett as an undergraduate at the College of William and Mary some three decades ago. First in a seminar paper and then in my senior honor's thesis, I sought to delve into the man apart from his famed charge. I had been intrigued a few years prior, after reading *The Killer Angels* as a New England teen. In the novel's epilogue, Michael Shaara says, "Pickett survives to great glory, but he broods on the loss."[1] I wanted to know more—not just what happened next but why and how. And I wanted to know what he was really like—the dandified white Southern man seemed like too much of a caricature to me. Why did he brood? What was he like before the battle? Could one event, even a battle so climactic as Gettysburg, embitter and change someone permanently?

Williamsburg was a short hour's drive to Pickett's gravesite at Hollywood Cemetery. In one of my early visits to Richmond, I had ventured to find him. Initially, I had no luck; this was long before ubiquitous iPhones or GPS, and I had no printed guide to the cemetery, only a vague sense that he was buried in the soldiers' section on Gettysburg Hill. At that time, there was a heavy overgrowth of trees, blocking easy access or a clear view from the pathway. I was nearly ready to give up, but then I found it: the monument marking Pickett's grave is large, some twenty-five feet high, foreboding in granite with bronze and copper tablets and a bronze funeral urn atop.

In fact, this monument was never meant to be in Hollywood at all; it was designed and commissioned by veterans from Pickett's division to be placed on the Gettysburg battlefield near the present day "clump of trees." When that location proved too controversial, the Pickett Division Association opted for Hollywood

Graves of George E. and LaSalle Corbell Pickett, Hollywood Cemetery, Richmond, Virginia (Photograph by Will Gallagher)

instead. As one newspaper explained, "It was then decided to place the monument over General Pickett's grave on Gettysburg Hill, in Hollywood Cemetery where the bodies of about twelve thousand Confederates, several hundred of whom were members of the historic division," were buried.[2] Five of the six bronze plaques on the monument list Pickett's brigades by regiment, including the artillery battalion commanded by James Dearing. The sixth memorializes Pickett as a soldier and commander, citing not only his Civil War record but also his Mexican-American War battles and experience on the San Juan Islands. Included is this poetic inscription, read aloud at the monument's dedication in 1888:

WHEREVER FIELD WAS TO BE
HELD OR WON,
OR HARDSHIP BORNE OR RIGHT
TO BE MAINTAINED,
OR DANGER MET OR DEED OF VALOR DONE,
OR HONOR, GLORY GAINED
WHERE MEN WERE CALLED TO
FRONT DEATH FACE TO FACE
THERE WAS ITS
RIGHTFUL PLACE.[3]

I remember thinking at the time that these jingoistic words celebrating Pickett and his men as selfless Confederate warriors seemed appropriate, yet also somehow ironic. Through my years of studying him, originally as an undergraduate and then for my doctoral dissertation, which became my first book, I found George Pickett to be much more complex than the caricature of a man depicted by Shaara. He was someone so steeped in Lost Cause mythology and postwar fabrication, much of it propagated by his wife, LaSalle, that it was difficult to discover the "real" George Pickett. Yet, in some ways, he probably would not have wanted it any other way. He was a soldier from the age of sixteen and never really considered other professions; the military was part of his identity as a Southern white male striving his whole life to prove, I believe, his worthiness. After July 3, 1863, he struggled to come to terms with what he deemed to be the wasteful destruction of his troops at Gettysburg. Nonetheless, his pride in being division commander grew with time. In one of his few postwar public addresses, Pickett told a crowd that included many veterans from his division, "I am proud beyond measure that it fell my lot to command such men as yourselves and your brother Virginians."[4] He spent his final years brooding over all he believed he had lost, at Gettysburg and beyond. When he died suddenly in July 1875 at the age of fifty, newspaper obituaries focused solely on his military service. The *Richmond Dispatch* called for a "shaft [to] be reared to his memory in Hollywood" in order to "perpetuate his martial figure so that future generations of Virginians may see what manner of a man he was, whose name is indissolubly linked with all the glory of Gettysburg."[5] Later that year, when he was laid to rest close to the remains of thousands of the Confederate dead in Hollywood, the paper observed, "No other burial place could have been as appropriate."[6] Indeed, I opened my undergraduate honor's thesis with an excerpt from an 1876 tribute to Pickett authored by his longtime friend Samuel Bell Maxey, who praised him as being "imperishably connected with the battle of Gettysburg, as a hero among heroes."[7]

One of the people most responsible for ensuring that the general's life was "imperishably connected" to Gettysburg was his widow, LaSalle "Sallie" Corbell Pickett, who outlived her husband by more than fifty years. She was a conspicuous presence at veteran commemorative activities, most notably the twenty-fifth anniversary of Gettysburg in 1887. "Mrs. Pickett," the *New York Times* reported, "was the centre of attraction on the field."[8] At the dedication of the monument to Pickett's division in 1888, a Richmond paper claimed that LaSalle was "deeply affected" by the ceremony, sobbing as she "stood leaning upon her son's shoulder."[9] Gettysburg was central to LaSalle's mythmaking, and she claimed authority on her husband not only personally but militarily as well. LaSalle eventually authored more than half a dozen books, including her own autobiography and fabricated letters between herself and George. She toured the country as the self-styled "child bride of the Confederacy," a label that exaggerated the age difference between her and her husband. By the time she died in 1931, LaSalle was as much a central figure in the promotion of the Lost Cause as the idealized image of her husband.[10] In her will, she referred to Pickett as "my late beloved husband, the distinguished Confederate soldier," adding, "in whose memory and to the preservation for posterity of his fame and accomplishments, I dedicated my life."[11]

When LaSalle died, family members sought to place her remains beside the general's grave at Hollywood. But Pickett's monument was located in the all-male "soldier" section of the cemetery, and the Ladies Hollywood Memorial Association, fearing the precedent such an action would make, rejected the request. The family was allegedly so upset they threatened to move George's remains from Hollywood and bury both Picketts in Arlington National Cemetery. Instead, George's grave was left untouched, and LaSalle's ashes were placed in the Abby Mausoleum on the outskirts of Arlington.[12]

The 1990s marked a decade of renewed public interest in George Pickett. This was due no doubt to a combination of factors, including Ken Burns's immensely successful 1990 documentary *The Civil War* and *Gettysburg*, a 1993 film version of Shaara's novel. Portrayed as "dashing" and "perfumed" and wholly devoted to his young love, the General Pickett whom viewers saw on the small and big screen bore little resemblance to the troubled and embittered man I discovered in my research.[13] But that mattered little to public audiences; this was the idealized image of "Her Soldier" that LaSalle Pickett had dedicated her life to promoting.

By 1997, plans were afoot to make marked changes to Pickett's gravesite. Over a six-month period, the Virginia chapter of the United Daughters of the Confederacy led efforts to raise funds to restore the monument and the grounds surrounding it. New landscaping was installed, including a flagstone walkway, and the monument was scoured and cleaned.[14] In addition, the UDC, along with Pickett descendants, organized to rescue LaSalle's remains and reunite her with her husband in Richmond.

The Arlington mausoleum that housed LaSalle's ashes had fallen into disrepair and neglect. In 1994 the *Washington Post* reported that police had discovered "dead cats, pentagrams, bloody handprints and other signs of Satanic worship" at the Arlington site. This particularly macabre incident in 1994 was the sixth time the mausoleum had been vandalized during a fifteen-year period. Vandals had also opened caskets, mounted skulls on sticks, and spilled ashes from urns.[15]

While all this was happening, I had become a newly hired assistant professor at Murray State University in Murray, Kentucky, and was close to completing my Pickett book. I had been in contact with members of the UDC who were busily planning a special ceremony to rebury LaSalle Corbell Pickett in Hollywood alongside George. At some point, the LaSalle Corbell

Reburial Committee contacted me and inquired about my speaking at the planned ceremony. But before anything definite had been determined, the invitation was rescinded. I recall learning that there was concern that I would not have anything "nice" to say about either Pickett.

The official rededication ceremony of the newly restored monument occurred on Sunday, March 22, 1998, the sixty-seventh anniversary of LaSalle's death, with the formal reinterment of her remains the day prior.[16] To mark the monument's rededication, the UDC awarded its "Order of the Military Cross" to the couple's great-grandson Chris Pickett and great-grandnephew William Pickett. Kathy Georg Harrison, then chief historian at Gettysburg National Military Park and coauthor of *Nothing but Glory: Pickett's Division at Gettysburg*, was the keynote speaker, selected by the Pickett family for having authored what they judged "the most fair and accurate account of Pickett's Charge."[17]

I did not attend these ceremonies, even though the organizers urged me to come despite the canceled invitation to speak. Later, though, I did receive a typed copy of Harrison's keynote address. She opened by recognizing the "boundary between historical fact and romantic fancy." "Who was this man," she asked her audience, "and does he really deserve for us to be here today?" She quickly answered: "You bet he deserves it." Harrison continued by describing Pickett as a "real and admirable gentleman who once walked the streets of his hometown." Defensive and laudatory, Harrison's speech characterized him as a passionate and dedicated commander yet a "moderate and loyal citizen," someone who did his duty and then some on July 3, 1863. "If anyone questions his leadership, the character, or the loyalty of George Pickett," she admonished her listeners,

"they need go no farther than the fields of Gettysburg. They need look no farther than Hollywood Cemetery." She closed by reiterating the appropriateness of Pickett's burial close to the remains of so many of his fellow Confederate soldiers: "The presence of General Pickett here at Hollywood, sharing the same sun and shadows that envelop the Gettysburg dead, finalizes that bond."[18] Harrison's speech made no mention of LaSalle, even though Pickett's widow was probably the key source for most of her remarks about the general.

Over the past two decades, the Pickett Society has largely claimed ownership of the Pickett graves at Hollywood and the physical space surrounding them. Formed the year after LaSalle's remains were reinterred in Hollywood, this not-for-profit organization funded a new gravestone and marker for LaSalle in 2010 to correct what they deemed errors in the original marker.[19] Two years earlier, in 2008, board member and actor Stephen Lang, who portrayed Pickett in the film version of *The Killer Angels*, donated a bench located close to the graves. The bench's inscription celebrates Shaara, who "so poignantly reminded us of the mortal sacrifice made by the soldiers who valiantly fought at Gettysburg, Pennsylvania, July 1st–3rd, 1863."[20]

Visitors to this place today will have an easier time finding Pickett's gravesite than I did thirty years ago. The landscape has changed, deliberately so, to convey a glorified narrative about a Confederate general, his division, and his devoted wife. And despite my own efforts, and those of others scholars, to understand these individuals as complex and faltering people, that mythology endures.

NOTES

1. Michael Shaara, *The Killer Angels* (New York: Ballantine Books, 1974), 358.

2. *Richmond Daily Dispatch*, October 6, 1888; see also Carol Reardon, *Pickett's Charge in History and Memory* (Chapel Hill: University of North Carolina Press, 1997), 105.

3. *Richmond Daily Dispatch*, October 26, 1888.

4. George E. Pickett, "Address delivered to this Company upon the completion of a flag by the ladies of Richmond," Henry H. Huntington Library, San Marino, Calif.; quoted in Lesley J. Gordon, *General George E. Pickett in Life and Legend* (Chapel Hill: University of North Carolina Press, 1998), 162–63.

5. *Richmond Dispatch*, August 2, 1875.

6. *Richmond Dispatch*, October 26, 1875.

7. Samuel Bell Maxey, "George E. Pickett," *Annual Reunion of the Association of the Graduates of the United States Military Academy* (West Point, N.Y.: USMA, 1876), 14.

8. *New York Times*, July 5, 1887. See also Gordon, *Pickett in Life and Legend*, 173–74; and Reardon, *Pickett's Charge*, 98.

9. *Richmond Dispatch*, October 6, 1888.

10. For more on LaSalle Pickett and her postwar efforts to promote not only her husband but also the Lost Cause, see Lesley J. Gordon, "'Let the People See the Old Life as It Was': LaSalle Corbell Pickett and the Myth of the Lost Cause," in *The Myth of the Lost Cause and Civil War History*, ed. Alan T. Nolan and Gary W. Gallagher (Bloomington: Indiana University Press, 2000), 170–84. See also Caroline E. Janney, "'One of the Best Loved, North and South': The Appropriation of National Reconciliation by LaSalle Corbell Pickett," *Virginia Magazine of History and Biography* 116 (2008): 370–406.

11. Quoted in Martha Boltz, "LaSalle Pickett's Battle to Buff Husband's Image," *Washington Times*, March 14, 1998.

12. Boltz, "LaSalle Pickett's Battle." See also Gordon, *Pickett in Life and Legend*, 180–81; and Mary H. Mitchell, *History of a Southern Shrine* (Richmond: Library of Virginia, 1985), 137–38.

13. Ken Burns, dir., *The Civil War* (PBS, 1990); Ronald F. Maxwell, dir., *Gettysburg* (Turner Pictures, 1993).

14. "Pickett Monument Undergoing Restoration Work," Virginia Division, United Daughters of the Confederacy, http://vaudc.org/pickett.html (accessed August 11, 2017).

15. See Peter Y. Hong, "Vandalism in Va. Mausoleum said to Indicate Satanism," *Washington Post*, June 23, 1994, https://www.washingtonpost.com/archive/local/1994/06/23/vandalism-in-va-mausoleum-said-to-indicate-satanism/48627374-9ee1-49be-a2ae-dcf66c28498d/?utm_term=.43cd2018d000 (accessed August 4, 2017).

16. Apparently, Hollywood did not allow Sunday burials. See Deborah Fitts, "Pickett's Wife to Be Reburied and His Grave Rededicated in March," *Civil War News*, February/March 1998, 27.

17. Unattributed quotation from Fitts, 27.

18. Kathy Georg Harrison, "Address on the Occasion of the Rededication of Pickett Monument, Hollywood Cemetery" [March 22, 1998], typed copy in possession of author.

19. See "Commemoration of General George E. Pickett's 185th Birthday, January 23, 2010," The Pickett Society, http://www.pickettsociety.com/185/2010_01_23.html (accessed August 11, 2017).

20. Blogger Kevin M. Levin observes, "The inscription has nothing whatsoever to do with Pickett other than to acknowledge one of the most popular works of historical fiction and its author." Kevin M. Levin, "Why Does Hollywood Cemetery Need a Michael Shaara Memorial Bench?," Civil War Memory Blog, January 22, 2009, http://cwmemory.com/2009/01/22/why-does-hollywood-cemetery-need-a-michael-shaara-memorial-bench/ (accessed August 11, 2017). See also "Dedication of Michael Shaara Memorial Bench donated by Stephen Lang, July 3, 2008," The Pickett Society, http://www.pickettsociety.com/events/2008_07_03/index.html (accessed August 11, 2017).

The tours that I lead at Arlington National Cemetery begin here. We are standing in Section 27, a location in the northeastern corner of the cemetery bordered by the wall to our right that separates this hallowed ground from the Marine Corps Memorial, popularly known as the Iwo Jima Monument. This is a silent corner of the cemetery, far from the tourists who stream up the hill to the Kennedy gravesite and the Arlington House. Breaking the contemplative quiet are the occasional maintenance vehicles that keep the cemetery pristine, as well as the Netherlands Carillon next door that tolls the time in Big Ben fashion. But the headstones make the greatest impression as they sweep up, then down, and then up again along the rolling terrain. Puzzling to a newcomer are the words "citizen" and "civilian" on the headstones in what is supposed to be a military cemetery. Yet they tell a story central to Arlington and mirror an even larger story of black Americans who lived through the transitions from slavery to segregation.

Here rest roughly 3,800 people whose individual stories likely will never be reclaimed and whose actions during a crucial moment in our past shaped the definition of freedom. Many of the headstones contain no name. The situation frustrates me because, whether the bodies have been identified or not, the people within these grounds did not leave records that allow doing justice to their memory. We know only that they were African Americans who died in the vicinity of Washington. More can be teased out of the military records of another 1,500 who fought with the U.S. Colored Troops and who also lie in this section. But we cannot learn much about Samuel Anderson, "Citizen," or what brought him here. We can merely situate him within a broader movement of people who either fled

Headstone, Arlington National Cemetery, Virginia
(Photograph by Will Gallagher)

the bonds of slavery or struck out on their own as free blacks to seize a greater range of choices opened by the Civil War. Section 27 evokes a past containing the experiences of the enslaved who lived here, the contrabands who congregated during the war here, and the emancipated citizens who earned their subsistence until evicted from here. This sweep of black history at Arlington from 1802 to 1900 even offers surprises: a sister-in-law of Robert E. Lee was a freed slave who lived most of her life on what is now patriotic ground.

Although I do appreciate the cemetery for its wider purpose, I cannot help but recognize that the place owes its existence to a slave plantation founded in 1802 by George Washington Parke Custis. It has been common to say that he built the mansion that sits on the heights overlooking the Potomac River and Washington, but this labor was accomplished primarily by his slaves. Custis inherited them from his natural grandmother the widowed Martha Dandridge Custis, whose second husband was George Washington. The father of the nation also became the adoptive father of Custis, giving him parental advice that betrayed exasperation over the lackadaisical manner in which the boy pursued his studies. With bequests from the Mount Vernon estate, which included nearly 200 slaves spread across three plantations, Custis lived a fairly comfortable life.

Most contemporaries considered Custis an indulgent master, an assessment that both acknowledged him as a good person and criticized him as a loose manager. He does not seem to have been overly harsh, yet even this judgment must be tempered by the reality of life under a master-slave relation. At least half a dozen slaves ran away from Arlington over the years before he died in 1857. And there was an incident with an overseer on one of Custis's three plantations (not Arlington) in which slaves may have been drowned, although the person accused claimed it was nothing more than accidental. Whatever the truth, the master of Arlington does not seem to have been culpable.

He also was a leader in the American Colonization Society, a movement considered to be progressive at the time. The assumption was that white and black people could not live together, that freedom for the enslaved necessitated voluntary relocation to countries like Liberia. This was about as far as progressive Virginians could go without adopting the radical policy of widespread abolition. Here again, Custis was typical of slave owners in arguing for colonization not from recognition of the humanity of his charges but as an effort for white people to avoid being overwhelmed by an ever-increasing, and potentially hostile, black population.[1] His belief in this effort allowed for the immigration of one of his enslaved families to Liberia— William and Rosabella Burke, who sent letters about their experience to Mary Custis Lee, the wife of the future Confederate general. Contemporaries and historians have noticed the affection that was shown to Mary in the letters from former slaves. This appeared to be heartfelt and represents one side of a complicated relationship in which white people considered black people as property while living in a world in which master and slave confronted each other personally.

The other side of this master-slave relationship lies in the story of Maria Syphax, one of the more famous former slaves on the Arlington plantation/cemetery. In 1826, Custis freed Syphax and her family and gave them seventeen acres of ground on the plantation. He had also hosted her marriage with Charles Syphax, a household slave, in the Arlington mansion—a rare occurrence. It turns out that Custis had fathered Maria with Ariana Carter, a household slave of his mother at Mount Vernon. The U.S. Congress in 1866 recognized

Maria's claim to the property, granted out of Custis's "paternal instinct," in legislation that allowed her to live out her life on the grounds until her death in 1886.[2] The illegitimate birth resulted from a relationship we can scarcely reconstruct, but even if it contained tenderness on the part of the slave it occurred within a power relation difficult to separate from sexual molestation. It was a common situation throughout the antebellum South. Thomas Jefferson may be the most famous transgressor with Sally Hemings, but he had company. Historians place the number of mulattoes in the South at between 10 and 12 percent in 1860, although the product of mixed-race unions constituted more significant proportions of city dwellers: 39 percent of free blacks and 20 percent of slaves. These were the numbers reported in a society that publicly frowned upon amalgamation of the races. There were certainly more mixed-race offspring than appear in the record.[3] The union made Maria the half-sister of Custis's only surviving white child, Mary, who became the wife of Robert Edward Lee in a ceremony at Arlington in 1831.

Often away on military duties, Lee reentered the Arlington picture in 1857 with the death of his father-in-law. Custis left the duties of executor of his estate to Lee, who confronted a situation that required him to act like a typical Southern planter. Custis had amassed enormous debt and left the responsibility of sorting out the family's fortunes to his son-in-law. This was not an easy task. Custis had not only stretched his finances but also promised his heirs more proceeds than the estate could fulfill. At the same time, his will ordered that the slaves who constituted the labor force, and main asset beyond land, be freed in five years. Although we do not know for certain if this happened, some of Custis's slaves contended that he told them they would be freed immediately upon his death. Remaining in slavery angered them, as did being driven harder by the departed master's son-in-law to recoup losses. Not surprisingly, some ran away, setting up an inevitable confrontation.

In recent decades the story of these runaways has grown in the scholarly literature on Lee, which depicts him as supervising the whipping of three recaptured fugitives from Arlington. The account rests upon the testimony of former slave Wesley Norris in 1866, but the story appeared before the war in Northern newspapers. Lee administered punishment to slaves as many of his class did—by using a third party. The punished included the sister and cousin of Norris, who said that Lee also ordered the whipper to wash their scars in brine to enhance the pain. After the war, Lee privately called the report untrue but did not refute the allegation publicly. Historians today accept the account as accurate in the larger details.[4]

Because of these stories, Arlington has provided a terrific site for me to convey to touring groups, which have included schoolteachers, that this place features elements very common to slave plantations in the Upper South. Here we encounter runaways, mixed-race offspring, whippings to enforce order, kindness toward slaves, harshness toward them, crushing debt, frustration on the part of the masters and the enslaved, paternalistic ideals by white people, experiments with the colonization movement, and the fact that the columned Arlington House that we admire today exists because of laborers who had little choice other than to build it. None of this was extraordinary.

The Civil War changed the equation and ushered in an era when formerly enslaved people, in conjunction with U.S. military forces, created on these grounds one of the more successful government-supported programs for black people in U.S. history.[5]

As the war came to Washington, so did the contrabands. The term was coined by Major General Benjamin F. Butler for slaves escaping from masters and reaching Union hands. As a way to circumvent the Fugitive Slave Law, Butler defined fugitives as contraband because they allowed whites to go to war while black labor produced the matériel to conduct it. Particularly after Congress banned slavery in the District of Columbia in April 1862, contrabands from Maryland and Virginia flowed to the nation's capital. And they kept coming until they overflowed the camps in the city, causing cramped conditions and diseases that claimed the lives of many. Someone who witnessed this firsthand was Harriet Jacobs, a famous escaped slave whose story gained renewed interest during the war. She was among the many who saw the need for greater relief in the Alexandria and Washington area.

The chief quartermaster of Washington looked over the river for a solution and chose Arlington to relocate these refugees. Founded in May 1863, the Freedman's Village was intended to be a temporary way station to teach freed people self-sufficiency. The government also used the labor of able-bodied men and women to support the operation. While providing workers with ten dollars per month plus rations and living space, the army taxed them five dollars per month to be put toward a contraband fund for the support of people too young, too old, or too infirm to labor. By January 1864, dwellings had been constructed along with a church, hospital, and home for the aged—all aligned on well laid-out streets with a park in the center. Workshops included blacksmiths, wheelwrights, carpenters, tailors, and shoemakers. But the larger concern was agriculture, with the villagers in their first season producing 200 tons of hay and 191 tons of corn fodder, as well as potatoes and other vegetables.

Conflict, nonetheless, existed that showed that African Americans would follow their own minds and, when necessary, resort to collective protest. Danforth B. Nichols, a civilian superintendent of the village appointed by the army, angered many who considered him overly restrictive and abusive. Former slaves testified that he drank and treated them unkindly. One slave indicated, "Mr. Nichols was not kind to the people under him in the camp; he used to knock them about and kick them right smart." He added, "I can not tell the number of persons he used to abuse, but there were a great many."[6] Matters improved little when Nichols was replaced by a military officer in the Quartermaster Department. African Americans petitioned to higher authorities for redress. They also protested the manipulation of rents, or one to three dollars per month charged on top of the contraband fund. The pushback led army officials to consider the experiment a failure and, after the war, to try to disband the village.

But the village endured. By 1865, it had come under control of the Freedmen's Bureau, a government-funded agency run by the military to aid the transition of slaves to freedom. In 1868, an effort to shut down the village was launched. Black people resisted, aided by the fact that Northerners did not mind the delicious irony of black people prospering on the property of General Lee, whose leadership had caused so many Union deaths. Four years earlier, the grounds also had become a national cemetery, with Quartermaster General Montgomery C. Meigs determined to bury bodies as close to Arlington House as possible to discourage the Lees from returning. By 1888, 170 families (nearly 800 individuals) were still living in the village.

The village did not exist in isolation but nourished black activism as part of the greater Alexandria County community. As the war ended, villagers and community blacks petitioned for the right to vote. By the summer of 1867, because of Radical Reconstruction, most black males in Alexandria County were voting Republican. Arlington estate straddled two of Alexandria County's three districts, giving the Freedman's Village political clout at the local level. Blacks held council seats, the county treasurer's office, the county clerk's office, and more.[7] This led to an effort in 1888 by Democrats to break this power by purging villagers from the voting rolls, claiming that living on a military reservation did not make them residents of the state of Virginia. Despite their activism, black people could not control the burial of their race at Arlington. Leaders like Frederick Douglass bristled at the segregation, asserting that black soldiers should lie with the white heroes of the Union. But this area became known as the "lower cemetery," which all understood to mean the colored section.

Development pressure coupled with the political climate that turned against African Americans spelled the demise of the Freedman's Village.[8] The cemetery needed to expand, and the village lay in the southeast area of the grounds. Prime property. A government study calculated what residents had put into their homes and came up with the figure of $75,000 to reimburse them. This compensation came in 1900 as the villagers were evicted and the buildings torn down. Today, not a trace of the village remains.

Such are some of the stories that wash over me as I stand in Section 27, a place that allows for discussion of a wide range of black history that engages with the Civil War. It bothers me that there are no signs that can inform visitors who lie here, although I am the first to admit that something done without proper thought could mar the sanctity of the spot and the cemetery in general. It is not an easy solution. It also saddens me that we will never know the personal stories of the people whose headstones appear before us. Many undoubtedly improved their lives; some likely died disappointed. The fact that these graves exist testifies to the determination of a people who tried to change their lives. They seized a moment, for good or for ill.

And their headstones have left behind a comment that undoubtedly was unintentional. "Citizen" was adopted by bureaucrats to distinguish these dead from soldiers, and nothing more. But the historian in me cannot help but note an ironic statement being made. In 1857, the U.S. Supreme Court declared in the *Dred Scott* decision that people of sub-Saharan African descent were not citizens. It pleases me to see a word carved on the stone of Samuel Anderson, a stone that lies in a U.S. government facility, that declares otherwise.

NOTES

1. *The African Repository, and Colonial Journal* 3 (February 1828): 356–60.

2. *Boston Daily Advertiser*, May 19, 1866; *Lowell Daily Citizen and News*, May 22, 1866; *U.S. Statutes at Large*, 39th Cong., 1st Sess. (Washington, D.C., 1866), 589–90.

3. Robert William Fogel and Stanley L. Engerman, *Time on the Cross: The Economics of American Negro Slavery*, 2 vols. (Boston: Little, Brown, 1974), 1:132; James Ford Rhodes, *History of the United States from the Compromise of 1850 to the McKinley-Bryan Campaign of 1896*, new ed. (New York: Macmillan, 1920), 340. See also *Population of the United States in 1860, Compiled from the Original Returns of the Eighth Census* (Washington: Government Printing Office, 1864), x.

4. John W. Blassingame, ed., *Slave Testimony: Two Centuries of Letters, Speeches, Interviews, and Autobiographies* (Baton Rouge: Louisiana State University Press, 1977), 467–68. For the best analysis of this instance, see Elizabeth Brown Pryor, *Reading the Man: A Portrait of Robert E. Lee through His Private Letters* (New York: Viking, 2007), 269–72.

5. For a good study of the evolution of Arlington through

Freedman's Village, cemetery, and beyond, see Micki McElya, *The Politics of Mourning: Death and Honor in Arlington National Cemetery* (Cambridge, Mass.: Harvard University Press, 2016).

6. Ira Berlin et al., eds., *Freedom: A Documentary History of Emancipation, 1861–1867*, ser. 1, vol. 2, *The Wartime Genesis of Free Labor: The Upper South* (New York: Cambridge University Press, 1993), 295.

7. Joseph P. Reidy, "'Coming from the Shadow of the Past': The Transition from Slavery to Freedom at Freedmen's Village, 1863–1900," *Virginia Magazine of History and Biography* 95 (October 1987): 403–28.

8. Reidy makes this most sensible conclusion, situating the demise of the village within a broader context.

Nineteenth-century Americans loved cemeteries. They thought of them as places where authentic feelings could well up and one could quietly contemplate the meaning of human existence while surrounded by the mysteries of death. That's why they made them so beautiful. Mount Auburn Cemetery in Cambridge, Massachusetts—the final resting place of Nathaniel Bowditch—is more beautiful than most. Beneath statues of soaring white angels, towering obelisks, or decorative urns lie the remains of thousands of New England elites—from Henry Adams and Edward Everett to Charles Sumner and Julia Ward Howe—their graves bordered by almost 200 acres of naturalistic gardens, crisscrossed by serpentine pathways and dotted with lakes overhung with flowering dogwood and weeping birch. This particular burial ground is renowned for launching the rural cemetery movement that reflected the growing romanticization of nature and death itself. But what drew me to Mount Auburn was my desire to see the grave of a soldier whose story figured prominently in my first book—a study of how Civil War Northerners contemplated and memorialized suffering.[1] It felt right to pay respects to the Bowditch family for having left behind such an abundance of material documenting their wartime struggles. I expected to doff my cap at Nathaniel's grave and move on. But instead, I experienced an unexpected surge of anger and sadness as I stood before his headstone.

Of all the historical subjects that I've come across over the years, Nathaniel Bowditch is the one whose story has affected me most. I used to feel guilty about this fact, since he came from such an elite Boston family. They were certainly worthy elites, who had risen from modest beginnings and gone on to support

(previous page)
Grave of Nathaniel Bowditch in Mount Auburn
Cemetery, Cambridge, Massachusetts
(Photograph by Will Gallagher)

abolitionism and donate their time to the less fortunate, but they were nonetheless incredibly privileged. They socialized with Boston Brahmins and had servants to see to their daily needs. All the Bowditch men went to Harvard. And each summer, the whole family decamped for their second home to escape the city's stifling heat and to avoid the regular outbreaks of cholera that killed up to 10 percent of their poorer neighbors' children. Usually my sympathies aren't engaged by people who enjoyed such disproportionate advantages.

But I empathized with Nathaniel in part because, for all his opportunities, he struck me as profoundly ordinary. At the same time, his story seemed to encapsulate something more universal about this war in particular and about manhood in general. Bowditch never appeared to meet his family's oversized expectations, and I had the impression that he was more or less goaded into war by his circumstance and social pressure. At least initially, he found the military to be a brutal and alien world, and he worried that he lacked the qualities required to lead men—an understandable anxiety, given that he was only twenty-two when commissioned as a second lieutenant. There were times when he desperately wanted to come home. Yet Bowditch also shared the elevated patriotism of the day, proclaiming his willingness to die for an honorable cause. Along with the rest of his family, he was adamant that slaveholding needed to end. The Bowditches believed—as do I—that so far as any war could be just, this war to end slavery and preserve democratic republicanism was morally defensible. The white South was never going to end slavery on its own; only war could have brought an end to one of the evilest systems of oppression the world has ever seen.

As a historian, I know this is true. But as someone who teaches not only the history of the Civil War but also the history of war in general, I find myself torn over the sheer stupidity and waste of armed conflict as a means of solving any issue. The more I ponder the idea of settling an argument by putting masses of mostly young people into uniforms, sending them off to massacre a bunch of strangers, and then declaring that those who massacre the most have won, the less I comprehend how war continues to be justified, given that it guarantees lasting bitterness and continuing violence, profits for those who equip armies, and terror and suffering for the rest. We talk very little about the illogic of war in the modern era, and even less about war's ultimate costs—a frightening and depressing subject to contemplate, highlighting how each war tends to bleed into the next, strengthening the structures, mindsets, and divisions that have kept Americans fighting one enemy or another from the moment of the country's founding to now. This is one of the great dilemmas of studying the Civil War for me: it means trying to balance two contradictory ideas—that this specific war was necessary and that war in general is absurd.

More than any other wartime death, Nathaniel Bowditch's encapsulates both of these ideas in my mind. He was a war hero who died in a noble cause, yet in reality, he might just as well have stayed at home. His death had no significance in the grand scheme of things. He wasn't killed in a decisive battle where his presence helped turned the tide toward victory; he died in a minor skirmish while charging toward the enemy, possibly because he'd lost control of his horse. But having recently faced an insinuation of cowardice, he may have simply been too afraid to retreat; like millions of young men before and after him, the fear of being labeled unmanly may have propelled him forward in the face of death. Whenever historians pay homage to heroism and noble wartime sacrifice, I worry that we're complicit in reinforcing the logic that leads to such deaths. And yet how else can we honor the antislavery motives of a soldier like Bowditch?

The fact that the Bowditches left behind so much material no doubt made it easier to empathize with them than with others who left far more fragmentary archives. Civil War historians are unusually fortunate in having a vast mass of material written by ordinary people. Studying the social worlds and experiences of nonelites at other points in the nineteenth century often necessitates making do without many original voices, yet almost everyone sent and received letters during this war, and tens of thousands of soldiers kept diaries. Caught up in events thought worthy of preservation, veterans tucked these chronicles away, while their families stored letters and mementos for future generations. But even so, it's still the case that most of what we find in the archives are truncated collections containing only a handful of letters or a partially completed diary, hurriedly recorded and often hard to read, and typically mute on the writers' pre- and postwar lives.

The collection containing Nathaniel Bowditch's wartime correspondence is different.[2] His father, Henry, was a committed record keeper and genealogist who had kept everything relating to his own father, the famed astronomer and mathematician Nathaniel Bowditch, after whom he named his firstborn son. Following this son's death, Henry spent a decade creating folio-sized memorial volumes dedicated to his legacy, which contained letters dating back to Nathaniel's time as a schoolboy in the 1850s, correspondence sent and received during the war, and every message of condolence the family received. He created another memorial volume for Nathaniel's

wartime fiancée, Katherine Day Putnam, upon her death, while his other two sons—Charles and Vincent—left their own scrapbooks, memoirs, and collections of personal papers to provide additional insight into this family's history. All of this material made it relatively easy to conjure the Bowditches in my mind—to track their connections and get a sense of Nathaniel's social and personal milieu in a way that's much more difficult for any of the other Civil War participants who have populated my work over the years.

But curiously, the more I discovered about this family, the less I felt capable of doing justice to their experiences. Before I started writing, I spent six months in piecing together a time line detailing everything that could be known about where and how various Bowditch family members spent their time, including tracking Nathaniel's cavalry regiment and figuring out the larger social scene in which he moved. I did this to be able to contextualize the sentiments appearing in their voluminous correspondence, which shifted in interesting ways throughout the war, particularly in terms of how Nathaniel felt about his officers, the progress of the war, and his suitability for military life. But I also felt like I'd learned things during this process that were impossible to "prove" given the conventions of historical writing. I could hint but not state outright my sense of Nathaniel's inner conflicts over being a son who always tried but never quite managed to come up to the mark—an impossible standard established by his famous grandfather and constantly reiterated by both of his parents. I could suggest but not confirm that Henry Bowditch was motivated to construct such elaborate memorials to his son because he needed to repress his own role in forcing his son to remain at war. And I felt stymied in fully charting the wartime roles of the women in Nathaniel's life because they appear to have destroyed their correspondence (it's clear that Katherine burned her letters prior to her death, but for unknown reasons almost nothing survives from the hand of Nathaniel's mother or sister).

I was fascinated by the glimpses that this collection nonetheless allowed of how a single wartime death affected some of the women and children closest to Nathaniel. I had the sense that his mother, Olivia, was the family's anchor, tempering his volatile father and shoring the rest of the family up in the wake of Nathaniel's death. Katherine Day Putnam, who contracted a secret engagement with Nathaniel during the war, seemed equally important in his decision to enlist and in his experience while in the service. After he was killed, she went on to live out what had become a standard plot in wartime poetry, literature, and drama—a wife or sweetheart who is so overcome by a soldier's death that she literally pines away after hearing the news—creating herself as a perfect embodiment of female patriotism.

Katherine was seventeen when Nathaniel enlisted in late 1861 and nineteen when he died, and she wrote poetry suggestive of someone striving earnestly to live by the tenets of Victorian womanhood—selfless, modest (she wrote anonymously), and extremely earnest. Henry Bowditch initially clung to his son's fiancée, viewing her as the one person who could understand the depths of his grief. They embarked on an emotional exchange that was intense, even by Victorian standards. At first, she was "My darling Nat's Kate" and "most precious Kate, Bride of my darling's heart." Later, Henry began referring to her as "my own darling little daughter" and to idealize her as one who had wielded an "almost divine influence" over his son. Asserting that neither of them would ever "get over" Nathaniel's loss, even if others did so, Henry appeared to cast Katherine permanently in a mourning role. It is obvious that she embraced this position at first, probably for reasons as complex as those that kept Nathaniel at war—to embody noble womanhood, as an outlet for her heartache, or as a form of war service—but it was not a role that could simply be shrugged off over time. Whereas Henry eventually went back to work as a professor of clinical medicine at Harvard, Katherine's options were limited either to casting Nathaniel's memory aside or devoting her whole life to grief. She chose the latter, dying single in 1875 at the age of thirty-one.

So many aspects of this story called out for speculation. Why did both Katherine and Nathaniel's sister, Olivia, who lived until the late 1920s, remain unmarried? They were friends who buoyed each other up in the face of wartime losses. But I wondered how much guilt the war left behind in women like these. When Nathaniel was sick and wanted to come home, Katherine apparently urged him not to resign. Before burning her letters, she showed them to Henry, who later wrote about her begging Nathaniel to "be patient, under whatsoever suffering" the war might bring; telling him that if he died it would be in a "holy fight"; and urging him "not to shrink from any danger or any duty, through fear of pain or the pangs of death." Other family members, including Nathaniel's mother, apparently did so too. In their pleadings, these women lived up to the family's patriotic ideals, and in the immediacy of the war they were confident in their decision. But how did they feel once the war was over and others had come home?

Why did Nathaniel's youngest brother, Vincent, who wrote in a rather passionate vein to Katherine after his brother's death, also remain single and then spend his last decades memorializing their father? I didn't know much about Vincent, except that, as a young boy, during the Civil War he dressed in a military uniform and pretended to be Nathaniel. He seems to have idolized his older brother. I knew that he would have witnessed his father's return from the front lines, devastated by his brother's death, and that he lived many of his formative years while his father worked on a series of memorials to Nathaniel, which were then locked away in a memorial cabinet kept in the family parlor. These memorials included pages from Henry's journals. One of these, written a few years after Nathaniel's death, read, "How much has all the beauty of life gone from me. I seem to have nobody to look forward to as my successor, and the sweet hopes I had formed of him are all vanished." It seems that Henry had enshrined his dead son in the role of his "successor" in a way that left no room for Vincent. If Katherine Putnam lived in the shadow of the war to the end of her life, then surely Nathaniel's brother did too, as the war created ripples that silently worked their way outward, resonating long into the future.

In looking at Nathaniel's grave, I felt both sadness and anger, partly because of the way this one individual was memorialized and partly because of the way we memorialize war. When I finally found Nathaniel's grave, the first thing that struck me was its size: given the lavish attention his father had spent in constructing memorials, I'd expected an elaborate headstone befitting the heroic story his father had created. Instead, Nathaniel's stone is small and flat—humbler than it appears in the accompanying photograph. Even more poignant is the fact that this stone is set into the ground a few feet away from the towering figure of Nathaniel's grandfather. Upon the death of the original Nathaniel Bowditch, British sculptor Robert Ball Hughes cast a life-size bronze figure in his honor—the first of its kind to be made in the United States—and seated him atop a lofty pedestal in white granite with an octant and celestial globe at his feet to remind the world of his scientific prowess. The burden of this famous ancestor—and what I suspected was the crushing weight of family expectations to live up to his memory—seemed writ in stone here, as Nathaniel lies forever at his grandfather's feet. The older man died at a ripe old age after a lifetime of accomplishments. We have no idea what deeds Nathaniel might have achieved if he'd lived through the war, or how many children he and Katherine might have had, or what those children might have gone on to do. We will never know how the war affected all the younger brothers who could never measure up to the dead, just as we don't know how many amazing thinkers, artists, inventors, or inspirational people died on battlefields, in contraband camps, or military hospitals. We commemorate individual deaths, but war kills possibilities as well, and there are no memorials to that.

NOTES

1. Frances M. Clarke, *War Stories: Suffering and Sacrifice in the Civil War North* (Chicago: University of Chicago Press, 2011).

2. Henry Ingersoll Bowditch Papers, Massachusetts Historical Society, Boston. Collections relating to various other members of the Bowditch family are held at the same repository.

III MEMORIALS
PLACES OF MEMORY

13 SOLDIERS AND SAILORS MEMORIAL HALL
A PLACE FOR QUIET REFLECTION

CAROL REARDON

oldiers and Sailors Memorial Hall in the Oakland section of Pittsburgh awes visitors more than it welcomes them. In 1891, a committee of delegates from Allegheny County's twenty-eight Grand Army of the Republic posts determined to build a memorial "of a character so imposing and impressive as to represent the wealth, intelligence, and patriotic sentiment of our great industrial center." Those attending the building's dedication in October 1910 validated the success of the planners' vision, declaring the edifice to be "among the most costly and magnificent military memorials in the world," one that reminded many of the Mausoleum of Halicarnassus, one of the Seven Wonders of the Ancient World.[1]

As a child, I cared nothing about Soldiers and Sailors Memorial Hall's founding. I did not know about the unpredictable shifts in state and local political support confronting the project's commissioners at every turn, the legal challenges to various state and local funding schemes, and the unprecedented vote in 1905 by Allegheny County residents to impose upon themselves a special tax to raise the $1.7 million needed for construction to begin in 1908. I knew nothing of the building's weeklong dedication in October 1910 that included a grand parade with over 2,000 Civil War veterans, two regiments of the Pennsylvania National Guard, Spanish-American War veterans, and a group called the "Military Order of the Medal of Honor Legion." Only the name of the president of that last-named organization, one-time Union major general Daniel E. Sickles, might have sparked a bit of recognition.[2]

No, I knew none of this when, after a Pittsburgh Pirates baseball game at old Forbes Field, my grandmother took me to our bus stop, then situated in

(previous page)
Soldiers and Sailors Memorial Hall,
Pittsburgh, Pennsylvania
(Photograph by Will Gallagher)

94

front of this imposing and distinctive building. The green space the founders managed to secure in front of Soldiers and Sailors—the local nickname for the edifice—allowed the main entrance to the building to sit atop a slight hill far back from busy Forbes Avenue. The long bricked walkway to the imposing bronze doors contributed significantly to Soldiers and Sailors' power to both intimidate and impress. The large artillery shells and siege guns that flanked the walkway immediately caught my eye. I desperately wanted to get a closer look at Frederick Hibbard's larger-than-life bronze portrait statues—*Parade Rest*, featuring a Union infantryman, and *Lookout*, portraying a Civil War sailor—that conspicuously guarded the main entrance. My grandmother, who I could rely upon to support anything of an educational nature that captured my interest, quickly promised to take me into Soldiers and Sailors after a future ballgame.

My first visit inside the grand sandstone and terra cotta hall a few months later made a lasting impression on me. A stone tablet near the entrance announced Soldiers and Sailors' mission to extend "appreciation of the courage, the loyalty to the government, and the devotion to freedom" of Allegheny County's Civil War combatants.[3] Of course, I did not understand the emancipationist tone of these words until years later. My grandmother and I may have been the only visitors in the quiet, cavernous building that day. Thus, I felt free to peek through the doors of the large auditorium that filled the center of the hall's first floor. Designed to seat approximately 2,300 guests, it featured a wide stage; originally an immense battle mural was to provide a thematic backdrop for that platform, but when costs became prohibitively high, the planners opted instead for the words inscribed there still today: Abraham Lincoln's Gettysburg Address. An inscription

on the auditorium wall also acknowledged the role of Pittsburgh's Subsistence Committee that organized local civilian support for the war effort between August 1861 and January 1866, its work "sustained by voluntary contributions of the citizens."[4] I looked into several smaller rooms, originally designed as meeting rooms for Allegheny County's GAR posts, still decorated with flags and military-themed artwork. On one wall of the Gettysburg Room hung an impressive oil painting; in the summer of 2017 I finally learned its subject was Brigadier General Alexander Hays, a longtime Pittsburgh resident whose division helped to repulse Pickett's Charge in July 1863 and who fell dead ten months later in the battle of the Wilderness.

My grandmother soon found a comfortable bench and let me roam at my own pace through the main corridors that trace the outline of the building. By tradition, they are called the West, North, East, and Main Halls, because uncompromising Union veterans who first staffed the building after its dedication simply refused to apply "South" to any part of a hall dedicated to the valor of Northern soldiers. Far more than the auditorium or the meeting rooms, the contents of the glass cases that lined these corridors endlessly fascinated me. Relics as nondescript as pieces of wood from Civil War battlefields—a piece of oak from Gettysburg, or cross-sections of tree trunks that revealed embedded bullets—provided little in the way of informative narrative or historical context, but I did not mind. Other cases displayed rifles, bayonets, bugles, swords, cap boxes, artillery shells, Bibles, canteens, and much more that offered small glimpses into life and death in wartime. The personal connections between relic and individual soldier drew my greatest interest. Most Pennsylvania regiments had served in Virginia, but the 77th and 78th Pennsylvania Infantry that included large contingents of Allegheny County volunteers served entirely in the Western Theater; the family of Samuel H. Croyle of the latter unit donated his pocket watch, its unique chain made from mussel shells gathered from the Tennessee River. I found a colorful Confederate drum captured at Spotsylvania and then carried throughout the rest of the war by musician Robert Y. Thompson of Pittsburgh's 61st Pennsylvania Infantry quite appealing. I could not pry my eyes from the kepi worn by First Lieutenant James T. Harbison of Pittsburgh's 139th Pennsylvania Infantry, especially the hole made in it by the bullet that killed him at Salem Church in May 1863. Tattered battle flags once carried into battle or on parade by Pittsburgh's 102nd Pennsylvania Infantry—stored along with items belonging to its commander, Colonel John W. Patterson, slain at the Wilderness not far from General Hays—filled another case. Most memorable of all, a segment of tree trunk from Chickamauga with two cannonballs embedded in it sat on the floor of the corridor unprotected by glass, so I could touch it![5]

But in the end, I left that first visit to Soldiers and Sailors thoroughly obsessed not with these evocative relics but with a burning, very personal question. Sixty-one large metal plaques lined the walls of the hall's corridors, each representing a Pennsylvania regiment with Allegheny County soldiers in its ranks, including all their names. My family had lived in the Pittsburgh area for generations, I believed. Did I have an ancestor named on one of those plaques?

My unrelenting search for an answer soon became a family annoyance. Neither of my parents knew if they had Civil War ancestors; their memories of family military service went back only to World War I. My grandmother, now somewhat regretting that she had taken me to Soldiers and Sailors at all, remembered only vaguely that her grandfather had a sword and "a funny hat" she later recognized as a kepi. Finally, however, she contacted her aunt Blanche—at ninety-nine, our oldest living relative—and asked for her help. I can still remember the big smile on my grandmother's face as she told me that my great-great-grandfather fought in the Civil War! His name was Joseph Garver, and he served as a corporal in the 14th Pennsylvania Cavalry.

Surprisingly, I received the news with mixed feelings. On one hand, I was entirely elated to know that I had a direct family connection to the Civil War. I remembered seeing a plaque to the 14th Pennsylvania Cavalry at Soldiers and Sailors, so I just knew I would see one familiar name there. On the other hand, I could find no evidence that Corporal Garver fought at Gettysburg, Antietam, or Spotsylvania, or in any of the Civil War's major battles. With no research skills at my command, the only reference to the 14th Pennsylvania Cavalry I recalled seeing on my visit to Soldiers and Sailors was a conspicuous oil painting featuring Colonel James M. Schoonmaker leading the regiment in a charge at Third Winchester in the 1864 Shenandoah Valley campaign, an action for which he received the Medal of Honor. I had trouble concealing my dismay in learning that my ancestor served in what I then deemed a relative backwater of the war.

Nonetheless, I still wanted to return to Soldiers and Sailors to find Corporal Garver's name on the 14th Pennsylvania Cavalry's plaque. When the opportunity came, however, my lingering dismay turned to utter devastation. I rushed through the front door, found the regimental plaque, and read the names, and when I reached Company L, I found bronze letters spelling out a name I did not expect to see: Private John Garver. No other soldier surnamed Garver appeared on the plaque.

I stood there, utterly stunned. They got his rank wrong! Worse, they got his first name wrong! How could anyone make such an egregious error for any soldier who fought for his country, let alone for MY soldier? Try as I might, the bitterness of that disappointment quashed all enthusiasm to ask more questions. I did not care to dig deeper. Indeed, I did not go back to Soldiers and Sailors again for years.

Still, the emotional distress of that day at Soldiers and Sailors may well have been essential to my ultimate decision to become a historian. I did not follow a direct path, to be sure. After I graduated from Brentwood High School, I went on to Allegheny College to major in biology. I continued to read about the Civil War, mostly about my favorite Eastern Theater leaders and battles, still upset that my family apparently played no role in them. The Civil War had become my hobby. One day, however, on a small balcony in Reis Library at Allegheny, I found some marvelous treasures I never had seen before. Along with a full set of the war's official records, I found Samuel P. Bates's *History of the Pennsylvania Volunteers*. Those five thick volumes, first published in 1870, reignited the nearly extinguished flame of my historical curiosity and helped to heal the scars of my last visit to Soldiers and Sailors.

Perusing Bates's volumes revealed important information that put me back on the right track. For starters, the index included a soldier named Joseph Garver. He had enlisted initially in April 1861 as a private in Company B, 9th Pennsylvania Infantry, a three-month regiment raised shortly after Fort Sumter. He mustered out in July 1861, but he waited until November 1862 to reenlist in the 14th Pennsylvania Cavalry. Perhaps because of his previous service, he mustered in as a corporal.[6] This perfectly fit the information Aunt Blanche gave my grandmother more

than a decade before! I pushed on, now suspecting that I had greatly erred when I accepted Private John Garver of Company L, 14th Pennsylvania Cavalry, as my Civil War ancestor. Bates confirmed that Corporal Joseph Garver was an entirely different individual, one who served in Company M of that same regiment. Now excited, and with history professors to guide me, I began to dig deeper. Dr. Jay Luvaas, soon to become my historical mentor, pointed me toward *Allegheny County, Pennsylvania in the War for the Suppression of the Rebellion*, which confirmed that the plaques in Soldiers and Sailors included only the names of soldiers who enlisted in Allegheny County. I quickly realized that Bates's volumes credited Company B of the 9th Pennsylvania Infantry, Joseph Garver's first unit, to Armstrong County, just northeast of Allegheny County. Bates also confirmed that the 14th Pennsylvania Cavalry included a large contingent of Armstrong County recruits. At a family reunion that summer, I learned that Joseph Garver, in fact, had enlisted in Kittanning in Armstrong County. The pieces came together! Short bursts of enlightenment—at Soldiers and Sailors, on a library balcony, at a family picnic—finally gave me my answers. The plaque at the memorial hall contained no error. The fault for the mistaken identity rested on me alone. I felt I had to atone for that!

Even as I completed my biology degree, I continued to hone the fine art of Civil War soldier research. History had hooked me, whether I knew it or not. I obtained a copy of Corporal Joseph Garver's compiled service record from the National Archives. Bates had listed him as "Not accounted for" at muster out, and I feared that perhaps my ancestor had deserted. After all, his regimental history noted that, after Appomattox, when soldiers in the 14th Pennsylvania Cavalry who still owed service received orders to duty in Kansas, "a large number of the boys—brave boys who had never failed to face the death dealing cannon in battle—left their commands and stole away to their homes at this time."[7] So I felt great relief to learn that Corporal Garver received an honorable discharge in June 1865 and returned home to his family. The change in my career path that took me from biology to history started soon after this discovery.

Since my initial explorations in the early 1960s, Soldiers and Sailors has expanded its mission to salute Allegheny County veterans of all wars. In 1963, about the time of my first visit, its commissioners opened the "Hall of Valor" to honor local residents who received the Medal of Honor from the Civil War to the present, as well as those who received the Distinguished Service Cross, Navy Cross, Air Force Cross, and Silver Star in twentieth- and twenty-first-century conflicts. The hall now includes displays on Allegheny County's pre–Civil War military history and local civilian contributions in wartime. It also remains a quiet place for reflection tucked in among the University of Pittsburgh, Carnegie Mellon University, the Carnegie Museum of Natural History, and a sprawling Veterans Administration medical complex. Most of all, it also continues to be my personal touchstone as the place I first began my journey to becoming a historian.

NOTES

1. Quoted in Memorial Hall Board of Managers, *Soldiers and Sailors Memorial Hall* (Pittsburgh, Pa.: Allegheny County Graphics Department, 1988), 3; *National Tribune*, September 20, 1910.

2. *National Tribune*, September 20, 1910.

3. Samuel M. Evans, comp., *Allegheny County, Pennsylvania, in the War for the Suppression of the Rebellion, 1861–1865* (Pittsburgh, Pa.: Board of Managers, Soldiers and Sailors Memorial Hall, 1924), 8.

4. Evans, *Allegheny County*, 9.

5. Memorial Hall Board of Managers, *Soldiers and Sailors Memorial Hall*, 16, 18.

6. Samuel P. Bates, *History of the Pennsylvania Volunteers, 1861–5; Prepared in Compliance with Acts of the Legislature* (1869–70; 10-vol. repr. with new 4-vol. index, Wilmington, N.C.: Broadfoot, 1993–94), 1:90, 8:892.

7. Rev. William Davis Slease, *The Fourteenth Pennsylvania Cavalry in the Civil War*, reprint ed. (Butler, Pa.: Mechling Associates, 1999), 286.

STEPHEN CUSHMAN

No escape from the rhythm of events.
—*Marcus Aurelius,* Meditations

Regilded in 2013 with a layer of 23.75-karat gold leaf, then repaired in 2014 after the new gilding showed the fine cracks called "crazing," there he sits on his golden stallion, perhaps Duke, his favorite horse during the war, trailing the Angel of Victory in triumph down Fifth Avenue. As a young Connecticut Yankee I had fewer daily brushes with reminders of the war than peers in Southern states. But every childhood or adolescent trip to New York held out the chance to stand at the southeast corner of Frederick Law Olmsted's Central Park, in Grand Army Plaza, and stare at this equestrian epic, the last major work of Augustus Saint Gaudens.[1]

An intriguing name, that resonant hybrid of Roman imperialism and French Christianity. He insisted on no hyphen, though his son Homer preferred and used it when editing *The Reminiscences of Augustus Saint-Gaudens,* published in 1913 by the Century Company. Also intriguing was the sculptor's directive, in 1888, the year he began teaching modeling at the Art Students League on West Fifty-seventh Street, on the correct pronunciation of his name: "'gau' as in 'gaudy,' 'ens,' as in 'enslave.'"[2] Enslave? Was there no other word for the Dublin-born immigrant, his parents fleeing the Great Famine six months after his birth in 1848, to choose? Ensconce, ensnare, ensue?

The Civil War, which began the year he turned thirteen, takes up small space in Saint Gaudens's *Reminiscences.* Where it appears, recollections of it consist mostly of "great visions and great remembrances." From a window on the first floor of a building on Broadway, just north of Eleventh Street, the young New Yorker saw "virtually the entire contingent of New England volunteers on their way to the Civil War, a spectacle profoundly impressive, even to my youthful

(previous page)
Statue of William Tecumseh Sherman, New York City
(Photograph by Will Gallagher)

imagination." He recollected "a vision of General Grant himself on horseback, with his slouch hat, during some great parade in New York City," adding parenthetically, "(his face I liked because of its kindliness)." And he had one other vision: "But, above all, what remains in my mind is seeing in a procession the figure of a tall and very dark man, seeming entirely out of proportion in his height with the carriage in which he was driven, bowing to the crowds on each side." Having withheld the name for dramatic effect, Saint Gaudens closed the paragraph with artful understatement: "This was on the corner of Twentieth or Twenty-first Street and Fifth Avenue, and the man was Abraham Lincoln on his way to Washington."[3]

The apparently unified group of Sherman riding Duke in the wake of Victory, unveiled at last on Memorial Day, May 30, 1903, turns out to be an assemblage of disparate parts, each with its distinct provenance and history. First—begun in the fall of 1887—came the bust of the complicated man who would soon be the only surviving four-star general in the U.S. Army, Ulysses S. Grant having died in 1885 and Philip H. Sheridan about to follow in the summer of 1888. The celebrated architect of the March to the Sea, recently moved to New York, was irascibly outspoken about "being pestered with damned sculptors" and adamantly refused to pose for any, including Saint Gaudens, who finally secured Sherman's consent through the persuasive mediation of Whitelaw Reid, successor to Horace Greeley as editor of the *New York Tribune*. In his *Reminiscences*, Saint Gaudens called his bust of Sherman, the product of eighteen sittings of two hours each, "a labor of love, for the General had remained in my eye as the typical American soldier ever since I had formed that idea of him during the Civil War." Robert Louis Stevenson, who was sitting for Saint

Gaudens at the same time as Sherman, petitioned the sculptor for an introduction. When the meeting took place at Sherman's apartment on Twenty-third Street, the general immediately asked Stevenson whether he was "one of his boys" in the army and appeared to lose interest in the interview after learning he was not, only to become reanimated when told that his visitor was the author of *Dr. Jekyll and Mr. Hyde* (1886), then "creating a sensation in New York" on the stage. An avid theatergoer all his life, Sherman pronounced on the subject of Stevenson's popular work, "The man who wrote that is no fool."[4]

Calling the sittings with Sherman "a memorable experience," Saint Gaudens regretted "nothing more than that I did not write down a daily record of his conversation, for he talked freely and most delightfully of the war, men and things." Of the Grand Review in May 1865, for example, Sherman recounted that when asked whether he wanted his soldiers to clean themselves up as those of the Army of the Potomac had done, he replied, "By no means. Let them be seen as they fought." According to the artist, the general "was an excellent sitter, except when I passed to his side to study the profile. Then he seemed uneasy ... as if he was watching out for his 'communications to the rear.'" Excellent sitter or no, Sherman could be volatile. Urged at one point by Saint Gaudens to button his coat collar in the manner of Bismarck and von Moltke, Sherman fired back, "I don't give a tinker's damn how men chose to wear their coats, but I want you to know that the General of the Army of the United States will wear his coat any damn way he pleases." Sherman's open collar, from which his thick cloak ripples back in late-autumn Georgia darkening toward winter solstice, is one of the best small details of the finished product.[5]

The bust of Sherman became the core of the monument, which was not commissioned until 1891, the year of the general's death and the year in which Saint Gaudens unveiled naked *Diana*, the highest statue in the city, 347 feet above the street, atop Stanford White's Madison Square Garden. Between the 1891 commission and the 1903 unveiling of Sherman, Saint Gaudens was busy, and increasingly unwell, working on, among other major projects, the Robert Gould Shaw memorial, also equestrian, unveiled on the Boston Common in May 1897. In October 1897 he sailed for Paris with his wife, Augusta (Gussie), seventeen-year-old Homer, and an ambition to bring his work to the attention of Europe. At the Salon of 1898 he exhibited a plaster cast of the Shaw memorial, and at the Salon of 1899 he followed with a plaster cast of Sherman on horseback but without the Angel of Victory, who appeared first with a palm frond in a small model of the complete group, which he also submitted. The Salon gave the place of honor to the Sherman cast, with copious honors following.[6]

Neither Saint Gaudens nor his wife liked Paris, and the sculptor become increasingly depressed and homesick. He worked fitfully on Sherman until the advent of young James Earle Fraser, a talented young artist whose work Saint Gaudens had admired in the Salon of 1898. Fraser became a disciple, soon finding himself assigned to the Sherman work, along with another young assistant, Helen Mears. Finally, the monumental group came together. Alexander Phimister Proctor, whose specialty was animals and who had provided the horse for Saint Gaudens's John Logan memorial in Grant Park, Chicago, produced for the Sherman group the well-endowed stallion now potently treading Charles Follen McKim's polished granite pedestal. But what of the Angel of Victory? An early model for her head is said to have been Elizabeth Cameron, who had posed in New York, but the nude

model in Paris was, according to Saint Gaudens, "a young woman from Georgia, dark, long-legged … certainly the handsomest model I have seen of either sex."[7]

Told by his French doctors that he was seriously ill with cancer of the lower intestine, the sculptor sailed for New York on July 18, 1900. Undergoing two operations at Massachusetts General Hospital later that year, he found himself recovering at his residence in Cornish, New Hampshire, where, according to Homer, "his first serious occupation … was the completion of the Sherman monument." A cast of the monument occupied the place of honor at the Paris Exposition of 1900, "while a plaster duplicate had gone to the French foundry," Thiébaut Frères of Paris. But Saint Gaudens was still unsatisfied and set up a third replica in Cornish, first in an enclosed shed and then "in the field back of his house, to the delight of the farmers, that he might experiment with the pedestal and supervise the application of the patine." The greatest changes sent on to the Paris foundry, from which the monument was shipped to New York in sections in December 1902, were not in the figure of Sherman himself, who "evolved smoothly," but in the figure of Victory, who did not.[8]

No wonder. Female allegorical figures were nothing new in the work of Saint Gaudens. There was his marble *Silence* (1874) at the Masonic Soldiers' and Sailors' Hospital in Utica, New York. There was the winged angelic Victory hovering over the men of the 54th Massachusetts in the Shaw memorial. There was the haunting hooded figure he called *The Mystery of the Hereafter or the Peace That Passeth Understanding* on the memorial for Marian "Clover" Hooper Adams, erected in 1891 in Rock Creek Park, Washington, D.C. Wife of Saint Gaudens's friend Henry Adams, Clover, who suffered from depression, had committed suicide in 1885 at the age of forty-two. The popular name for the hooded figure, androgynous in the eyes of some beholders, was and still is "Grief," a designation to which Adams strenuously objected in a letter of January 24, 1908, to Saint Gaudens's son: "Do not allow the world to tag my figure with a name! Every magazine writer wants to label it as some American patent medicine for popular consumption—*Grief, Despair, Pear's Soap*, or *Macy's Men's Suits Made to Measure.* Your father meant it to ask a question, not to give an answer; and the man who answers will be damned to eternity like the men who answered the Sphinx."[9]

Saint Gaudens meant to ask a question, not to give an answer: fair enough in the case of *The Mystery of the Hereafter* but surely not in the case of Victory leading Sherman. Victory proclaims, she celebrates, she is certain, she is the answer. Perhaps so, but for many, beginning in the 1980s, she has raised plenty of questions, foremost among them, Who was she? With Burke Wilkinson's 1985 biography, *Uncommon Clay: The Life and Works of Augustus Saint Gaudens*, one new answer emerged: she may have been based partly on Albertina Hulgren (or Hultgren), whom Saint Gaudens nicknamed Davida and who subsequently called herself Davida Johnson Clark. A Swede, she was his model, his mistress, his muse, the mother of his son Louis, and in Wilkinson's formulation "his beautiful obsession," whose "traits appeared in all the idealized women in his sculpture."[10] But since the appearance of Wilkinson's biography, with its revelation about Davida, another Victory, or another contributor to Victory, has emerged. She was Harriette Eugenia Anderson, known as Hettie. She was not from Georgia; she was from Columbia, South Carolina, born there in 1873. She was also the model for the ten- and twenty-dollar gold coins Saint Gaudens designed for the United States Mint. She was the dark, long-legged model in Paris, handsomest Saint Gaudens had seen of either sex. And she was African American.[11]

A "nigger as such is a most excellent fellow, but he is not fit to marry, to associate, or vote with me, or mine." So wrote Sherman in a letter dated at his field headquarters at Goldsboro, North Carolina, March 24, 1865. He had already followed Victory into Savannah three months before. He had followed her into Hettie's hometown, which burned, under circumstances still debated and contested, the previous month. In another month, after surrender negotiations with Joseph E. Johnston in the Bennett farmhouse west of Durham Station, he would follow her from North Carolina through the battlefields of Virginia, which he particularly wanted to see, and on to the Grand Review in May.[12]

In one of his notes to his father's *Reminiscences*, Homer repeated the sculptor's exasperated statement, made with respect to his Sherman monument, "I am sick of seeing statues look like stove pipes." Homer continued that his father "longed for the unusual combination of gilded bronze on a cream-colored base. The plan was not wholly feasible, as he failed to obtain the stone he desired for the pedestal. But at least he covered the 'Sherman' with two layers of gold-leaf; and if the 'Marcus Aurelius' on the Capitoline Hill in Rome is a test, that gold-leaf will remain on the 'Sherman' for some centuries." But the original gold leaf did not remain on Sherman, and equestrian Marcus Aurelius was not melted down only because medieval Christian Romans incorrectly identified him as Constantine.[13]

Although hardly intended by him, Saint Gaudens's Victory asks another question: Just what is it, this Victory? If she is the artist's mistress (the head of Sherman's Victory, her lips parted as though she is speaking, looks more like photographs of Davida than photographs of Hettie), is there something inescapably adulterated about it? Could one say the same of History in general? If she is deemed unfit or unacceptable by those she would guide, her feet sandaled and her left leg forward, the shape of her strong thigh against the thin tunic surely another labor of Saint Gaudens's love, is Victory, or History, nothing but mirror on mirror mirrored, in William Butler Yeats's phrasing, each generation choosing to "remember" in its own way?

Returning to the United States in 1904 for ten months, after twenty years of expatriation, Henry James visited Grand Army Plaza, calling it "the heterogeneous, miscellaneous apology for a Square," where his acutely discriminating aesthetic eye dwelt on the "best thing in the picture, obviously": "Saint Gaudens's great group, splendid in its golden elegance and doing more for the scene (by thus giving the beholder a point of dignity for his orientation) than all its other elements together ... the comparative vulgarity of the environment drinking it up, on the one side, like an insatiable sponge, and yet failing at the same time sensibly to impair its virtue." Saint Gaudens acknowledged this high praise in a letter of February 8, 1906, written to James after his comments appeared in the *North American Review*.[14]

But James's praise was elaborately qualified, nuanced, oblique. He had a bone to pick with Saint Gaudens's monument: "I should have risked another word or two, have addressed perhaps even a brief challenge to a certain ambiguity in the Sherman." The "certain ambiguity" that irked James was the "equivocal" idea of Saint Gaudens's image, or more precisely its doubleness: "the image being, on the one side, and splendidly rendered, that of an overwhelming military advance, an irresistible march into an enemy's country—the strain forward, the very inflation of

drapery with the rush, symbolizing the very breath of the Destroyer. But the idea is at the same time ... that the Destroyer is a messenger of peace, with the olive branch too waved in the blast and with embodied grace, in the form of a beautiful American girl, attending his business."

Henry James misread the palm frond of Victory as an olive branch, and his misreading led to the question, How could the Destroyer be at the same time a messenger of peace? There is much to savor about James, of all people, rejecting ambiguity, equivocation, and doubleness, as he goes on to call for their opposite: "I would have the Destroyer, in intention at least, not docked of one of his bristles. I would have him deadly and terrible, and, if he be wanted beautiful, beautiful only as a war-god and crested not with peace, but with snakes. Peace is a long way round from him, and blood and ashes in between.... I would have had a Sherman of the terrible march ... not irradiating benevolence, but signifying, by every ingenious device, the misery, the ruin and the vengeance of his track."[15]

Regilded Sherman redresses at least one of James's complaints. The golden warrior has plenty of new bristles, long metallic quills that spike from his hatless head, from his boots, from Duke's ears, from Victory's wings and right middle finger, from the pine boughs and pine cones stepped on by the horse's right rear hoof to symbolize the conquered South, from every horizontal surface on which desecrating, corrosive pigeons could otherwise land. Even without these freshly discouraging barbs, if James had been the sculptor, guests exiting the Plaza Hotel, which opened to the public two months after Saint Gaudens's death, would have encountered a vastly different, far more terrible vision.

Among the thousands of people who walk by the

Sherman monument each day, it is doubtful many share James's "lapse of satisfaction in the presence of the interweaving" of apparent contradictions. Many of them probably would agree with James's conclusion that "monuments should always have a clean, clear meaning," but does Saint Gaudens's image give any casual passerby or photo-clicking tourist immediate reason to miss a clean, clear meaning?[16] Here is a victor, and this is how victory looked to the late nineteenth century. But James did make a crucial point, though for reasons he could not have known and would not have endorsed: Saint Gaudens's image of Sherman and his Victory is indeed ambiguous, equivocal, double. What is more important, ambiguity, equivocation, and doubleness are some of its cleanest, clearest meanings. They are clear and clean because Sherman's Victory, like the larger history of which it is a much-mythologized part, has turned out to be something more complex and changeable than what James demanded, something continually crazing in the rhythm of events, something in need of constant regilding.

NOTES

1. For background on the regilding and the subsequent repair, see David W. Dunlap, "It's General Sherman's Time to Shine, but Not Too Much," *New York Times*, June 18, 2013, http://cityroom.blogs.nytimes.com/2013/06/18/its-general-shermans-time-to-shine-but-not-too-much/?_r=0; and "A Gilded Monument Is Mysteriously Shedding Its Brand-New Gold," *New York Times*, June 18, 2014, http://www.nytimes.com/2014/06/19/nyregion/william-tecumseh-sherman-monument-mysteriously-sheds-its-brand-new-gold.html?_r=0 (accessed May 16, 2016). For more on Duke as Sherman's favorite horse during the war, see his letter of November 7, 1888, to E. F. Andrews, William Tecumseh Sherman Miscellaneous Manuscripts Collection, Rutherford B. Hayes Presidential Center, http://www.rbhayes.org/hayes/manunews/paper_trail_display.asp?nid=170&subj=manunews (accessed May 19, 2016).

2. Burke Wilkinson, *Uncommon Clay: The Life and Works of Augustus Saint Gaudens* (New York: Harcourt Brace, 1985), xvii.

3. Augustus Saint Gaudens, *The Reminiscences of Augustus Saint-Gaudens*, ed. Homer Saint-Gaudens, 2 vols. (New York: Century, 1913), 1:41–42.

4. Saint Gaudens, *Reminiscences*, 1:378–83; Wilkinson, *Uncommon Clay*, 177–82. Wilkinson cites Lloyd Lewis, *Sherman: Fighting Prophet* (New York: Harcourt, Brace, 1932), 646.

5. Saint Gaudens, *Reminiscences*, 1:378–83; Wilkinson, *Uncommon Clay*, 177–82.

6. Wilkinson, *Uncommon Clay*, 209–10, 291–92.

7. Wilkinson, *Uncommon Clay*, 304–5.

8. Wilkinson, *Uncommon Clay*, 310–12, 315; Saint Gaudens, *Reminiscences*, 2:289–94.

9. Henry Adams to Homer Saint-Gaudens, January 24, 1908, in Henry Adams, *Selected Letters*, ed. Ernest Samuels (Cambridge, Mass.: Harvard University Press, 1992), 483. For the angel in the Shaw memorial, which some interpret as Victory, some as Fame, and some as Death, see, for example, Charles Lewis Hind, *Augustus Saint-Gaudens* (London: J. Lane, 1908), viii; and Robert L. Gale, *The Gay Nineties in America: A Cultural Dictionary of the 1890s* (Westport, Conn.: Greenwood Press, 1992), 316.

10. Wilkinson, *Uncommon Clay*, 138–42.

11. For more on Hettie Anderson, see Catherine Gaich et al., *Augustus Saint-Gaudens, 1848–1907: Un maître de la sculpture américaine* (Paris: Somology, 1999), 135–39; and William E. Hagans, "Saint-Gaudens, Zorn, and the Goddesslike Miss Anderson," *American Art* 16 (Summer 2002): 66–89.

12. William T. Sherman, *Sherman's Civil War: Selected Correspondence of William T. Sherman, 1860–1865*, ed. Brooks D. Simpson and Jean V. Berlin (Chapel Hill: University of North Carolina Press, 1999), 833 (see also 3, 677–78, 727, 740, 796, 900).

13. Saint Gaudens, *Reminiscences*, 2:294; John Baskett, *The Horse in Art* (New Haven, Conn.: Yale University Press, 2006),

17. Saint Gaudens's *Reminiscences* includes examples of his "regard for other equestrian statues both ancient and modern," but the Capitoline *Marcus Aurelius* is not among them. Instead, "to his eyes come before all the others the 'Gattamalata' by Donatello in Padua, then the 'Colleoni' by Verrocchio in Venice, and then the 'Jeanne d'Arc' by Paul Dubois in Rheims." For modern examples he admired, as well as some he did not, see *Reminiscences*, 2:301–5.

14. Henry James, *The American Scene*, introduction with notes by Leon Edel (Bloomington: Indiana University Press, 1968), 171–72; Saint Gaudens, *Reminiscences*, 2:296, 299. James's comments on Saint Gaudens's Sherman monument appeared first in "New York: Social Notes, I," *North American Review* 182 (January 1906): 19–31.

15. James, *American Scene*, 173.

16. James, *American Scene*, 173–74.

15 MEMORY'S PAST AND FUTURE
HARVARD'S MEMORIAL HALL

DREW GILPIN FAUST

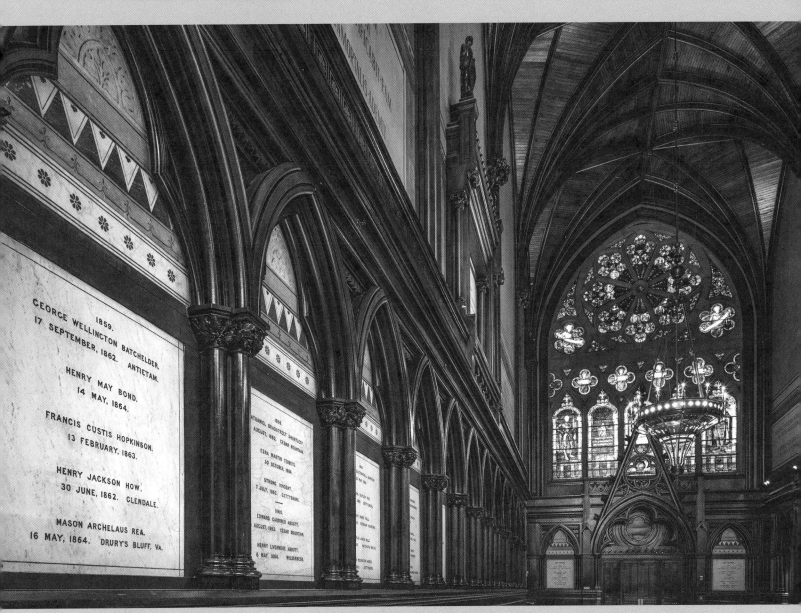

One hundred thirty-six names are inscribed on the walls—each with a date of death, most with a final battle. These are Harvard's Union dead—Robert Gould Shaw, killed leading the African American troops of the Massachusetts 54th at Fort Wagner; Wilder Dwight, who died on what he described as a beautiful "misty moisty morning" at Antietam; Nathaniel Bowditch, left untreated on the field for hours after being mortally wounded in 1863 at Kelly's Ford; Sumner Paine, the youngest Harvard student to die in the war, barely eighteen when he perished at Gettysburg; James Amory Perkins, described in the 1857 Class Book as "not over bright" and "long, thin, and ugly," killed at Morris Island in 1863; Charles Russell Lowell, who had thirteen horses shot from under him before his death in 1864 in the Valley campaign.[1]

This is the vestibule of Harvard's Memorial Hall, 30 feet wide and 112 feet long, conceived to mimic a cathedral transept with marble floor and stained-glass windows at either end. "The effect of the place," Henry James wrote in *The Bostonians*, just a little more than a decade after Memorial Hall's dedication, "is singularly noble and solemn, and it is impossible to feel it without a lifting of the heart. It stands there for duty and honour, it speaks of sacrifice and example, seems a kind of temple to youth, manhood, generosity. Most of them were young, all were in their prime, and all of them had fallen; this simple idea hovers before the visitor and makes him read with tenderness each name and place." A bivouac of the dead, assembled at the center of a building that is at the vibrant heart of today's university. Every spring, on the evening before commencement, the vestibule is crowded with nearly 500 faculty, alumni, and guests, sipping wine and eagerly awaiting entry into

(previous page)
Interior of Harvard's Memorial Hall,
Cambridge, Massachusetts
(Photograph by Will Gallagher)

the adjoining hall where the names of those receiving honorary degrees will at last be revealed at a dinner in their honor.[2]

This adjacent space was originally called Alumni Hall but has been known as Annenberg since a 1996 gift from that foundation enabled its restoration. It is nearly twice again as large as the vestibule, its walls decorated with portraits, prints, and busts, almost all of soldiers and statesmen from the Civil War era. Stained-glass windows commissioned by nineteenth-century Harvard alumni classes depict stories and allegories of military courage, public sacrifice, and moral triumph, embracing and extolling such figures as Epaminondas, Charlemagne, Dante, and Chaucer.

This space too reflects the original conception of a secular cathedral enunciated by the university's governing body when in 1878 it officially accepted Memorial Hall as a gift from its alumni. The structure would, Harvard's Corporation proclaimed, combine "daily usefulness and moral significance," as it honored the sons of Harvard who had served the Union cause. Critics dubbed this combination of transcendence and pragmatism a tribute to "Yankee shrewdness" in serving the dead and the living simultaneously.[3]

From its earliest days, the large hall was intended to serve as a "vast refectory," as Henry James described it. After a hiatus between the 1930s and the final years of the twentieth century, it serves that nourishing purpose once again—now as the dining hall for first-year students in the college. It regularly hosts as well a number of university celebrations, like the honorary degree dinner the evening before commencement. For me, the most unforgettable of these occurred when J. K. Rowling received a degree in 2008, and Annenberg was transformed, quite easily in fact, into a credible facsimile of Hogwarts, complete with exploding food.[4]

One mid-nineteenth-century alumnus complained that he "did not care to eat his dinner in a mausoleum." But today the balance of utility and memory tilts decidedly toward the former. The soldiers peering down from the walls are silent witnesses to people and times preoccupied with their own crises and challenges—and celebrations. Surrounded by relics and inscriptions, today's denizens of Memorial Hall reflect only in passing on those it was built to honor.[5]

The opposite side of the vestibule opens to Sanders Theatre, the apse of the cathedral design. Here for decades a far smaller university celebrated commencements. Now Sanders has capacity for only the diploma ceremony for graduate students in arts and sciences. Throughout the year, undergraduates gather here for some of the college's most popular, iconic courses: First Nights, an exploration of the premieres of five famous musical compositions, from Monteverdi's *Orfeo* in 1607 to Stravinsky's *Rites of Spring* in 1913; Justice, an introduction to moral and political philosophy; CS 50, the introduction to computer science; and Ec 10, the basic course in economics. Winston Churchill, Teddy Roosevelt, Teddy Kennedy, Booker T. Washington, Martin Luther King, Jr., e. e. cummings, and Seamus Heaney have all spoken here; John Gielgud, Siobhán McKenna, and Marcel Marceau have performed; Leonard Bernstein and John Adams have conducted; Yo-Yo Ma and Wynton Marsalis are among those who have played. When Marsalis gave a series of six lecture-concerts in Sanders between 2011 and 2014, he remarked to me that performing inside the theater's wooden walls was like playing inside a violin.

How did Memorial Hall's combination of pragmatism and transcendence come into being? And how has it weathered to survive into our own time? In 1967, one observer despaired, the building seemed "neglected ... unappreciated—a sorry example of the shortness of human memory." A twentieth-century Harvard president even developed a secret plan to tear it down. Yet today, Harvard without Memorial Hall is almost unimaginable. It is, an administrative report from the 1990s stated in proposing its renovation, "literally and psychologically at the heart of the University."[6]

The idea for a Civil War memorial was first articulated by James Walker, Harvard's president in 1863, but the notion began to receive focused attention only when alumni gathered in the summer of 1865 to celebrate the war's end and to honor its veterans. A preliminary Committee on a Permanent Memorial was followed by a Committee of 50 that included alumni from classes reaching back to 1806. By early 1866, the group had produced a plan that became the basis for a fund-raising campaign. Henry Van Brunt and William Ware, Harvard graduates who had established a Boston firm in 1864, served as the building's architects, but in many ways the creation of Memorial Hall was a collective process, with committee members and alumni more generally exerting significant influence on the design. The cornerstone was laid in the fall of 1870, but fundraising challenges interrupted steady progress. After a somewhat premature dedication in 1874, the building was at last completed in 1878 at a cost of $387,000 and officially transferred from the alumni to the university. It was the largest collegiate building of its time, and it contained, Van Brunt proudly declared, the largest college dining hall in the world. Memorial Hall has been cited as the finest example of Ruskinian Gothic and the pinnacle of American High Victorian Gothic style, and indeed John Ruskin was a close friend of Committee of 50 member and Harvard professor Charles Eliot Norton. Architectural historians have also noted that,

in the words of Stephen Fan, who wrote an excellent study of Memorial Hall as his Harvard College senior thesis in 2006, "by the time of the building's completion, it was already out of style, a slightly anachronistic period piece."[7]

Charles William Eliot, often hailed as Harvard's greatest president and far and away its longest-serving (1869–1909), resigned from the committee when he assumed responsibility for the university. But he continued to play an important role in the building's development, embracing its scale and grandeur as a fitting symbol for the institution he intended Harvard to become. The memorial, he believed, should inspire all who saw it to "admire and love more than all things else courage, self-sacrifice, endurance and faith in freedom. It is to nurture men of this brave pattern," he continued, "that churches, schools, universities and free institutions themselves exist."[8]

Eliot also made clear that in his view, "men of this brave pattern" were not just Yankees. A substantial fraction of Harvard students in the prewar period came from the South—about one-third of the enrollment of the college, including Robert E. Lee's own son, and a similar proportion of the Law School. Serving in the Confederacy were 304 Harvard students and alumni, and 70 died as a result of the war. The exclusion of their names from Harvard's Civil War memorial has been a matter of contention from its conception to the present day. The alumni who transferred the property to the university in 1878 were quite explicit that its purpose should be to honor those who fought for the preservation of the Union, thus placing significant legal obstacles to adding Confederate names. But this has hardly silenced the controversy.[9]

Eliot's ambition to build a great national university made him eager for suppression of sectional differences and a rapid reconciliation of North and South. Many shared his view. At the dedicatory ceremonies for Memorial Hall in 1874, General William Francis Bartlett argued that men are ennobled not so much by the cause for which they fight but by the spirit of willing sacrifice and selflessness that carries them into battle. More than a decade later, Oliver Wendell Holmes Jr., who had almost died from wounds he received at Antietam, made a similar argument in a Memorial Day address: "Those who stood against us," he proclaimed, "held just as sacred convictions that were the opposite of ours, and we respected them as every man with a heart must respect those who gave all for their belief."[10]

But others vehemently disagreed. Colonel Nathaniel Hallowell speaking in 1896 would have none of such arguments. Reflecting his deep-rooted abolitionist principles, he remarked, "May this Memorial Hall stand for those who fought for liberty and not for slavery," he proclaimed. "Conviction," he continued, was "sometimes very far from praiseworthy.... Slavery and polygamy were convictions."[11]

In the years following the end of Reconstruction, national memory gradually erased—even denied—both the conflict's origins in slavery and the war's emancipationist purposes in order to advance a narrative more conducive to national reconciliation and the preservation of racial hierarchy. The judicial evisceration of the Reconstruction amendments and the emergence of Jim Crow offered white Americans North and South a foundation for agreement and national unity. Confederates and Yankees had all fought nobly for their differing and principled interpretations of the Constitution, the new story went; race and slavery would no longer play a central part in the account of union and disunion. The abandonment of the war's emancipationist purposes—of the "new birth of freedom" Lincoln had called for at Gettysburg—was the price the nation proved willing to pay for sectional reconciliation and the promise of the newly powerful, once again United States.[12]

Demands for the inclusion of Confederate names in Memorial Hall arose from this very desire for a restored national unity based in sentiment as well as on military conquest. The circumstances at Harvard may also offer an illustration of one factor that helped make the national abandonment of the war's principles and purposes possible. Many Harvard students and graduates regarded Confederates not as defenders of slavery but as their friends and erstwhile classmates—young men far more like themselves than any exploited, distant, and dark-skinned slave. But it was nevertheless the views of Hallowell that prevailed, for the inscriptions in Memorial Hall honor only those who "fought for liberty and not for slavery." Nowhere does it name the names of Harvard's Confederate alumni.

Yet it is at the same time notable that the building and the commemorative objects it contains make almost no mention of the antislavery origins and inspirations of so many of Harvard's Union dead. Invoking such commitments during the years of the late nineteenth century would have increasingly been seen as unnecessarily divisive in the context of the nation's new postwar agenda. Only one of eighteen window openings in Annenberg Hall contains no stained glass. In 1897, the Class of 1864 proposed a design for the space, "commemorative of the struggles of the country for the Preservation of the Union and the Emancipation of the Slaves." The Corporation never approved it.[13]

Efforts to honor the Confederate dead have continued to appear into our own time. The idea of some sort of memorial was bruited about at the time of the university's tercentenary in 1936, then again in the 1960s during the Civil War centennial, and again at the time of Harvard's 350th in 1986. In 1995, the Harvard Alumni Association appointed a committee to consider commemorating Southerners who had died in the war in nearby Memorial Church, where the dead of the two World Wars and the Korean and Vietnam Wars are honored. The clergyman who led the church was the Reverend Peter J. Gomes, an African American whose enthusiasm for the project encouraged many supporters of a Confederate memorial that their long-sought goal might be achieved. Gomes was eloquent, influential, and an iconoclast who took delight in never being predictable. "If we are always to be the 'enemy' and 'victor,'" he wrote in 1995, "with no hope of transcending those designations that kill and divide, then it appears we can take no profit from tragedy and that the future will always be held hostage to the past. A memorial is not merely an artifact of the past. By its very nature it is a key to the future." The university church, he believed, "should strive to tell a larger truth ... however painful or ambiguous it may be."[14]

But even Gomes's support could not carry the day. Perhaps the most vehement and effective opposition came from the Harvard Black Law Students Association, whose president declared the proposal "absurd and offensive." In face of such pressure, the university's Board of Overseers rejected the alumni association's plan, and Gomes withdrew his support.[15]

It would be surprising if the issue of honoring the Confederate dead does not rise again. As recently as 2010, an organization calling itself the Southern Legal Resource Center launched a "Harvard Confederate Memorial Initiative" as part of its commitment to "preserve southern heritage." Because of the deed of gift of 1878, designating Memorial Hall to those who

fought for the preservation of the Union, however, these intermittent efforts have been focused on other sites. Memorial Hall remains safely dedicated to its original purpose.[16]

The greatest threat to Memorial Hall's purpose in the near century and a half of its existence, however, came not from those who wished to reconcile Yankees and Confederates within its walls but from those who in the mid-twentieth century began to regard the structure as something of a white elephant. When Harvard initiated a residential house system for undergraduates in the 1930s, with a dining hall as the center of each house's life, Memorial Hall's role as student refectory was abandoned. Many alumni of the decades that followed remember taking final exams in the vast hall, but for the most part it stood without clear purpose and took on, one observer remarked, "the air of a disused lumber room." The building overall, one report from the early 1990s put it, "slipped into a long period of disrepair and neglect." In both a literal and figurative crowning blow, the Memorial Hall tower caught fire and burned in 1956 as a welder endeavored to make repairs. President Nathan Pusey was overheard remarking as he watched the fire, "Isn't it a pity that it didn't start at the bottom?" He was said to have developed a sealed plan to level Memorial Hall after the children of the donors died.[17]

Memorial Hall survived—both the fire and Pusey's plan—but it remained without a tower for more than two decades. "Looking sawed off, squatty, meaningless, the present stub of a tower," as Charles Sullivan of the Cambridge Historical Commission despaired, was regarded by many as an affront. At last, beginning in the late 1980s, Presidents Derek Bok and Neil Rudenstine, aided by several generous donors, restored Memorial Hall inside and out. Students—this time freshmen not yet assigned to Harvard houses—once again dine alongside the portraits and relics in the building's main hall. The replacement tower, fifty-eight feet tall, was lowered into place in 1999. Now it serves again as a landmark that can be seen for miles around, representing at once an old and a new Harvard.

And in the soaring vestibule, the young men's names still preside. I feel I almost know a number of them because I have read their letters, diaries, and biographies; I have mourned with their stricken families, who vividly recorded their grief; and I have visited their graves in nearby Mount Auburn Cemetery. But for many if not most people who use and even love Memorial Hall, the names go all but unnoticed. "A memorial is not merely an artifact of the past," as Peter Gomes put it. "By its very nature it is a key to the future." We still have important lessons for our future to learn from these young soldiers. Lessons about what we owe to our nation, cherished in their time as the "last, best hope of earth." Lessons about ideals that meant more to them than the trajectory of accomplishment on which their Harvard education had launched them. Lessons about selflessness and sacrifice. Lessons about fighting for justice, equality, and a new birth of freedom still not realized a century and a half after these men gave their lives. Lessons about what really matters, for we are the future for which they fought.[18]

NOTES

1. Wilder Dwight to his mother, September 17, 1862, Wilder Dwight Papers, Massachusetts Historical Society, Boston; on Perkins, see Class Book of 1857, Harvard University Archives, Cambridge, Mass., p. 271 (repository hereafter cited as HUA). More than half of Harvard's living graduates enlisted in the war. The number of dead was equivalent to the total size of two college classes. See Corydon Ireland, "Blue, Gray, and Crimson," *Harvard Gazette*, March 21, 2012, http://news.harvard.edu /gazette/story/2012/03/blue-gray-and-crimson/. My thanks to Ellen Morrissey Trudel for assistance with research and to Lars Madsen, as always, for assistance with everything.

2. Henry James, *The Bostonians* (1886; repr., New York: Penguin Books, 2000), 189.

3. "Acceptance of Hall by President and Fellows, July 8, 1878," *Proceedings of the Committee of Fifty, Harvard College*, 269, HUA; Judge Warren quoted in Walter Muir Whitehall, "Memorial Hall and the Shortness of Human Memory," *Harvard Graduate Society for Advanced Study and Research Newsletter*, May 17, 1967, 1.

4. James, *Bostonians*, 188.

5. Quoted in Stephen Fan, "Memorial Hall: Collective Memories and Constructions of Harvard's Civil War Legacy (1863–1897)," Harvard senior thesis, 2006, 35.

6. Whitehill, "Memorial Hall," 2.

7. Fan, "Memorial Hall," 2.

8. Eliot quoted in Fan, "Memorial Hall," 66.

9. Daniel R. Coquillette and Bruce A. Kimball, *On the Battlefield of Merit: Harvard Law School, the First Century* (Cambridge, Mass.: Harvard University Press, 2015), 259; Helen P. Trimpi, *Crimson Confederates: Harvard Men Who Fought for the South* (Knoxville: University of Tennessee Press, 2010), ix–xix; Ireland, "Blue, Gray, and Crimson."

10. Holmes, quoted in James McAuley, "Remembrance of Things Past," *Harvard Crimson*, November 11, 2010, www .thecrimson.com/article/2010/11/11/memorial-harvard-war -confederate/.

11. Hallowell quoted in Fan, "Memorial Hall," 128.

12. See David Blight, *Race and Reunion: The Civil War in American Memory* (Cambridge, Mass.: Harvard University Press, 2002).

13. Class of 1864 design proposal quoted in Fan, "Memorial Hall," 103.

14. Peter J. Gomes, "Civil Wars and Moral Ambiguity," *Harvard Crimson*, January 17, 1996, http://www.thecrimson .com/article/1996/1/17/civil-wars-and-moral-ambiguity-pand/.

15. Patience Singleton, "Kill Memorial for Confederacy,"

Harvard Crimson, December 5, 1995, http://www.thecrimson .com/article/1995/12/5/kill-memorial-for-confederacy -pwhile-i/.

16. Southern Legal Resource Center, "Special Harvard Confederate Update," June 25, 2010, http://shnv.blogspot.com /2010/06/special-harvard-confederate-update.html.

17. Whitehill, "Memorial Hall," 2; undated report [early 1990s], "File: MHPlanco.rpt.," HUA; Pusey quoted in "Inspiring Moment," *Harvard Magazine*, November 1999, https:// harvardmagazine.com/1999/11/jhj.html.

18. Lincoln, Annual Message to Congress, December 1, 1862, http://www.abrahamlincolnonline.org/lincoln/speeches /congress.htm.

IN THE THICKETS OF HISTORY AND MEMORY
USING CHARLOTTESVILLE'S CONFEDERATE MEMORIAL LANDSCAPE

GARY W. GALLAGHER

C harlottesville's Confederate memorial landscape did not come to mind when I first considered which place to select for this project. I initially thought in terms of the trans-100th-meridian West, where I grew up, to add some geographical balance to the book. But events that unfolded as I prepared to write persuaded me to abandon the plan to honor my Western roots. Long-simmering conflict over the equestrian statue of Robert E. Lee in Charlottesville, where I have taught at the University of Virginia since 1998, erupted into violence on August 11–12, 2017. I decided to devote my essay to Charlottesville—not in an effort to engage with the ongoing controversy but rather to explain how, as a teacher and historian, I have used the city's memorial landscape for almost twenty years.

As I write this, the future of all Confederate monuments in Charlottesville is uncertain. The city council, after a long period of review, voted in February 2017 to take down the Lee statue—a decision immediately challenged in court by opponents. The violence in August led to calls for removal of the rest of the Confederate memorial landscape—a process already completed in New Orleans and Baltimore and begun in other cities across the former slaveholding South. By the time this essay appears in print, the issue may be decided.[1] The fate of the American Republic does not hang in the balance. But should all the monuments go, the opportunity to draw lessons from a valuable interpretive resource regarding Charlottesville's connection to the Civil War and the conflict's long-term resonance will disappear. Absent potentially painful reminders of the past, the city's history will appear to be simpler. Historical understanding and simplicity, alas, are seldom compatible.

(previous page)
Confederate monument in University of Virginia Cemetery and Columbarium, Charlottesville (Photograph by Will Gallagher)

The question of how best to deal with Confederate monuments inspires honest disagreement among well-intentioned, well-informed people while also eliciting—from both ends of the political spectrum—vitriolic cant that has little to do with monuments, the Confederacy, or the Civil War. I see memorial landscapes as similar in nature and value to literary and graphic sources—all compose part of the historical record and should be interpreted as such. I favor adding text to situate monuments within the full sweep of how Americans have remembered the Civil War. I also support erecting new monuments devoted to previously slighted groups or events. But eliminating monuments is tantamount to destroying records or images, potentially inhibiting a real understanding of our past, warts and all, and obscuring important themes, movements, and eras. I readily concede that elements of the Civil War's memorial landscape offend some people, which is a useful reminder that history has hard and sometimes unpleasant edges. I will add, lastly, that local communities should have the final say, after an open process of discussion and evaluation such as that followed by Charlottesville with the statue of Lee, about whether to keep monuments in place.

Civil War sites, including memorial landscapes, have been an important part of my nearly lifelong fascination with Civil War–era history. I have used a great number of them—battlefields, houses and other structures, monuments, and cemeteries—in teaching thousands of students at Penn State University and the University of Virginia, as well as in working with hundreds of middle and high school teachers in summer institutes devoted to pedagogy. With both students and teachers, I discuss the difference between history and memory and argue that memory often trumps history in shaping how Americans understand the past. I also emphasize the

need to accept that however complicated we think some historical episode might have been, it almost certainly was far more complicated. Perhaps the greatest obstacle to achieving some degree of historical understanding is the strong inclination, almost universal among students in my experience, to find simple answers or reduce the past to stark black-and-white alternatives.

Charlottesville's Confederate memorial landscape has proved invaluable in illustrating my points about both history and memory and historical complexity. On walking tours, I discuss how the city's monuments and tablets highlight the Lost Cause, one of four major memory traditions created by the wartime generation. Together with the Union Cause (which celebrated saving the democratic republic fashioned by the founding generation as the war's most important outcome), the Emancipation Cause (which pronounced killing slavery the most notable result of four years of slaughter), and the Reconciliation Cause (which sought a middle ground celebrating American—as opposed to Northern or Southern—virtues highlighted during the conflict), the Lost Cause set in place arguments and interpretations that have ebbed and flowed from the aftermath of Appomattox to the present. Charlottesville also provides excellent evidence of the commemorative landscape's complexity, revealing the danger of flattening out Lost Cause memorialization to fit a single template of intention and impact.[2]

On the latter point, it mattered when monuments went up, who took the lead in creating them, and how they fit into larger trends. A widely held view attributes all Confederate monuments to a white supremacist desire, especially during the Jim Crow era, to intimidate African Americans. I make clear on my tours of Charlottesville that almost everyone who supported erecting the monuments held what we would deem white supremacist racial views — as did almost all white Americans from the nineteenth or early twentieth centuries. Deep prejudice, by our reckoning, should be taken as the baseline in exploring white America from the years of the Civil War through the 1920s, when the last spasm of monument building occurred in Charlottesville. The Jim Crow South, I explain, represented the most obvious manifestation of how former Confederates dealt with their failure to establish a slaveholding republic, and the monumental landscape, together with Confederate Memorial Day, placement of the war's dead in special sections of cemeteries, and other cultural features carried forward a sense of collective identity that had fueled the Confederacy's massive military effort between 1861 and 1865.

But white supremacy as a sole motivating factor does not convey an adequate understanding of Charlottesville's memorials. The city's five principal sites include two monuments to common soldiers (1893 and 1909), a pair of tablets on the Rotunda at the University of Virginia listing students who died in Confederate service (1906 — removed in September 2017), and equestrian statues of "Stonewall" Jackson and Lee (1921, 1924). The first three of the five, in substantial measure at least, sought to recognize human loss on a scale unmatched by any other white segment of American society. The Confederacy mobilized approximately 900,000 soldiers out of a white population of 5,500,000 and lost 260,000–300,000 dead — a percentage of between 4.7 and 5.5. By way of comparison, the loyal states in the Civil War lost about 1.8 percent and the United States in World War II about .3 percent of their entire populations. In World War I, often cited as an example of surpassing carnage, none of the major combatants — France,

Germany, Great Britain, and Russia — matched the Confederacy's loss as a percentage of total population. The two equestrian statues, in addition to singling out the most famous Confederate military commanders, also bring into play a powerful national impulse toward reconciliation in the 1920s.[3]

I begin my tour of Charlottesville's memorial landscape with a series of framing observations about the Lost Cause and how it departed from, and sometimes aligned with, the history of the war — in other words, I set up the tension between what happened and how it was remembered. Departures included, most obviously, a retrospective attempt to distance the act of secession and establishment of the Confederacy from the institution of slavery and to present the war as fundamentally an ideological fight for state rights against encroaching federal power. Lost Cause advocates also labeled Union victory inevitable because of superior manpower and resources. In reality, I stress, concern about the institution of slavery lay at the heart of secession and the Confederacy, and Union victory was by no means certain (though the rebels did have far fewer men and less matériel). Former Confederates who embraced the Lost Cause got Lee right in important ways — he was the most important wartime figure in the Confederacy and won some famous battles against very long odds — though they finessed his views about slavery and strained to absolve him of responsibility for defeat at Gettysburg and poor performances elsewhere.

My tour proceeds chronologically by date of the monuments' dedications. I interpret the first three as efforts, in significant measure, to remember a generation decimated by the Civil War. Women's groups took a leading role in all three instances — as they had in the process of reinterring Confederate dead in the immediate aftermath of the conflict. The earliest of the three monuments, unveiled on June 7, 1893, sits in a cemetery on UVA ground that contains 1,093 Confederates, most of them in unmarked graves, who died in Charlottesville hospitals during the war. The artist Caspar Buberl sculpted a soldier gazing forward with his hat in hand and the butt of his musket resting on the ground. The inscription on the front reads

Fate Denied Them Victory
But Crowned Them with
Glorious Immortality

Panels on each side list the dead by state, creating the effect of a Confederate national cemetery. The location in a soldiers' cemetery underscores the theme of youthful sacrifice, while the inscription conveys the Lost Cause idea of hopeless struggle. Who could win a war if Fate dictated otherwise?[4]

The two bronze tablets on the Rotunda, my second stop, contain no overtly political text. They list more than 500 names, approximately 250 on each, meant to serve as

The Honor Roll
In Memory Of
The Students And Alumni Of The University Of
   Virginia
Who Lost Their Lives In The Military Service Of
   The Confederacy 1861–1865

That text appears beneath a shield bearing the St. Andrew's Cross associated with the battle flag of the Army of Northern Virginia. The only other text, below the rosters of names, reads, "Erected by the Ladies Confederate Memorial Association of Albemarle County Virginia 1906." At this stop, I discuss the degree to which the war was a Confederate phenomenon for the university. More than 80 percent of the students enrolled at the beginning of the secession crisis enlisted in Southern units within a year, and approximately 2,500 UVA men across all graduating classes fought for the Confederacy. I also mention that tributes to alumni who fought or perished in the war, such as the tablets on the Rotunda, were not uncommon at colleges and universities, with Harvard's Memorial Hall being the most impressive.[5]

My third stop features a second bronze sculpture of a common soldier, this one in front of the Albemarle County Court House in downtown Charlottesville. Dedicated on May 9, 1909, it depicts an infantryman at the ready positioned above a large Confederate flag on the front of the base. Text on two sides lauds the Confederate rank and file and credits those responsible for the monument:

1909
Erected by
the Daughters of
the Confederacy,
Albemarle County,
and the City of Charlottesville
to Commemorate
the Heroism of
the Volunteers of
Charlottesville and
Albemarle County
"Love Makes
Memory Eternal"

And, in more emotional language,

Warriors:
Your Valor;
Your Devotion to Duty;

Your Fortitude
Under Privations:
Teach Us
How to Suffer
and Grow Strong.
"Lest We Forget."

A third side of the base offers a crucial Lost Cause claim:

Confederate Soldiers
Defenders
of the
Rights of the States

In addition to the mourning and Lost Cause aspects of the monument, I mention a reconciliationist dimension in the form of a pair of flanking cannon. The fieldpieces, manufactured in 1863 for the Union war effort, were donated to Charlottesville by the U.S. government after entreaties from local politicians.[6]

A walk of two blocks from the monument in front of the courthouse takes my tour groups to the equestrian statues of first Jackson and then Lee. Charlottesville native and UVA graduate Paul Goodloe McIntire financed both. A philanthropist who made his money in Chicago and New York City and gave substantial gifts to the city and university, McIntire commissioned Charles Keck to sculpt Jackson and Henry Shrady—whose work included the impressive statue of Ulysses S. Grant that overlooks the National Mall in front of the U.S. Capitol—to sculpt Lee (Leo Lentelli completed the statue after Shrady's death in 1922).

I preface my comments about the equestrian statues by addressing how they lack common characteristics shared by the three earlier examples of memorialization in Charlottesville. Planning and fund-raising for

the latter involved groups of people—women's and veterans' organizations and members of city and county government, many of whom had experienced the war—and honored men tied directly to the area, whether soldiers who died in local hospitals, UVA graduates who perished while in service, or citizens from the city and county who served in the Confederate army. Two of the three stood in places associated with the university that relatively few people would visit on a regular basis—the cemetery on the edge of campus and the exterior of the Rotunda. As already noted, the desire to remember a generation of young men ravaged by the Confederate war helped animate those who erected all three—a fact that aligned perfectly with impulses to embrace Lost Cause interpretive conventions and maintain and strengthen the racial hierarchy in the Jim Crow South. The statues of Jackson and Lee, in contrast, originated with a single individual who was just four years old when the war ended, honored famous men with no direct tie to the area, and occupied small parks in the busy heart of Charlottesville. The impetus behind the equestrian statues probably had less to do with the Confederacy or white supremacy and more to do with a wealthy individual's wish to leave his imprint on the city of his birth (McIntire also funded statues of Meriwether Lewis and William Clark and of George Rogers Clark, erected in 1919 and 1921 respectively and located along the avenue that connects the University of Virginia and downtown Charlottesville).[7]

Neither equestrian statue includes any Lost Cause inscriptions. Jackson's, dedicated on October 19, 1921, features the names of some of his most storied operations—Chancellorsville, the Valley campaign, and Manassas—as well as his full name and birth and death dates. Large male and female allegorical figures representing "Valor" and "Faith" dominate the front of the statue's base, with a shield bearing the St. Andrew's Cross between them. Keck captured a sense of martial energy, movement, and drama in his rendering of Jackson and his mount, a fact that likely contributed to a number of positive comments from contemporary and later art critics.

Lee's statue presents a more stolid, even clunky, figure. Devoid of any text except Lee's full name and birth and death dates, it includes a large eagle, wings extended above its head, on the front of the base and a wreath on the back. At the dedicatory ceremony on May 21, 1924, speakers offered the usual tributes to Lee's military skill, well-known Christian modesty, and postwar career as an educator at Washington College (now Washington and Lee University). Delivered at a time when rigid legal and social inequalities were firmly enforced and not at risk, their comments betrayed no fear for the future of Jim Crow and contained no mention of racial topics. In speaking about the statue, I quote reconciliationist language about Lee from the dedication, including this passage: "It was due to his overwhelming influence that the war ended at Appomattox and the nation was spared the endless horrors of guerrilla warfare. To his efforts and example, more than to those of any other leader, North or South, we owe the obliteration in a single generation of sectional bitterness, and the present harmony of our reunited nation under the flag of our fathers."[8]

That language regarding Lee, I point out, fits into a much larger phenomenon of sectional conciliation in the early and mid-1920s. A year after the statue went up in Charlottesville, Congress passed legislation, sponsored by Republican Louis C. Cramton of Michigan, authorizing the restoration of Arlington House as a national memorial to Lee. What other rebel leader in any civil war, I ask students and teachers, has

been so acknowledged? And what are we to make of that acknowledgment? Between January and March 1925, the United States Mint in Philadelphia issued a half dollar featuring a design by Gutzon Borglum, who had been working on a massive Confederate sculpture at Stone Mountain, Georgia. The obverse showed a mounted Lee and Jackson with the text "Stone Mountain," the reverse an eagle with the text "Memorial to the Valor of the Soldier of the South." Despite lobbying against the coin by the Grand Army of the Republic, which insisted it celebrated traitors, Congress had unanimously passed a bill authorizing the coin in March 1924.

While still at the Lee statue, whether with students or teachers, we revisit my opening topics of history and memory and historical complexity. We talk about the Lost Cause and reconciliation and how we have seen the two could overlap, which always elicits expressions of surprise from those who imagined a less complicated reading of the monuments and tablets. We also discuss white Unionists from the area, students from UVA who fought for the United States during the Civil War, and, most obviously, the nearly 14,000 African Americans in Albemarle County in 1860 (more than 50 percent of the county's residents), none of whom have a presence in the Lost Cause memorial landscape. I ask how we might redress that absence. Removal of monuments? Addition of new ones? The Union Cause and the Emancipation Cause could be added, I say, and the process could start with a tablet listing UVA students who served the Union and a monument to the more than 250 black men born in Albemarle County who joined United States Colored Troops units during the war. I often close by asking students and teachers to imagine standing near the Lee statue and seeing, across the small park, a memorial to the U.S. Colored Troops soldiers. What better way to engage with history and memory and the changing nature of historical landscapes?

NOTES

1. Three of the five major parts of Charlottesville's Confederate memorial landscape discussed in this essay have been particularly at issue. A pair of tablets on the Rotunda at the University of Virginia were taken down and placed in storage on September 17, 2017; earlier, in August, the city draped black plastic around the equestrian statues of Lee and Stonewall Jackson as an interim measure pending a court decision regarding the ultimate fate of the sculptures. A subsequent court ruling stipulated that the shrouds be removed. On the tablets, see "U.Va. Removes Confederate Plaques from Rotunda," *The Cavalier Daily* website, http://www.cavalierdaily.com/article/2017/09/u-va-removes-confederate-plaques-from-rotunda (accessed November 21, 2017). On the draping and court decision, see "Wrapped: Charlottesville Covers Confederate Statues in Black," AP website, https://www.apnews.com/cdcd452629cd40d3b9d5431a34f564d3/Wrapped:-Charlottesville-covers-Confederate-statues-in-black; and "Confederate Monuments Controversy: Judge Rules to Remove Tarps from Charlottesville Statues," *Newsweek* website, http://www.newsweek.com/shrouds-will-be-removed-confederate-statues-charlottesville-823163 (accessed respectively on November 21, 2017, and April 2, 2018).

2. For a brief overview of the four memory traditions, see Gary W. Gallagher and Joan Waugh, *The American War: A History of the Civil War Era* (State College, Pa.: Spielvogel Books, 2015), chap. 12.

3. For the traditional estimate of Confederate fatalities, see E. B. Long, *The Civil War Day by Day: An Almanac, 1861–1865* (Garden City, N.Y.: Doubleday, 1971), 711. For an argument revising the numbers upward, see J. David Hacker, "A Census-Based Count of the Civil War Dead," *Civil War History* 57 (December 2011): 307–48.

4. Robert Stiles, a major in the Army of Northern Virginia during the Civil War, gave the principal address at the dedica-tion. On the proceedings, see Homer Richey, ed., *Memorial History of the John Bowie Strange Camp, United Confederate Veterans …* (Charlottesville, Va.: Press of the Michie Company, 1920), 182–90; "Civil War Monuments in Charlottesville," *Magazine of Albemarle County History* 22 (1963–64): 205 (the articles in this special "Civil War Issue" of the journal are all unsigned); and A. Robert Kuhlthau and Harry W. Webb, "Sculpture in and around Charlottesville: Confederate Memorials," *Magazine of Albemarle History* 48 (1990): 1–58.

5. On the number of UVA students who fought for the Confederacy, see Philip Alexander Bruce, *History of the University of Virginia, 1819–1919*, 5 vols. (New York: Macmillan, 1920–22), 3:284–86. On the dedication of the tablets, see "Civil War Monuments in Charlottesville," 207–8; and Kuhlthau and Webb, "Confederate Memorials," 40–44. In 1963, the noted Civil War historian Bruce Catton delivered a speech on the Rotunda's portico in front of the tablets.

6. On the dedication, see Richey, *Memorial History*, 190–93; "Civil War Monuments in Charlottesville," 208–9; and Kuhlthau and Webb, "Confederate Monuments," 14–40. Former Confederates Carlton McCarthy and John Warwick Daniel (the latter a U.S. senator from Virginia) gave remarks, as did Samuel J. McCall, a former congressman and governor from Massachusetts.

7. McIntire's support of municipal parks and public statuary also fit comfortably within the City Beautiful movement—a topic beyond the scope of this essay.

8. Speech of Henry Louis Smith, in *Proceedings of the 37th Annual Reunion of the Virginia Division of the Grand Camp U.C.V. and of the 29th Reunion of the Sons of Confederate Veterans at Charlottesville, Va. May 20, 21, 22, 1924*, ed. John S. Patton (n.p.: Committee on Publication, [1924]), 66. See also "Civil War Monuments in Charlottesville," 209–10. In their article, Kuhlthau and Webb discuss neither of the equestrian statues—which they place in a category separate from the soldier monuments in the cemetery and in front of the courthouse and the tablets on the Rotunda. Kuhlthau and Webb, "Confederate Monuments," 1–2.

IN THIS TEMPLE
AS IN THE HEARTS OF THE PEOPLE
FOR WHOM HE SAVED THE UNION
THE MEMORY OF ABRAHAM LINCOLN
IS ENSHRINED FOREVER

have been doing it for as long as I've been coming to Washington. The National Archives doesn't open until ten, so there is always plenty of time to take a morning run to the Lincoln Memorial. The first thing I do is find a hotel, locate it on the map, and then plan my run so that I get to the memorial at about the halfway point, when I am getting my second wind and before I really start needing a coffee. This plan never disappoints—and neither does the Lincoln Memorial.

I prefer to get there early, so I can have his undivided attention. Just as the sun is coming up is the best time. No matter when I get there, he's always waiting. The room looks the same, too, everything just like I left it. The two urns out front, his shawl thrown over his chair, crooked bow tie, crumpled pants, the look of concern on his face. It is comforting.

Depending on the route, I enter the space with different emotions. This last time, I approached the memorial from behind, passing buildings I don't usually place in the space: the State Department, National Academy of Sciences, American Institute for Peace. From the front, my run takes me past the World War II Memorial with its compelling words about what those who served in that war fought for and against— "Here we mark the price of freedom"—their sacrifices represented by pillars for each state in the nation and the stars inside for those who died. Tracing the path on the left of the reflecting pool takes me past the haunting Korean War monument, with the squadron of statue-men in heavy boots and raincoats. I prefer the path on the right, because it feels less crowded. Then up the stairs, and there he is. Just where I expect to see him. His concerned face greeting me.

I read his words quietly to myself. The Gettysburg Address: "we can not dedicate—we can not

(previous page)
Lincoln Memorial, Washington, D.C.
(Photograph by Will Gallagher)

124

consecrate—we can not hallow—this ground. The brave men, living and dead, who struggled here, have consecrated it, far above our poor power to add or detract." But we have work to do, dedicating ourselves to the cause they fought for—or really caus*es*: "that this nation, under God, shall have a new birth of freedom—and that government of the people, by the people, for the people, shall not perish from the earth." Emancipation and Union. And in the alcove to Lincoln's left, his Second Inaugural. I always want to whisper these words, first, in that quiet temple because in them Lincoln's full emotional complexity is clear. I make myself start with November 1863 and then move to March 1865 and Lincoln's Second Inaugural. Just weeks before the end of the war, here is Lincoln struggling with war's great costs, trying to imagine a time afterward when the two sides are reconciled, and he's angry—or, rather, he is channeling an angry God. God is angry about slavery and at the nation that benefited from it for a hundred years. Not the South, but *the nation*. And if God wills this war go on until all of the wealth extracted from slavery is repaid in blood, then so be it. It is hard to imagine how it must have felt to hear—or perhaps more likely, to read—those words in the spring of 1865, that after hundreds of thousands had died and many more were wounded, the end of the war might not be close at all. Temperamentally cautious, Lincoln surely thought about how that would sound to war-weary Americans. But war had to mean something, and this one was about saving the nation for "the people," two words that Lincoln, invoking the Declaration of Independence, repeated three times. And it was a nation committed to a "new birth of freedom," one that was better now that it was shorn of slavery.

That worried face. Like his words, Lincoln's face reminds me that he took the act of waging war seriously. The reasons for it, the commitment to it once commenced, and ensuring that those who died fighting it were ennobled by the realization of the war's purposes. That's all there, in Lincoln's face and in his words about going into war reluctantly but, once there, committing to it unreservedly. After reading his words, I take a good long look at his face. This is comforting, and as I leave the temple, threading my way past the monuments to America's other wars, I hold on to the feeling that those who made the decisions to wage war subscribed to the same ideals.

At a high point of reconciliationism, all but one of the speakers at the 1922 ceremony dedicating the Lincoln Memorial remained silent about slavery. Robert Moton, president of the Tuskegee Institute, son of slaves, reminded the segregated audience that Abraham Lincoln "spoke the word that gave freedom to a race."[1] As Scott Sandage argued, "Even its Potomac River site opposite Robert E. Lee's former Virginia home bespoke sectional reunion."[2] This reconciliationism is reflected in the quote inscribed just above Lincoln's head, which dedicates the memorial to the "People for Whom He Saved the Union." Here the focus on unity and union implied letting bygones be bygones; there may have been differences between the two sides in that war, but with the ancestors of that generation having just fought side by side in a war in Europe, and with Jim Crow triumphant throughout the land, surely the temple should not revisit such things.

But where the memorial designers sought with these words to avoid opening up old wounds about the war's causes and its unfinished business—and in so doing to sanitize Lincoln for the ages—*Lincoln's* words undermine that effort. And, importantly, the memorial has been the platform on which generations of Americans have come to lay claim to be "the people," equal parts of a nation worth saving. To me, there is no better place to think about who we are as a nation and how we got there than this place.

Who are the people? And what sort of Union had been saved for them? These questions motivated black interactions with the memorial from the beginning, and in answering them, black activists adopted Lincoln's memory and his memorial to their purposes. This process began years before there was a memorial, when in 1876, at the dedication of another Lincoln statue, Frederick Douglass spoke to black Americans, whom he entreated to remember that "under his wise and beneficent rule, and by measures approved and vigorously pressed by him, we saw that the handwriting of ages, in the form of prejudice and proscription, was rapidly fading away from the face of our whole country."[3] Douglass's reference to the fading "handwriting of ages" captured his sense that Lincoln had changed during the war, revising his own opinions about slavery and racial equality, a sense that was supported by Lincoln's policies. If Lincoln had "considered it too humiliating to learn in advanced years," a formerly enslaved man recalled, "our race would yet have remained" enslaved.[4] To his contemporaries, Lincoln was a man on the move, evolving in his views toward race relations in the nation he saved.

In 1909, activists invoked Lincoln's one-hundredth birthday in the call to organize the National Association for the Advancement of Colored People. And, despite Douglass's memory of Lincoln's caution, his equivocation, Lincoln has never stopped being the black man and woman's president. They have been among his most vocal defenders. "The venomous snake of segregation reared its head," the *Chicago*

Defender reported of the 1922 dedication ceremony, "at a memorial to the Great Emancipator!"[5] The NAACP choreographed and managed Marion Anderson's April 9, 1939, Easter Sunday concert at the memorial that became a symbolic rebuke of segregation and American racism. Anderson came back to the memorial in 1963 when Martin Luther King delivered his "I Have a Dream" speech, borrowing from Lincoln's Gettysburg Address, at what was the largest civil rights demonstration to date at the Lincoln Memorial at the end of the March on Washington for Jobs and Freedom. "Five score years ago," King began, "a great American in whose symbolic shadow we stand today signed the Emancipation Proclamation." By then, Sandage says, African American civil rights activists had adopted the shrine as their own, turning it into the "Supreme Court of Public Opinion," for as protests in the South turned violent and activists were arrested, patriotism and pageantry reigned at the Lincoln Memorial.[6]

Some 500 Confederate monuments were erected in the South from 1865 to 1912, 300 of them in the last twelve years of the period, according to Gaines M. Foster.[7] Early twentieth-century monuments often portrayed a lone, anonymous Confederate soldier. Out of the cemeteries, these new pedestaled figures lined the streets of cities and took their places in front of courthouses and city halls. During this peak in monument building, statues funded by private groups such as the United Daughters of the Confederacy celebrated black disenfranchisement and the triumph of white supremacy. (Confederate memorialization spiked again in the 1950s and 1960s, with more new monuments, but in this later period, schools were named after Confederate leaders as black students entered them for the first time.)[8] The Lincoln Memorial was unveiled and dedicated at the tail end of the peak in Confederate memorialization, and its designers sought not to offend the Jim Crow sensibilities of the period.

I made my most recent trip to the Lincoln Memorial in August 2017, amidst a wide-ranging reconstruction of the country's commemorative landscape. On August 12, days before I arrived, a white woman was killed at a protest in Charlottesville, Virginia, when a group of young white men expressing a toxic mix of neo-Confederate and neo-Nazi sentiments descended on the college town to protest the planned removal of a statue of Robert E. Lee. The woman, Heather Heyer, was part of a counterprotest. Since August 12—in just nine days—by my count twenty-five Confederate statues, plaques, and other markers have been removed; others have been covered and slated for potential removal.[9] Congressmen have launched a petition to take down statues of Confederate president Jefferson Davis, Vice President Alexander Stephens, and Robert E. Lee, among others, from the capital; these statues arrived in Washington around the same time that Confederate statues were marching out of the graveyards and into the streets and when Daniel Chester French and Henry Bacon were designing a monument to Lincoln that appealed to segregationists. Likenesses of Davis and Lee also grace the monument at Stone Mountain—along with Stonewall Jackson—work for which began in the same year as the dedication of the Lincoln Memorial. "The figures when completed will appear to be moving across the face of the mountain rather than resting against its side," the *Tulsa Daily World* described the monument under construction outside of Atlanta. The sculptor, Gutzon Borglum, did not want his figures to look static but rather to appear to be in motion. "A memorial to a movement," he said, capturing the sense that when complete, his monument would place the Confederacy in the present instead of the past.[10]

And he was right to see himself as contributing to a movement. A statue of Stonewall Jackson was dedicated in Charlottesville, Virginia, in 1921, followed in 1924 with a statue to Robert E. Lee, planned and financed by the same person, Paul Goodloe McIntire, a Charlottesville native and University of Virginia dropout who nonetheless made his fortune in business. McIntire also donated money for segregated parks in the city.[11] According to the papers, a huge crowd turned out for the unveiling of Charlottesville's Lee monument, including "several thousand veterans of the army of northern Virginia" in town for their annual reunion and officials from both Washington and Lee University, where Lee had served as president, and the University of Virginia.[12] In a ceremony rich with symbolism, town and university officials stood alongside Lee family descendants to mark the segregated space and to remind the town's black residents that they did not belong, that they were not part of "the people" to whom the public places of the city were devoted. This was the movement that was afoot in the nation when the Lincoln Memorial was built, unveiled, and dedicated. Soldiers in gray uniforms—some living and others made of stone—were cheered and celebrated in the streets. It's no wonder that African Americans took a deep interest in the Lincoln Memorial and made the space their own, seeking the company of the man in whom Frederick Douglass had seen the fading of "the handwriting of ages." The memorial stood as a reminder that history could also move in the other direction.

We are at a critical moment in the history of American race relations, and it is no surprise that we are seeing it manifest in the very places that were once claimed by those who would deny rights to some of "the people." The day before I arrived in Washington, someone vandalized the Lincoln Memorial with spray paint. It is unclear if this event was connected to the protest in Charlottesville—or to anything, really—but it underscores the point that all commemorative spaces are contested, even the one dedicated to Lincoln. We make our own meanings there. Standing before the giant seated Lincoln makes me feel small, but it also fills me with comfort because of what he stood for, the words he chose so carefully at a time of great national peril, and his hope for what the nation would someday become.

NOTES

1. Quoted in Scott A. Sandage, "A Marble House Divided: The Lincoln Memorial, the Civil Rights Movement, and the Politics of Memory," *Journal of American History* 80 (June 1993): 141.

2. Sandage, "Marble House Divided," 140.

3. Frederick Douglass, "Oration in Memory of Abraham Lincoln," April 14, 1876, *Teaching American History*, http://teachingamericanhistory.org/library/document/oration-in-memory-of-abraham-lincoln/ (accessed August 22, 2017).

4. Quoted in Eric Foner, *The Fiery Trial: Abraham Lincoln and American Slavery* (New York: W. W. Norton, 2010), 334n26, 406.

5. J. LeCount Chestnut, "Mock Ideal of Lincoln at Memorial," *Chicago Defender*, June 10, 1922, 1, national edition.

6. Sandage, "Marble House Divided," 160.

7. Foster did not include in this count monuments to Confederate women or the boulders that were affixed with plaques. Gaines M. Foster, *Ghosts of the Confederacy: Defeat, the Lost Cause, and the Emergence of the Lost Cause* (New York: Oxford University Press, 1987), 273.

8. The Southern Poverty Law Center has compiled a list of 1,500 Confederate monuments and schools named after Confederates, which it presents on a time line. SPLC, "Whose Heritage: Public Symbols of the Confederacy," April 21, 2016, https://www.splcenter.org/sites/default/files/whoseheritage-timeline150_years_of_iconography.jpg (accessed August 22, 2017).

9. "Confederate Monuments Are Coming Down across the United States. Here's a List," *New York Times*, August 16, 2017 (updated August 22, 2017), https://www.nytimes.com/interactive/2017/08/16/us/confederate-monuments-removed.html?mcubz=1&_r=0 (accessed August 22, 2017).

10. "South's Stupendous Memorial to the Lost Cause to Be Carved on Stone Mountain, Near Atlanta," *Tulsa Daily World*, October 9, 1922, 7.

11. Mark Jacob, "How a Former Chicago Office Boy Built Charlottesville's Gen. Lee Statue," *Chicago Tribune*, August 17, 2017, http://www.chicagotribune.com/news/history/ct-charlottesville-robert-e-lee-statue-chicago-20170818-story.html (accessed August 24, 2017).

12. "Statue of Gen. Lee Unveiled as Hosts of His Men Look On," *Washington Post*, May 22, 1924, 3.

18 THE EMANCIPATION OAK COMMEMORATING FREEDOM, FAMILY, AND INTELLECTUAL PURSUIT

BRENDA E. STEVENSON

The Emancipation Oak, located on the historic grounds of Hampton University in southeastern Virginia, remains an iconic symbol to African Americans of much that was positive, and possible, about the outcome of the Civil War. Over the years, I have come to connect with it on a myriad of personal and professional levels. It represents freedom, family, and intellectual pursuit—both my investment in academic accomplishment and the subjects of African Americans, slavery, and the South that I have chosen to explore and elucidate.

Under the majestic limbs that reach upward and outward from this "southern live oak," black people escaping slavery from the surrounding Tidewater counties found their entrée to a new life of freedom, education, and future purpose. Local free blacks, steeped in their generations-old traditions of self-help, Christian fellowship, and racial uplift, stepped in to shape the efforts of the workers assigned by the American Missionary Association to provide material aid for the thousands of fleeing "contrabands"[1] in the form of housing, food, clothing, bedding, and medical attention; to create a primary school for educational instruction; and to foster spiritual uplift and moral guidance through Christian conversion and teachings.

I grew up in the neighboring city of Portsmouth, Virginia, and the lingering duality of the Emancipation Oak as a site of higher learning for African Americans *and* as the place of one of the first public readings of the Emancipation Proclamation (January 1, 1863) in the Confederate South played reassuringly in my imagination against the dim reality of black life in the segregated South where I resided.[2] It brilliantly undermined the two-step lessons of white supremacy and black inferiority that seemed to be everywhere

(previous page)
Emancipation Oak, Hampton, Virginia
(Photograph by Will Gallagher)

130

external to my segregated community—the "whites only" signs at restaurants and movie theaters, in the spacious waiting rooms at doctors' office, and on public bathrooms, water fountains, and buses; the grand Confederate monument in the center of our downtown—in the center of every local downtown; the special hours assigned for our use of the public library and the "nice" department stores; and the schools that I attended without libraries, science equipment, musical instruments, or art supplies.

Despite the obvious second-class status of our public school education and citizenship, my parents were determined that my sisters and I would fulfill their dreams for our bright future with a college degree as its foundation. They pointed to the elite education that young black adults could receive at Hampton Institute (formally Hampton Normal and Agricultural Institute) as precisely the intellectual experience they wanted us to have. Graduates of Hampton populated our community as its shining professional and social stars. They were our teachers, physicians, ministers, dentists, military officers, business leaders, and government employees. Their sororities, fraternities, Masonic lodges, women's organizations, mothers' clubs, athletic leagues, and historical societies undergirded our social world and littered the pages of our local black newspaper, the *Norfolk Journal and Guide*. Hampton Institute, we all knew, was a special place with a wondrous history exemplified by the image of its splendid Emancipation Oak.

My parents came of age in the Jim Crow South of the Depression era and regarded all of the region's historic black colleges, but particularly the campus of the Emancipation Oak, as inestimable resources for the national African American community and even the global African diaspora. Their places of birth in the rural Carolinas hardly boasted secondary schools for even the brightest of black youth, much less colleges. Indeed, one of my maternal aunts chose to remain in the eighth grade for three years while she waited for a high school for African Americans to be built in her hometown of Mullins, South Carolina. My grandfather Edmund Gerald contributed funds to and served on the "colored" board of a General Education Board school that all of the family attended—but it was only a one-room school that had to accommodate grades one through eight. It was this same grandfather who built my mother's family a spacious home on his modest tobacco farm, planting his own southern live oak in the middle of the front yard. It was his own "emancipation oak"—symbolizing his elevation to a landholder on some of the same property where his mulatto father had been enslaved and across the dirt road from the slave cemetery where his relatives were buried.

As a child, I was both awed and frightened by that giant tree's imposing limbs draped in wispy Spanish moss. Over the years, our own live oak in rural South Carolina provided front porch shade and comfort as generations of my maternal kin watched a parade of family weddings, funeral processions, birthday parties, and family reunions. "Oak Tree" reunions, my cousin Thurman, the family's contemporary patriarch, has labeled them, take place every Fourth of July. That familial landmark connected me, visually and spiritually, to the Emancipation Oak at Hampton that I saw occasionally when we visited relatives who lived near it.

My affection for and interest in the Emancipation Oak also are linked to the tree's visual beauty and its decidedly "Southern" identity—an identity that I own deeply, even though I have not been a true resident of the South since I left years ago for graduate school.[3]

The southern live oak (*Quercus virginiana*) is native to the southeastern region of the United States. Its location in lower Tidewater Virginia, where the Emancipation Oak grows, marks the northernmost part of its natural growing range, which extends south and west through the Carolinas, Georgia, Florida, and the Gulf of Mexico. At its maturity, the southern live oak is enormous, reaching 40 to 60 feet in height and 60 to 100 feet in the spread of its branches, with a trunk that can expand to 6 feet in diameter.[4] The oldest of these trees in the South, however, defies even these impressive dimensions. A 300-year-old southern live oak in Mobile, Alabama, known as the Duffie Oak, for example, has a limb span of 126 feet and a trunk of almost 31 feet in circumference.[5] The Emancipation Oak, which was planted in 1831, has limbs that today are more than 100 feet in width. Because of its age, its beauty, and certainly its historic significance, the National Geographic Society has designated Hampton's Emancipation Oak as one of the 10 Great Trees of the World. Likewise, the U.S. Department of the Interior selected it as a National Historic Landmark.[6]

Ironically, the southern live oak at Hampton University that marks the beginning of the end of slavery in the American South also is an iconic symbol of the "Old South" and all that label suggests with regard to legends of brave cavaliers, beautiful belles, and complacent, if not "happy-go-lucky," slave men, women, and children. Indeed, these magnificent trees still adorn the grounds of richly endowed agricultural estates that are impressive architectural landmarks from the eighteenth and nineteenth centuries. In Virginia, George Washington planted live oaks on his Mount Vernon estate.[7] His neighbor Richard Fitzhugh named his Georgian-style home "Oak Hill" in 1790 because of the two live oak trees that still remain on the property.[8] And there is no better example of antebellum splendor in the Deep South than Oak Alley Plantation, the famed sugar estate on the Mississippi River in southern Louisiana. The name was inspired by a double row of overarching southern live oak trees, purportedly planted in 1810, which lead away from the mighty Mississippi to the front of the Greek Revival mansion. Initially owned by the "King of Sugar," Valcour Aime, Oak Alley became the property of Aime's brother-in-law Jacques Roman in 1836. Legend has it that Roman actually chose that particular site for his estate's mansion not because of its strategic location next to the most important trading corridor in North America but because of the beautiful and imposing oaks that already were flourishing there when he acquired the property.[9] Likewise, Chicora Wood rice plantation in the Low Country of South Carolina, in 1860 the home of Governor Robert Allston and more than 600 slaves, also boasted beautiful southern live oaks draped in Spanish moss. Not surprisingly, the White House of the Confederacy in Richmond, Virginia, also had an imposing southern live oak in its back garden, allegedly planted on the occasion of the 1824 visit of the Marquis de Lafayette to its owner at the time.[10] While the presence of Lafayette, of American Revolution fame, and Jefferson Davis, president of the Confederacy, determined the historical importance of this particular southern live oak in Richmond, the Emancipation Oak in Hampton has retained its prominence as a Civil War monument in its own right because of the early wartime efforts of three persons in particular—Lewis C. Lockwood, Benjamin F. Butler, and Mary S. Peake.

The Reverend Lewis C. Lockwood arrived at Fort Monroe in early September 1861, as the first representative of the American Missionary Association, a racially integrated organization created in 1846 in part to oppose slavery.[11] The treasurer of the AMA, noted abolitionist Lewis Tappan, had written to Major General Benjamin F. Butler,[12] Union commander at Fort Monroe, on August 8, 1861, regarding what the organization could do to help protect and advance the cause of the "contraband of war," as Butler labeled the freedom-seeking slaves who were arriving daily behind Union lines in southern Virginia and elsewhere in the South.[13] The AMA, as well as other abolitionist organizations, feared that these self-liberating bond people would be harmed or returned to slavery. The group also realized that most of those camped around Fort Monroe were in dire material support since Confederate soldiers, under the command of Major General John B. Magruder, and local sympathizers had burned much of Hampton.[14]

General Butler wrote back to ensure the AMA that the "contraband" would be protected from being returned to slavery or abused by Confederate sympathizers. He noted as well that he planned to have them either employed in the government's service or put to work on confiscated land so they could support themselves. General Butler's response prompted the AMA to send the Reverend Lockwood to Fort Monroe to establish and administer a mission with a mandate to address the material, spiritual, and educational needs of regional blacks, free and contraband.[15] One of the first persons Lockwood met, befriended, and came to rely on for the success of his plan was local free woman of color Mary Peake.

Mary Smith Kelsey was born in 1823 in Norfolk, Virginia. She was the daughter of a free biracial mother and a Frenchman.[16] As a young child, Mary's mother sent her to live with an aunt and uncle in Alexandria in order for her to be formally educated.[17] Virginia had passed stringent laws banning black education and restricting the movement of free blacks on the heels of the Nat Turner rebellion of August 1831, as part of a bevy of legislation meant to discourage free black state residency and to diminish white fears of a free black emergent status.[18] Virginia had ceded Alexandria as land that could be used for the nation's new capital in 1791, which meant that the state's antiliteracy laws did not hold sway there. It still was not part of Virginia in 1830 when Mary moved there, and elite free persons of color sent their children to free black and Quaker schools that were located there. Classmates remembered Mary as "very amiable" and a "good student."[19]

Her first teacher was a free woman of color, undoubtedly providing a role model for Mary's later work in Norfolk and Hampton. Local Quakers administered her second school. Mary came to acquire strong literary skills, including mastery of reading, writing, spelling, and grammar; basic mathematics; and the "female arts"—embroidery, knitting, pattern making, sewing, and music. Her female relations introduced her to Christianity, and she acquired a pronounced expertise in Bible scriptures. Virginia reannexed Alexandria in 1846, removing the education option for free people of color like Mary. Forced to end her formal academic pursuits by congressional legislation prohibiting education for free people of color in the District of Columbia, Smith, at the age of sixteen, returned to her family in Norfolk.[20] Five years later, she married Thomas Peake, a formerly enslaved man who had memorable blue eyes, dark wavy hair, and skin light enough for him to pass for white.[21] Like many enterprising men in the bustling port city, Thomas worked in the service of the merchant marine, he as a "wardroom boy."[22]

Mary probably never stopped developing academically, no doubt continuing a course of self-education throughout her young adulthood, as did many free women of color of her era, both in the South and in other parts of the nation. Soon after taking up residence again in Norfolk, she began to teach free blacks and also enslaved people clandestinely. Additionally, she contributed to local moral reform efforts by becoming a religious "exhorter" and by providing her community with a benevolent society that she created—the Daughters of Zion.[23]

Sometime during the 1850s, Thomas Peake moved Mary, their young daughter, Hattie, and his mother-in-law to Hampton. The family seemed to flourish there among the small number of free people of color (201 in 1860) and acquired an elite social profile and two homes—one worth $2,200, the most expensive owned by a free black family in the city. Thomas worked in a local hotel. In Hampton, as in Norfolk, Mary Peake busied herself with service to the poor and sick within her community and carried on her teaching of black children.[24]

Soon after escaped slaves began to arrive at Fort Monroe, Union officers under the direction of Edward L. Pierce of the 3rd Massachusetts Infantry began to employ them, and also local free people of color, to work on rebuilding the artillery battery that had been partially destroyed.[25] They also had to build housing for themselves that too had been destroyed, including Peake's home and furniture, which Confederate troops had burned during an operation in the vicinity of Hampton.[26] As a missionary, Lockwood was dedicated intently to the Christian conversion of those he encountered and wanted the contrabands to become literate. He readily admitted that he "aimed to teach self-development" and "proposed to commence Sabbath and week-day schools," although he did not expect these tasks to be easily accomplished. Lockwood

acknowledged to the AMA that he, some among the Union Army at the fort, and the contrabands were "trying the very highest experiment." "They [the contrabands] are here emphatically 'turned loose,' and are shifting for themselves," he reported. "It is not to be expected that on the 'sacred soil of Virginia,' this experiment should be carried out without encountering difficulties."[27]

Mrs. Peake, probably with the blessing of General Butler and through her own commitment, already had been in the business of teaching some of the local parents and youth under the large oak tree near the fort. Her students asked Lockwood to recruit her to teach for his organization. The reverend recalled that he soon realized that Mrs. Peake indeed was a "teacher of the choicest spirit."[28]

Mary Peake conducted her first AMA-sanctioned classes under what was to become the Emancipation Oak on September 17, 1861.[29] Within a few days, the number of students she taught grew from about a dozen to more than fifty day-pupils and twenty adults at night. Peake continued to hold her classes under the shade of the large oak during the hot and humid days of the early fall while other accommodations could be arranged. Records indicate, for example, that she also began to teach classes at the "Brown Cottage," a small two-story building that faced the missionaries' seminary building. Peake gave lessons in literacy, math, geography, Christianity, and choral music.[30] With Lockwood's support, Mary Peake became the first AMA teacher in Hampton and the first black teacher paid by that mission organization, which would come to dominate black southern education over the next several decades.[31]

Reverend Lockwood recognized not only that Mrs. Peake was a fine teacher and exemplary Christian but also that she was physically frail. On February 22, 1862, five months after they met, Mary Peake died from complications related to pulmonary disease. She taught almost to the day of her demise.[32] Neither she nor Butler nor Lockwood could have imagined that "emancipation" for the contrabands would come so shortly thereafter. Still, on January 1, 1863, teachers, soldiers, local free blacks, and townspeople gathered under the "Emancipation Oak" to hear the reading of President Lincoln's Emancipation Proclamation.[33]

That same year, the school that Mary Peake had helped to found became the Butler School for Negro Children—named after Benjamin Butler, who had given a large donation for that purpose—and was built next to the Emancipation Oak. It accommodated 600 students.[34] Five years later near the same site, the American Missionary Association opened the doors of Hampton Normal and Agricultural Institute under the leadership of Brigadier General Samuel C. Armstrong. The mandate that the organization established for Hampton was one that Lockwood, Peake, and Butler had articulated when Peake's first classes were held under the Emancipation Oak—to prepare black Southerners to be of sound moral character and financially independent and to supply teachers who would carry out these instructions in lower schools.[35]

The Emancipation Oak remains a recurring stop on my biannual visits to my Virginia home. My husband, who is a native Hamptonian and grew up playing in the shadow of the oak, and I have introduced our daughter to the endearing, enduring, and inspirational leafy memorial. She has circled it with her cousins while hearing the stories of the contrabands, missionaries, teachers, and soldiers who helped to bring emancipation and education to her ancestors. The Emancipation Oak at Hampton University is a Civil War monument that beautifully commemorates the values of freedom, family, and intellectual pursuit.

NOTES

1. Regarding the "fugitive slaves" who escaped behind Union lines and into Union-held military bases and life in the Hampton area during the Civil War, see, for example, Robert Engs, *Freedom's First Generation: Black Hampton, Virginia, 1861–1890* (New York: Fordham University Press, 2004); and Howard Westwood, *Black Troops, White Commanders and the Freedmen during the Civil War* (Carbondale: Southern Illinois University Press, 1992), 39.

2. Freedmen aid society workers and the Union military officers also had the Emancipation Proclamation read in Beaufort, South Carolina, on that same date with similar pomp, circumstance, and celebration that included the participation of local contrabands. See, for example, Charlotte Forten's description in her diary of public reading along with the joint contraband/Union troops' celebration of the Emancipation Proclamation at Camp Saxton at Port Royal (Beaufort County), South Carolina, on January 1, 1863. Charlotte Forten Grimké, *The Journals of Charlotte Forten Grimké*, ed. Brenda Stevenson (New York: Oxford University Press, 1988), 428–32.

3. The National Arbor Day Foundation actually named the oak tree (the southern live oak is one of sixty species of oak that grow in the United States) as the official "National Tree" of the United States in 2004. See "Oak Becomes America's National Tree," Arbor Day Foundation Press Release, December 10, 2004, https://www.arborday.org/media/pressreleases/pressrelease.cfm?id=95.

4. Edward F. Gilman and Dennis G. Watson, "*Quercus virginiana*: Southern Live Oak," *Fact Sheet ST-564* (October 1994), United States Department of Agriculture, Forest Service, http://hort.ifas.ufl.edu/trees/QUEVIRA.pdf.

5. Rick Holmes, "On the Road with Rick Holmes: Off the Beaten Track in Mobile, Alabama, the Duffie Oak Endures," *Carbondale (Ill.) News*, May 18, 2017, www.thecarbondalenews.com/opinion/20170518/on-road-with-rick-holmes-off-beaten-track-in-mobile-alabama-duffie-oak-endures.

6. "Emancipation Oak," Hampton University website, http://

www.hamptonu.edu/about/emancipation_oak.cfm (accessed June 15, 2017).

7. "Ten Facts About the Landscape at Mount Vernon," George Washington's Mount Vernon, http://www.mountvernon.org/the-estate-gardens/gardens-landscapes/ten-facts-about-the-landscape-at-mount-vernon/ (accessed June 15, 2017).

8. Kathy Orton, "Oak Hill Was a Haven for Jefferson and Confederate Cash," *Washington Post*, March 24, 2017, https://www.washingtonpost.com/news/where-we-live/wp/2017/03/24/oak-hill-was-a-haven-for-jefferson-confederate-cash/?utm_term=.e43683cff3f6.

9. "History of Oak Alley Plantation," Oak Alley Plantation website, http://www.oakalleyplantation.org (accessed June 23, 2017).

10. The house was then the home of Dr. John Brockenbrough, president of the Bank of Virginia. Lafayette visited the home twice in 1824. Legend has it that the marquis might have planted the tree himself. See "The Stories of the Historic Trees at the White House of the Confederacy," American Civil War Museum White House Wednesday Column, https://acwm.org/blog/white-house-wednesday-story-historic-trees-white-house-confederacy (accessed June 23, 2017).

11. Reverend Lewis C. Lockwood, *Mary S. Peake, the Colored Teacher at Fortress Monroe* (Boston, Mass.: American Tract Society, 1862), 12.

12. Michael Thomas Smith, "Benjamin F. Butler (1818–1893)," *Encyclopedia of Virginia*, https://www.encyclopediavirginia.org/Butler_Benjamin_F_1818–1893#contrib (accessed June 23, 2017).

13. Michael T. Smith, "The Beast Unleashed: Benjamin F. Butler and Conceptions of Masculinity in the Civil War North," *New England Quarterly* 79 (June 2006): 250, 252.

14. Engs, *Freedom's First Generation*, 19.

15. Reverend Lewis C. Lockwood, "Appendix," *Mary S. Peake, the Colored Teacher at Fortress Monroe* (Boston, Mass.: American Tract Society, 1862), An American Antiquarian Society Online Exhibition, Curated by Lucia Z. Noles, 2006, http://www.americanantiquarian.org/Freedmen/Manuscripts/marypeakeappend.html .

16. Engs, *Freedom's First Generation*, 9.

17. Lockwood, *Mary S. Peake*, 7.

18. Brenda E. Stevenson, *Life in Black and White: Family and Community in the Slave South* (New York: Oxford University Press, 1996), 289.

19. Lockwood, *Mary S. Peake*, 7.

20. Stevenson, *Life in Black and White*, 289–90; Lockwood, *Mary S. Peake*, 7–8.

21. Engs, *Freedom's First Generation*, 8–9.

22. Lockwood, *Mary S. Peake*, 11; Kay Ann Taylor, "Mary S. Peake and Charlotte L. Forten: Black Teachers during the Civil War and Reconstruction," *Journal of Negro Education* 74 (Spring 2005): 128.

23. Lockwood, *Mary S. Peake*, 10–11.

24. Engs, *Freedom's First Generation*, 9.

25. James Oakes, *Freedom National: The Destruction of Slavery in the United States, 1861–1865* (New York: W. W. Norton, 2013), 140–43. Pierce would go on to expand his "experiment" among the contrabands of Beaufort County, South Carolina.

26. Engs, *Freedom's First Generation*, 15; Taylor, "Mary S. Peake and Charlotte L. Forten," 129.

27. Lockwood, *Mary S. Peake*, 28–29.

28. Lockwood, *Mary S. Peake*, 31.

29. "Emancipation Oak."

30. Lockwood, *Mary S. Peake*, 20–21.

31. Taylor, "Mary S. Peake and Charlotte L. Forten," 126.

32. Lockwood, *Mary S. Peake*, 45.

33. "Emancipation Oak."

34. "Emancipation Oak"; Ludwell H. Johnson, "Contraband Trade during the Last Year of the Civil War," *Mississippi Valley Historical Review* 49 (March 1963): 641.

35. "Emancipation Oak"; Eng, *Freedom's First Generation*, 29.

IV BUILDINGS
ENDURING PLACES

19 FORGING THE CONFEDERACY

EDWARD L. AYERS

The subtle grays, blacks, and whites of Will Gallagher's skillfully framed photograph capture a scene that often evokes nostalgia: a gently turning waterwheel, gravity, and flow moving wooden beams, leather belts, and heavy stones to grind wheat and corn. The wheel in this image, however, was not part of such a comforting scene. Instead, it powered the machinery of a hot, loud, and rough industrial enterprise in the middle of a raucous city, firing furnaces to produce hundreds of cannon for a Confederacy that had few other sources of the crucial armament.

The wheel in this photograph turns at the Tredegar Iron Works in Richmond, Virginia, the largest and most important industrial enterprise in the slave South and in the Confederacy. The artifact serves as a centerpiece of the American Civil War Museum, built within the ruins of the Tredegar works, telling the story of our nation's defining conflict. As a trustee of that museum, I have sometimes paused to watch the turning of the wheel, taking encouragement from knowing that such wheels have turned at this site next to the James River for nearly two centuries. The museum, drawing on the expertise of talented historians, curators, and educators, uses the wheel to power curiosity and imagination rather than the tools of war.

The Tredegar Iron Works had been something of an oddity before secession, the embodiment of an entrepreneurial spirit in a society that claimed to disdain such a spirit. The foundry drew its power from the James River as it descended from the Blue Ridge to the Tidewater at Richmond, the river's rush channeled into a canal crossing the ground above the works. From the canal, water coursed down a raceway to the waterwheel, which in turn drove a solid cast-iron

140

flywheel over fifteen feet wide and weighing six tons. Belts carried the force of the water to machines and bellows across the works.

Tredegar began in the 1830s when a group of Virginia investors, eagerly assessing the iron ore and coal near the falls, ambitiously named their project after a famous ironworks in Wales. They imported skilled workers from Britain to help build and labor in the industry that was both heavy and subtle. Tredegar struggled in its first years but then came to prosper under the leadership of Joseph Reid Anderson. A native Virginian, Anderson graduated fourth in his class from West Point in 1836, where he trained as an engineer. Anderson plunged into business, beginning as a commercial agent for Tredegar in 1841. Within seven years he had become its owner.

Throughout the 1840s and 1850s Tredegar grew, through boom and bust, into a major producer of iron for the nation. Tredegar, running day and night, grew into the largest employer in Richmond, employing up to 350 men and attracting emigrants from England, Ireland, and Germany. The enterprise expanded into six buildings stretching along the James, producing everything from decorative iron flowers for the new St. Paul's Church to heavy arms for the U.S. government.

The Tredegar Iron Works also produced the machinery of the new age, the heavy iron spikes, undercarriages, and wheels of the locomotives spanning more of the United States each day. Tredegar forged cannon for the nation's nascent army and navy, taking advantage of lucrative contracts born of Anderson's connections through West Point. Anderson declared himself a Whig, devoted to using the federal government to foster internal improvements and tariffs protective of American business.

Even as Tredegar became ever more tightly tied to the markets and capital of the Northeast, however, the works grew into one of the largest employers of enslaved men in the South. The company purchased some men and Anderson rented the labor of others from slave owners across the city and neighboring counties. While Tredegar was forced to pay high wages to white workers to keep them from leaving for larger enterprises in the North, Anderson could hire enslaved men for only about $100 a year. Those men, of course, could not leave, no matter how hard they were worked or how disgruntled they became.

Recognizing the advantages of slavery, Anderson sought to transfer the knowledge of his skilled white workers to his enslaved workers through training on the job. But white workers rebelled. The Irish and Welsh workers who knew the complex mysteries of the furnaces demanded that they pass on their skills only to their sons, not to slaves. The white workers went on strike, demanding higher wages as well as the expulsion of African American men from the places where skilled crafts were practiced. Anderson had no choice but to relent. Enslaved men would work at Tredegar for as long as slavery endured but would never become apprentices.

Tredegar grew most profitable in the years just before 1860. The works continued to produce cannon for the United States into 1860—nearly 900 in the fifteen years before secession, including those that fired on Fort Sumter—but Anderson had already begun marketing to Southern states and their militias as a proudly Southern enterprise. Anderson moved from Unionist to secessionist, calculating profit and loss as well as patriotism. When, after prolonged debate, Virginia seceded in April 1861, Anderson led a procession through Richmond's streets down the steep hills to Tredegar on the James. There, the State Armory Band played "Le Marseillaise" as Tredegar's workers raised a Confederate flag over the works.

Anderson sent his son Archer to Montgomery, Alabama, the capital of the new and growing Confederacy, to offer to sell or lease the ironworks to the new nation. Jefferson Davis's government declined and Tredegar remained the property of Joseph Anderson and his family throughout the war, maintaining an advantageous relationship with the Confederate government that desperately needed Tredegar and Anderson. The white workers at Tredegar were commissioned as a home unit in the Confederate army, stationed at the works yet available for defense of the city. Several times over the course of the war those workers left the ironworks to defend Richmond as soldiers.

Anderson, based on his military training, requested and received an appointment as a brigadier general. The Confederate government and Robert E. Lee were not eager to see Anderson leave Tredegar for the field, for other men could lead soldiers but only one man could provide the cannon that could win the war. Anderson did serve, however, and commanded well until he was wounded in mid-1862, fighting outside of Richmond in the Seven Days Battles. For the rest of the war Anderson aided the Confederacy by arming its troops. Tredegar's labor force surged to 800 men, white and black, native and foreign-born, free and enslaved.

Tredegar immediately and repeatedly proved its worth to the Confederacy. The foundry cast the iron to sheath the new nation's first ironclad, the CSS *Virginia*, a recovered United States vessel. Early experiments showed that iron an inch thick would not stop the shells of U.S. warships, and so Tredegar forged plates twice that thick, with the iron weighing 723 tons. The rapid innovation at Tredegar prevented the USS *Monitor* from taking Hampton Roads in March 1862.

The foundry operated at breakneck pace across the four years of war. The works in Richmond produced about half of all Confederate cannon—473 siege cannon and 626 pieces of field artillery—ranging from portable mountain howitzers that fired shells weighing six pounds to huge cannon used for coastal defenses that launched shells weighing up to forty-two pounds. Anderson continually innovated as supplies dwindled and as captured Union blueprints or artillery supplied critical information about improvements. Young white girls worked on nearby islands to make the friction primers that would fire the cannon. A horrifying explosion and fire killed dozens in 1863, but the work continued.

Tredegar's frantic production, though, could not supply the greatest deficiencies of the Confederacy: men and the transport of food to sustain those men. Neither could Tredegar's cannon prevent Richmond from being overrun by U.S. forces in April 1865. Fleeing Confederates set fire to tobacco warehouses in the city, and the conflagration rapidly roared out of control. The fire consumed the core of Richmond's business district and burned to the very edge of the Tredegar site. There, the Tredegar Battalion fought the flames and drove away looters in the chaos before the U.S. Army arrived and helped extinguish the fire and bring order to the devastated city.

After the war Joseph Anderson once again moved quickly to adapt to the new situation. Under Union orders, Tredegar's waterwheel groaned back into motion to make iron for the bridges across the James. Anderson applied for and received a pardon from President Andrew Johnson, the iron maker proclaiming his desire for Virginia to reunite with the Union in peaceful prosperity. Though Tredegar had been damaged and worn by war, within a few years the site had successfully converted from boring cannon to forging iron railroad spikes to tie the expanding nation together. Anderson soon employed 2,000 men, and Tredegar rose again to become Richmond's largest enterprise. The good economic times continued until 1873, when a depression devastated the railroad industry and much of the American economy with it. The company narrowly survived, passing into receivership to weather the prolonged crisis of the late 1870s.

Tredegar recovered once again in the New South era, producing streetcars as well as horseshoes. Black men continued to work at Tredegar, finding rare opportunities for skilled jobs in the increasingly segregated South. Tredegar sought niches in markets increasingly dominated by vast new steel mills in the North and Midwest. The company considered turning to steel production but decided to focus instead on stability and longevity. Leadership of the business passed from one Anderson to the next, surviving lean times and benefiting from good years, such as when Tredegar rapidly expanded again to produce shells for World War I and World War II.

The waterwheel continued to power Tredegar for nearly a century after the Civil War. A long legal battle in the 1930s over the amount of water the works diverted from the James River demonstrated how critical the waterwheel remained even in the era of electricity. Tredegar finally fell silent in the 1950s, however, victim of national and international markets that left the once-innovative works a relic of long-vanished eras. The buildings and grounds became overgrown, victim to fire and flooding. The raceway for the waterwheel rotted away, and the canal dried and crumbled.

The Gottwald family of Richmond, acquiring the site in the 1960s as part of a larger business arrangement, preserved Tredegar for its historic value, shoring up walls and clearing vines in anticipation of a compelling use for the evocative location. And, indeed, the American Civil War Museum broke ground in 2017 to construct a new building on the Tredegar site, set into the hillside and enclosing the ruined wall from the Civil War era. The waterwheel operates there once more, reminding visitors that the struggles of the battlefield depended on hundreds of men, black and white, slave and free, who labored beside the wheel's ceaseless turning.

20 CEDAR HILL FREDERICK DOUGLASS'S PERSONAL CIVIL WAR MUSEUM FOR A PUBLIC MAN

DAVID W. BLIGHT

With a $6,000 loan in 1877 from a black friend and former abolitionist, Robert Purvis, Frederick Douglass purchased Cedar Hill, the house on a fifteen-acre estate on the heights in Anacostia in the southeast part of the District of Columbia. He and his wife Anna and parts of his large extended family had already moved permanently to Washington in 1872 in the wake of an arsonist's fire that destroyed their home in Rochester, New York. Some forty yards or so out behind the big house, beyond the lawn where friends and family played games of croquet, Douglass constructed his "growlery," a small, single-room stone structure, with no windows and a small fireplace, complete with a writing desk and a chaise lounge. The desk may have been that of Charles Sumner, a keepsake the orator had received upon the senator's death in 1874. He borrowed the name for his writer's retreat from Charles Dickens's *Bleak House*. In the novel, Mr. Jarndyce established such a "little library of books and papers" as the "refuge" in which he hid when "out of humor" and the place "I come and growl." When besieged by his large family of four adult children and eventually twenty-one grandchildren, siblings real and fictive, his increasingly ill wife, and assorted others, Douglass escaped to his growlery.[1] Major parts of *The Life and Times of Frederick Douglass*, his third autobiography, published in 1881, were likely written there.

In *Life and Times*, Douglass narrated and probed the meaning of the entire epoch of the Civil War and Reconstruction era in his eventful life. At the end of that work, Douglass declared that he had "lived several lives in one: first, the life of slavery; secondly, the life of a fugitive from slavery; thirdly, the life of comparative freedom; fourthly, the life of conflict and

"Cedar Hill," Frederick Douglass's house, in Washington, D.C. (Photograph by Will Gallagher)

battle; and fifthly, the life of victory, if not complete, at least assured."[2] The stages Douglass gave to his life are instructive, but they are the categories of an aging man summing up his public life and attempting to control his historical reputation. They also give a certain symmetry to a story of transformative turmoil and struggle. He lets us see the self-image of the fugitive slave risen to racial and national leader, the person and the nation regenerated in the blood sacrifice of civil war. But his effort to impose order on time by such a shaping of his career masks the equally compelling, if hidden, dilemmas of his personal life. In that realm, about which he wrote so little, Douglass experienced plenty of pain and frustration about which to growl.

Born a slave as Frederick Augustus Washington Bailey in Talbot County, on the eastern shore of Maryland, in February 1818, Frederick Douglass (he took the name from a character in Walter Scott's epic poem *Our Lady of the Lake*) was the son of Harriet Bailey, one of five daughters of Betsy Bailey, and in all likelihood his mother's white master. Douglass hardly knew his mother and never knew the true identity of his father. Hence, for life, he was an orphan in the fullest sense. Douglass lived twenty years as a slave and nearly nine years as a fugitive slave subject to capture; from the 1840s to his death in 1895, he attained international fame as an abolitionist, reformer, editor, orator of almost unparalleled stature, and author, especially of three classic autobiographies. As a public man, he began his abolitionist career two decades before America divided in a civil war over slavery. He lived to see black emancipation achieved with enormous bloodshed in a war for which he was a virulent propagandist, to work actively for women's equality, to realize the civil and political rights successes

and failures of Reconstruction, to forge an abolitionist historical memory of the Civil War era, and to witness America's economic and international expansion in the Gilded Age. Douglass lived until the beginning of the age of Jim Crow and the prolonged crisis of lynching, when American society collapsed into retreat from the very revolutions in race relations he had helped to win. He captured and analyzed this history and his personal experience in thousands of speeches and editorials and in the voice of memoir. The man of words and public affairs, though, needed a safe retreat.

During the final seventeen years of his life, 1878–95, Douglass made Cedar Hill his home. It was a place of refuge for a man dealing with excessive public attention, a haven of workspaces, and the scene of what he called many family "joys and sorrows." His wife Anna died in 1882, he lost his son Frederick Jr. at age fifty-one in 1891, and a dozen of his grandchildren died of disease and epidemic during his years in Anacostia; all were given funerals that began in Cedar Hill's front parlor. The house had been built in 1855–59 for an architect, John Welsh Van Hook. Douglass purchased the property in September 1877 with nine acres; over the next sixteen years, he acquired six more adjoining acres and expanded the structure from fourteen to twenty-one rooms, adding a large new kitchen wing and remodeling the attic into new bedrooms. On a visit in October 1878 a close friend, Ottilie Assing, could not stop "marveling at it." It was "one of the most beautiful places" in America, she enthused, high "on top of a hill, with magnificent old trees."[3] The view included the U.S. Capitol itself across the bridge over the Anacostia River. With a squint of the eye and a little imagination, one could almost see to the Chesapeake Bay, across which Douglass had been born in slavery. The grounds and stables included horses, cows, and other animals. In time Douglass's family planted an orchard that gave them fresh apples and peaches in season.

Over these last years of his life the patriarch of the hilltop estate became known in the District of Columbia and beyond as the "Sage of Cedar Hill." The moniker reflected Douglass's ownership of such a mansion despite his slave roots, but especially his exalted place as the most important African American man of letters, as an itinerant orator heard by perhaps more people than anyone else in the nineteenth century, and as a Republican Party loyalist who achieved two major federal government appointments: President Rutherford B. Hayes made Douglass marshal of the District of Columbia in 1877, and President James A. Garfield appointed him recorder of deeds for the District in 1881. In both of these positions Douglass moved from his status as a radical political outsider, which he endured through the war and early Reconstruction years, to a party insider, albeit one who still possessed little real power except that of his pen and voice.

For Douglass, Cedar Hill became a place of memory, a site of both repose and reflection on his own past, which he kept revising and reimagining. In the summer of 1881, during the drama of the assassination of Garfield and the president's prolonged and highly publicized deathbed watch, Douglass finished and published his *Life and Times*. The book garnered considerable publicity and fanfare even as its sales were disappointing. The return to telling his narrative a third time was as renewing as it was risky and difficult. *Life and Times* would be an aging man's journey into and out of his memory. That constant quest in writing to grasp and explain his personal past may tell us much

about why Douglass clung so fiercely to his views on black self-reliance, on faith in voting and political solutions, and on forging an abolitionist memory of the Civil War epoch. That memory was both retrievable and not; it was bracing and startling and somehow had to be harnessed in the service of a narrative about increasing fame and achievement. And at times, he understood that he was losing the memory struggle against the narrative power of the South's Lost Cause ideology.

This search for himself again in the storybook of his life was never as easy to achieve as he wished. In *Life and Times* he ceases his rich description of experience at one point and reflects, "When one has advanced far in the journey of life … and has had many and strange experiences of shadow and sunshine, when long distances of time and space have come between him and his point of departure, it is natural that his thoughts should return to the place of his beginning … to revisit scenes of his early recollection, and live over in memory the incidents of his childhood."[4] It was as though he hoped that telling his story once again, and constantly revising it, might bring symmetry to his life in the present. Douglass robustly lived looking ahead in real time, while he also lived, as a writer, inside the inscrutable if magical power of memory. Cedar Hill was the place from which Douglass sought out all the other pivotal places that had shaped his life.

Life and Times has always been at least two remarkable, if confounding, things: first, an indispensable source for at least the last forty years of Douglass's life, and second, a repeatedly revised, alternately exhilarating and torpid memoir about the accomplishments of a Gilded Age gentleman who conquered some if not all racial boundaries and who rose from radical outsider to insecure insider. So much of what we know about Douglass's dramatic role in the Civil War era comes from his recollections in this book: his deep and nearly fatal relationship with John Brown and the Harpers Ferry raid; his three memorable meetings with Abraham Lincoln during the war and his profound response to the president's assassination; his tortured reflections on recruiting his own sons into the famous 54th Massachusetts Regiment; the "vast changes" his life and work underwent in the wake of the war; his testy relationships with Ulysses S. Grant and other crucial Reconstruction era politicians; his conception of a "regenerated" America out of the revolution of emancipation; his eleven-month tour of Europe and the Mediterranean world with his second wife, Helen Pitts, in 1886–87; and his difficult tenure as U.S. minister to Haiti in 1889–91. In the course of all the new chapters of *Life and Times*, Douglass transformed from a revolutionary to a diplomat—proudly, knowingly, but never with ease.

A reader is likely never to forget Douglass's moving reminiscence of emancipation night, January 1, 1863, at "an immense assembly convened in Tremont Temple" in Boston. Waiting all day for the word over the telegraph wires that Lincoln had indeed signed the Emancipation Proclamation, Douglass described the transcendent scene. "It was not logic, but the trump of jubilee," he wrote, "which everybody wanted to hear. We were waiting and listening as for a bolt from the sky, which would rend the fetters of four millions of slaves; we were watching, as it were, by the dim light of the stars, for the dawn of a new day; we were longing for the answer to the agonizing prayers of centuries. Remembering those in bonds as bound with them, we wanted to join in the shout for freedom, and in the anthem of the redeemed." When the telegraphic word

finally arrived late in the evening, Douglass described a friend and preacher named Rue leading the jubilant crowd in the old anthem "Sound the loud timbel o'er Egypt's dark sea, Jehovah hath triumphed, his people are free!"[5] Any teacher who may read this passage as a way of conveying the meaning of emancipation, as I have so many times, may wish to contemplate that Douglass summoned it from his amazing memory while sitting one morning at Cedar Hill some eighteen years after the event. The Civil War and emancipation never left his consciousness.

On most of the 620 pages of *Life and Times* Douglass sought a unity, or a completeness, and he hoped to make his own life a kind of monument, an edifice so strong that no surge of racism, no embittered rivalry, no lynch mob, no conservative Supreme Court decision, no Lost Cause romance, nor even the ravages of time could tear down. *Life and Times* is memoir as a living literary museum designed to repudiate the unpredictable fates of America's racial history. Whatever might occur in the future, whatever forms white supremacy might take, Douglass wanted to be sitting there for us to gaze at, his story there as bold refutation. His house was big and imposing, but his story looms even larger.

Douglass believed that the United States had undergone apocalyptic regeneration in the Civil War; so too, as the autobiographer kept trying to demonstrate, had his own life. In the parlor, in the study, and throughout hallways at Cedar Hill, Douglass assembled his own personal museum of artifacts, heroes, and colleagues. Visually he made his home a statement of victory for abolitionism and the cause of emancipation in the very time those crusades faced violent resistance and counterrevolution. When one walked in the front door of the house, a large parlor off to the right contained many images important to Douglass's life and sense of legacy. The largest was a portrait of Lincoln directly over the mantle, visible the moment one entered. A photograph of Wendell Phillips, the abolitionist, sat prominently on an easel. Other objects included a statuette of a Grecian slave woman in chains as well as a wooden bust of John Mercer Langston, a black law professor at Howard University and member of Congress from Virginia, who ironically became a fierce rival of Douglass's. The parlor moreover contained a piano, on top of which Douglass displayed his violin, which he was very fond of playing with his grandson Joseph, who indeed was a talented musician and a concert violinist. Paintings or photographs of the writer Alexandre Dumas, Haitian president Florvil Hyppolite (leader of the island nation while Douglass was U.S. minister), and a scene from Shakespeare's *Othello* adorned the walls. Douglass cultivated a lifelong fascination with Shakespeare's most famous black character, one steeped in tragedies the great orator had come to understand.[6]

Elsewhere on the first floor of Cedar Hill, in the left parlor, Douglass owned a large bust of himself, as well as a large painting of a standing Douglass holding a scroll. The same room contained a photograph of Anna Murray Douglass wearing a pendant with an image of Toussaint L'Ouverture. In the front hallway between the parlors Douglass displayed a Kurz and Allison print of the painting *Storming Fort Wagner*, an image of the climactic moment of the 54th Massachusetts and its tragic glory at Charleston Harbor in July 1863. Douglass's oldest son, Lewis, was badly wounded in that battle and endured many months of recovery. At other places in the hallways were portraits of the women suffragists Elizabeth Cady Stanton and Susan B. Anthony, his friends and sometimes antagonists. To the left and more toward the rear of the house, reached

through the left parlor, was Douglass's study. There he mounted around the walls pictures of the abolitionists William Lloyd Garrison, James Birney, Henry Highland Garnet, and Gerrit Smith. A print of the famous Thomas Hovenden painting *The Last Moments of John Brown* also hung in the study, as did a portrait of Cinqué, the leader of the celebrated slave rebellion aboard the ship *La Amistad* in 1839. And in one corner two images appeared of German thinkers Ludwig von Feuerbach, the religious skeptic and atheist, and David Friedrich Strauss, the liberal Protestant theologian who wrote of the distinction between the historical and biblical Jesus.[7] In such an exhibition of somewhat eclectic personal and philosophical influences on his life, Douglass marked his own place in American history.

On February 20, 1895, a destitute African American named Lucius Harrod wrote to the Sage of Cedar Hill from just down the road in Hillsdale, D.C. Harrod was feeble, was in ill health, and had not worked since 1888. He had no coal for heating fuel in the winter. "I am poor and needy, yet the Lord thinketh upon me," he confessed, directly quoting Psalm 40:17 to the great man up on the hill. "If you can do me any good in whatever way." The letter included at bottom a postscript: "Often read 32nd ch. Isaiah, 2nd v of your 1862 July." Harrod may have remembered a Douglass speech he had read that included the Isaiah passage, but on this day of all days, to reference Isaiah, which Douglass had done so many times himself, gives a special poignancy to the moment: "And a man shall be as an hiding place from the wind, and a covert from the tempest; as rivers of water in a dry place, as the shadow of a great rock in a weary land."[8] Harrod had no idea he had suggested an apt epitaph for the man whose aid he sought.

At approximately seven o'clock that evening, at age seventy-seven, Douglass fell to the floor in the front hallway of Cedar Hill, dead from an apparent heart attack. He first sank slowly to his knees and then spread out on the floor. Helen Douglass, whom he had married in 1884, was right at his side, alone. She went to the front door and cried for help. In a short while a Dr. J. Stewart Harrison was at the stricken man's side and pronounced him dead. The man of millions of words had gone cold and silent. He was scheduled to give a lecture that evening in a local black church in Hillsdale, and the carriage arrived just as he fell dead. Lucius Harrod never received a reply as he searched for a "covert" that winter from his travail. He did find work, however, as a pastor in 1896.[9] Douglass's joyous and turbulent tempest was over.

That morning, February 20, Frederick and Helen had taken a carriage down into the middle of Washington. Helen went to the Library of Congress while Douglass attended for most of the day a meeting of the National Council of Women at Metzerott Hall on Pennsylvania Avenue (at the location of today's FBI Building). May Wright Sewall presided, and Douglass sat on the platform next to his old friend Susan B. Anthony. Douglass seemed in good health through the day among the fifty delegates, although one woman later reported that he continually rubbed his left hand as though it were "benumbed"; he did not make an address. He returned home to Cedar Hill around 5 P.M. The news of his death spread rapidly through Washington that evening and across the country. At the National Council of Women's meeting that evening Sewall announced that Douglass had died. Anthony, in agony, could not continue. The next day, with bitter opposition from white Southern members, the U.S. House of Representatives passed a resolution by 32 to 25 to adjourn out of respect for Douglass.[10]

One final feature of the main parlor at Cedar Hill, not immediately recognizable until closely inspected, were the cords tying back the draperies at the entryway: they were specially made balls and chains. The former slave not only had a sense of humor but insisted on some reminder of his own past in bondage. Douglass had a keen sense of place, and both his roots as a slave on the eastern side of the Chesapeake and his famous homestead on a hill in the nation's capital on the western side were never far apart.

NOTES

1. Notes, conversations, and tour with Ka'Mal McClarin, museum curator, Frederick Douglass National Historic Site, National Park Service, September 28, 2014; Charles Dickens, *Bleak House* (1853; repr., New York: Penguin, 2003), 117.

2. Frederick Douglass, *The Life and Times of Frederick Douglass* (1892; repr., New York: Collier, 1962), 479.

3. On Cedar Hill, see National Park Service, Frederick Douglass National Historic Site website, http://www.nps.gov/frdo/learn/historyculture/places.htm; Ottilie Assing to Sylvester Koehler, October 6, November 12, 1878, Koehler Papers, Archives of American Art, Washington, D.C.

4. Douglass, *Life and Times*, 444–45. On the perpetual revision or the "seriality" of the autobiographies, see Robert Levine, *The Lives of Frederick Douglass* (Cambridge, Mass.: Harvard University Press, 2016), 1–30.

5. Douglass, *Life and Times*, 353.

6. Notes, conversations, and tour with Ka'Mal McClarin. This was an after-hours tour and visit to Cedar Hill in which the curators allowed me a relatively free run of the house. I was able to hold several of Douglass's books, with gloves, and to sit in his desk chair.

7. Notes, conversations, and tour with Ka'Mal McClarin.

8. Douglass to Frank Hacker and Henry Haigh (president

and secretary of the Michigan Club), February 19, 1895, and L. Harrod to Douglass, February 20, 1895, Frederick Douglass Papers, Library of Congress, Washington, D.C.; Isaiah 32:2 (King James Version).

9. *New York Times*, February 20, 1895; *New York Tribune*, February 21, 1895. See also John Muller, *Frederick Douglass in Washington: The Lion of Anacostia* (Charleston, S.C.: History Press, 2012), 165–67. Muller's research in the Washington, D.C., City Directory for 1896 found Harrod's survival, employment, and first name.

10. *New York Times*, February 20, 1895; *New York Tribune*, February 21, 1895; *Daily Gazette for Middlesbrough* (England), February 22, 1895, and reprinted in many other foreign papers.

21 SURRENDER GROUNDS
THE MCLEAN HOUSE AT APPOMATTOX

ELIZABETH R. VARON

The McLean House in the village of Appomattox Court House in central Virginia, the site of Robert E. Lee's surrender to Ulysses S. Grant on April 9, 1865, was owned in 1865 by Wilmer McLean, a man whose improbable life story has become familiar Civil War lore. At the start of the war, McLean, a slaveholding merchant, resided on his plantation in Manassas, Virginia. When the first major battle of the war happened there in July 1861, McLean agreed to let the Confederates commandeer his property as a military hospital, and he moved his family away from the war-torn area; after living in a variety of Virginia localities, the McLeans settled, in the fall of 1863, in quiet Appomattox Court House, where McLean purchased a handsome brick Greek Revival–style house, the finest residence in the village. McLean was able to afford it because he was amassing a tidy sum during the war as a speculator in the sugar market, selling the precious commodity to the Confederate army. The house was chosen as the surrender site by Lee's aide-de-camp Charles Marshall, who was at Lee's side (and the only other Confederate at the scene) for the April 9 conference with Grant. Grant had a robust entourage with him for the meeting, symbolizing the might of the Federal army. The image of the patrician Lee, bedecked in his fine dress uniform, surrendering to the commoner Grant, in his mud-spattered uniform, is among the most iconic of Civil War set pieces. And the fact that Wilmer McLean resided on the first and last major battlefields of the war has come down as one of the war's most curious footnotes.[1]

My own relationship to Appomattox has been shaped by three especially memorable visits to the site. The first came in April 2007 as I was contemplating a possible research project on the April 9 surrender. I was

McLean House, Appomattox Court House, Virginia
(Photograph by Will Gallagher)

accompanied by my dear friend Julie Campbell, editor of Washington and Lee University's alumni magazine. It was a warm spring weekday and the national battlefield park was nearly empty—serene and stately in its simplicity. It was very difficult for me on that day, picnicking amid the small cluster of buildings that make up the historic village, to picture the dramatic events of the surrender: the battle on the morning of April 9, the armies raising flags of truce, Lee and Grant converging on the McLean House, the troops receiving the news of the surrender terms. I was keenly aware that popular memory cast this landscape as a site of reconciliation and national regeneration. But the very stillness of the site that spring day hinted at a different story. Part of the charm of Appomattox for me, that first time I visited it, was the sense that it was something of a well-kept secret.

The second most memorable among my visits to Appomattox came in May 2011, when I had committed to writing about the surrender and set up a daylong tour of the site with National Park Service historian Patrick Schroeder. Again it was a weekday, and tourists at the park were scarce. But this visit was different from the first. Patrick's expertise brought the site to life for me—he explained the lay of the land and the flow of events; provided me with hard-to-access primary sources; and encouraged me to develop a theme in which we had a shared interest, namely the role of African American Union soldiers in the Appomattox campaign. I decided on that day that my book on Appomattox would try to reconstruct the surrender and its immediate aftermath in fine detail, paying close attention to how competing accounts of the surrender scene differed from each other and to the interpretive patterns that emerged from the varying perspectives of soldiers, civilians, journalists, freed people, politicians, and so on.

Appomattox was from that point on a seat of knowledge for me, representing the collective wisdom of Patrick and his colleagues and all of the stories that the landscape, the artifacts, and the documentary record might yield up.

My book, published in 2013, peeled back the myth of Appomattox as a place of healing and showed instead that the surrender instantly became a touchstone in heated political debates over the meaning of the war and the nature of the peace: Unionists insisted that the surrender signified the providential victory of right over wrong, and Confederates countered that it signified the illegitimate victory of might over right. These early debates foreshadowed an enduring ambivalence. Americans, I came to understand, have always had a fraught relationship with Appomattox. The fate of the McLean House itself reflects the complexity of this relationship. In the moments after the surrender, Union soldiers and then local civilians rifled through the house for relics of the momentous occasion, carrying away furniture and various household goods; it seems that McLean sold some souvenirs, including his own autograph, but parted with others of his possessions unwillingly. With his own financial situation precarious, McLean and his family left the house in 1867 and returned to Northern Virginia, and the house was sold at auction in 1869. After changing hands repeatedly, it was purchased by a New York speculator who planned to dismantle it and reassemble it for display at the 1893 World's Columbian Exposition in Chicago. Legal and financial setbacks scotched the plan, and the deconstructed house languished in Appomattox as a pile of bricks and rotting lumber, "prey to vandals, collectors, and the environment for fifty years," to quote the Appomattox NPS website. The village of Appomattox Court House too fell into disrepair in the 1890s, even as national battlefield parks were successfully established at Shiloh, Gettysburg, and Vicksburg.[2]

In 1893, the War Department began to take measures to stake out Appomattox as a historic site, swapping the makeshift wooden signs that locals had placed there to guide the few tourists who strayed into the region with descriptive iron markers at points of interest like the McLean House location. But the renovation efforts hit a series of roadblocks and took time to gain momentum. In the lean years before the historic site was established, newspapers around the nation periodically featured stories with titles such as "Little Left of Old Appomattox," "Sleepy Appomattox," and "Appomattox, Then—Now," lamenting its downcast state. A correspondent of the *Philadelphia Times* observed in an 1886 article that the village seemed "to have become tired of its existence away back in the early part of the century and to have settled into a Rip Van Winkle sleep, from which it only once awoke, shaken by the thunder of cannon and the tread of armed men, only to relapse into a more profound slumber." A 1915 article in the *Washington Times* observed ruefully that the McLean House site was a "foreboding looking, dank, dark spot in the woods, overgrown with tall, foul-smelling weeds, saplings and underbrush," while a 1916 article in an Ohio newspaper noted that Appomattox had "gone backward in fifty years," its houses having "fallen into decay or disappeared" and its fields having "grown up to pine."[3]

Some veterans lent their voices to this chorus. Union major general Joshua L. Chamberlain, who had presided over the stacking-of-arms ceremony at Appomattox on April 12, 1865, returned to the site in the fall of 1903 only to find the McLean House a "dismal heap of ruin" and the village itself "uncared

for and forlorn." He mused that Southerners had little inclination to cherish "the scenes and tokens of the last days of their glory." He was onto something: proposals by the federal government to erect a "peace monument" at Appomattox in the 1920s and 1930s foundered on the opposition of white Southerners who were loath to memorialize Union victory and Confederate defeat and for whom Appomattox represented the onset of the "tragic era" of Reconstruction. As the historian Caroline Janney has explained, these same Southerners finally acceded in 1935 to the creation of a national battlefield park with the restored McLean House as its centerpiece, reckoning that the house (unlike a federally sponsored monument celebrating Grant's triumph) could be seen as "an inoffensive historical site open to interpretation." After a number of delays, the restored McLean House welcomed its first visitors in April 1950.[4]

A revealing time line of images of the McLean House on the NPS website allows visitors to picture this evolution—there one finds wet plate and stereoscopic photographs from 1865 to 1893 showing the intact house before it was dismantled; postcards from 1920 showing the deconstructed house (including one with a photograph titled *School Children among the Ruins of the Old McLean House, Surrender Grounds*); pictures of the site reverting to nature, overgrown with brush and honeysuckle; images from the 1940s, tracing the painstaking archaeological and architectural reconstruction of the site; a photo of U. S. Grant III and R. E. Lee IV cutting the ribbon at the dedication ceremony of the restored house in April 1950; and the image of the site thronged by spectators at the April 1965 centennial commemoration of the surrender.[5]

That final image is in a sense misleading. Except during the centennial, Americans have not, over the years, flocked en masse to Appomattox to partake of the spirit of reconciliation. In the decades since the national park site was opened, it has attracted markedly fewer visitors than such popular battlefield parks as Gettysburg, Fredericksburg, Shiloh, and Antietam. The remote, rural setting; the (mistaken) sense that the battle of Appomattox Court House was a minor affair and foregone conclusion rather than a significant engagement; the sense that the battle and surrender represented a stark finality rather than a series of "what ifs" that could be endlessly reimagined and debated—all of these factors help explain why the site has lagged behind other major Civil War sites in visitation. Like all national parks, Appomattox has also been vulnerable to the vicissitudes of partisan politics. The federal government shutdown of the fall of 2014, for example, led to reduced hours and employee furloughs at the park, resulting in a drastic decline in total visitors during October (usually the fourth busiest month of the year, thanks to traffic from tourists out to see the fall colors). Finally, broad cultural and lifestyle changes have resulted in a marked decrease, in the twenty-first century, in Americans' overall attendance at historic sites. Factors often cited to explain this trend include the high cost of travel; shrinking education budgets, especially for humanities (as opposed to STEM) subjects; a resulting decline in historical literacy in the general public; the proliferation of digital entertainments and distractions such as social media; and the generally overscheduled nature of family life and of childhood, leaving less time for recreational excursions. In Virginia, these factors are compounded by the fierce competition among the state's many historic sites, all drawing on the same shrinking demographic pool.[6]

But such sobering realities faded into the background on April 9, 2015, the date of my most recent and most memorable visit to Appomattox. Between April 8 and 12, 2015, Appomattox Court House National Park hosted more than 20,000 visitors at a series of Civil War sesquicentennial commemorative events it sponsored. The events were a triumph for the Park Service. The mood of the spectators who thronged the park by the thousands on April 9 was thoughtful and upbeat, and these visitors seemed to be deeply appreciative of the rich range of programming—speeches by eminent historians such as David Blight and dignitaries such as Virginia senator Tim Kaine; living history encampments; a reenactment of the meeting between Grant and Lee; and a culminating ceremony in honor of Hannah Reynolds, an enslaved woman who was mortally wounded at Appomattox just as the war's end was bringing the dawn of freedom—that the Park Service offered up. Many of the participants knew or sensed that history was being made that day: that in the future, historians would analyze the sesquicentennial, seeing it as a window into the evolution of Americans' attitudes toward the Civil War. I felt a keen fellowship that day with all the park rangers, curators, preservationists, archaeologists, reenactors, and other history devotees who teamed up to make the sesquicentennial events so memorable.

And yet, even as Appomattox has served in the modern day as a site of recreation, education, and commemoration, there remains something profoundly melancholy about the place. All Civil War battlefields are solemn settings. But Appomattox, perhaps more than any other battlefield site, asks us to confront the totality of the war: the capacity of human beings to inflict suffering and endure sacrifice; the price of pride, greed, and hypocrisy; the frailty of life and capriciousness of death; the elusiveness of sectional reconciliation and of social justice. Will Gallagher's photograph of the McLean House perfectly captures the stark beauty and enduring mystique of Appomattox and why it is my favorite Civil War site.

NOTES

1. Frank P. Cauble, *Biography of Wilmer McLean* (Lynchburg, Va.: H. E. Howard, 1987), 28–33.

2. Elizabeth R. Varon, *Appomattox: Victory, Defeat, and Freedom at the End of the Civil War* (New York: Oxford University Press, 2013); Cauble, *Biography of Wilmer McLean*, 41–59; "The McLean House—Site of the Surrender," National Park Service, Appomattox Court House National Park website, https://www.nps.gov/apco/mclean-house.htm.

3 *Philadelphia Times* as quoted in *Galveston Daily News*, October 14, 1886; *Galveston Daily News*, November 26, 1893; *Washington Times*, September 26, 1915; *Greenville (Ohio) Journal*, May 25, 1916.

4. See National Park Service, Appomattox Court House National Park website, https://www.nps.gov/apco/mclean-house.htm; Caroline E. Janney, *Remembering the Civil War: Reunion and the Limits of Reconciliation* (Chapel Hill: University of North Carolina Press, 2013), 296–300; Caroline E. Janney, "War over a Shrine of Peace: The Appomattox Peace Monument and Retreat from Reconciliation," *Journal of Southern History* 77 (February 2011): 91–120; *Appomattox and Buckingham Times*, November 23, 1893; William Marvel, *A Place Called Appomattox: Community at the Crossroads of History* (Chapel Hill: University of North Carolina Press, 2000), 310.

5. "A Time Line of Images of the McLean House," National Park Service, Appomattox Court House National Park website, https://www.nps.gov/apco/upload/McLean-House-timeline.pdf.

6. For statistics on national park visitation, see "Annual Park Recreation Visitation (1941—Last Calendar Year)," National Park Service, NPS Stats website, https://irma.nps.gov/Stats/Reports/Park/APCO. On the government shutdown's impact on visitation, see Katrina Koerting, "Government Shutdown Left Fewer Visitors at Appomattox Court House," *The News & Advance* (Lynchburg, Va.), March 6, 2014, *News & Advance* website, http://www.newsadvance.com/news/local/government-shutdown-left-fewer-visitors-at-appomattox-court-house/article_e4e52f02-a5ab-11e3-a6fc-0017a43b2370.html. On the general decline in attendance at historic sites, see, for example, Humanities Indicators, a Project of the American Academy of Arts & Sciences website, http://humanitiesindicators.org/content/indicatordoc.aspx?i=101.

STEPHEN D. ENGLE

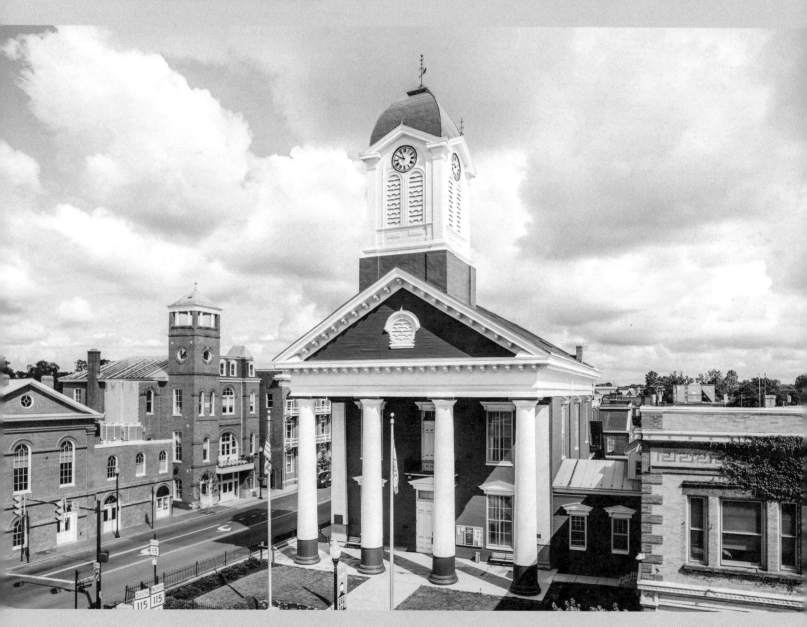

was born and raised in Charles Town, West Virginia, a hamlet named for Charles Washington, the youngest brother of the nation's first president. My maternal grandfather, Henry Cecil Allnutt, lived at 518 South Mildred Street, and as a youngster I relished spending time with him. Indeed, when I was six years old, he introduced me to the quixotic crusader John Brown. H. C.'s backyard ended at the alleyway that separated his lot from the small knoll between Mildred Street and Samuel Street, where Brown was executed, then a vast meadow known as Rebecca Hunter's farm. In the evenings, we would sit outside on the balcony of his second-floor bedroom that overlooked the courtyard, and H. C. would regale me with stories of "Old Man Brown."

When I was a little older, my father expanded my knowledge of Old Man Brown by taking me to the Jefferson County Courthouse, located at the northeast corner of George and Washington Streets, a furlong from the scaffold site. It is an unpretentious building in an unassuming town in the most storied valley of the American Civil War. Today, a green cupola and refurbished red brick mark the Georgian-style building fronted with four plaster Doric columns, and a clock tower adorning all sides of its square dome is topped by a weather vane. The ravages of the Civil War destroyed much of the original 1837 courthouse, and years later residents restored the structure, gave it a second floor, and relocated the judicial chambers upstairs. Nonetheless, it was the spot where Brown stood trial from October 25 through November 2, 1859. One summer afternoon, my father, who worked in the local post office located on the site of the jail that had housed Brown, took me across the street and walked me onto the legendary judicial ground where jurors tried and convicted the abolitionist for treason, conspiracy, and

Jefferson County Courthouse in Charles Town, West Virginia (Photograph by Will Gallagher)

murder. He told me the jury returned a guilty verdict within an hour, and Circuit Judge Richard Parker read the sentence in the criminal trial *Virginia v. John Brown*.[1]

My father often said that history was made in these chambers. The trial garnered national attention, and Harpers Ferry and Charles Town soon became synonymous with John Brown. The room, the furniture, and the history of the place fascinated me, but the immortal words Brown spoke at the trial's conclusion stuck with me. Recovering from his wounds, he stood and responded to his fate. "Now," he proclaimed, "if it is deemed necessary that I should forfeit my life for the furtherance of the ends of justice, and mingle my blood further with the blood of my children and with the blood of millions in this slave country whose rights are disregarded by wicked, cruel, and unjust enactments, I submit; so let it be done!"[2]

The story of Brown and his men who descended on the Federal armory and arsenal at Harpers Ferry on the moonless Sunday night of October 16, 1859, commenced a most memorable history that became fodder for serious scholarship as well as sensational legends. In the arsenal superintendent's office the next day, weak, haggard, bleeding, and lying next to his dead son, Brown spoke to reporters and his captors, including Lieutenant James E. B. "Jeb" Stuart, Lieutenant Colonel Robert E. Lee, and Governor Henry A. Wise, and prophesied what he believed lay ahead for Americans. "I think, my friend," he said to one Southerner, "you are guilty of a great wrong to God and against humanity. You had better—all of you people of the South—prepare yourselves for a settlement of this question."[3]

Those words and the forty-seven days that followed propelled Brown and his cause to new heights—indeed, they became legend. Although his Cromwell-like raid was ill conceived and poorly planned and executed, Brown's attack, subsequent trial, and execution became central to the American Civil War and, more personally, became central to my life as I grew up appreciating the unique combination of spectacular scenery and stunning human drama presented by my native grounds.[4]

For me, the courthouse came to symbolize the gulf that existed between abolitionists and slavery's supporters. Brown's trial polarized the nation. Governor Wise appointed local attorney Andrew Hunter to assist commonwealth attorney Charles B. Harding in prosecuting Brown and his coconspirators. Defending Brown was complicated, especially because he rejected an insanity plea. Nonetheless, the court appointed prominent Virginia attorney Lawson Botts to act as lead defense counsel and, at Brown's request, Charles Town mayor Thomas C. Green. Abolitionist John Albion Andrew of Massachusetts, soon to be the state's next governor, helped raise funds for Brown's defense. Once the trial got underway, Wise stationed more than a thousand militia soldiers at the courthouse and throughout Charles Town to protect against crop burners, barn burners, Brownites, assassins, and vigilantes threatening mob violence either against or in favor of Brown's actions. Jefferson County was part of a wealthy plantation region, but many of its residents were pro-Northern, and jurors experienced hardships for their part in the proceedings.

During the trial, well-known actor John Wilkes Booth rushed to join the Richmond Greys, who were heading to Charles Town. While there, he entertained audiences with dramatic Shakespearean recitations at the Episcopal Reading Room at the corner of Liberty and Lawrence Streets and at the Zion Episcopal

Church on Congress Street (where I attended church). When Brown exited the courthouse on the day of his execution, he added more drama to the already sensational episode by passing a plain but prophetic note to a guard: "Charlestown, Va, 2d, December, 1859. I John Brown am now quite *certain* that the crimes of this *guilty, land: will* never be purged *away*; but with Blood. I had *as I now think*: *vainly* flattered myself that without *very much* bloodshed; it might be done."[5]

When Virginia seceded and the Civil War erupted, county authorities transported the courthouse records up the Shenandoah Valley to Lexington and in February 1865 relocated the county seat thirteen miles to the north to Shepherdstown, so that Union troops stationed along the Baltimore and Ohio Railroad could safeguard the buildings. The courthouse, however, succumbed to the conflict, reduced to a skeleton of what it once was. A few years after the war, famed newspaper correspondent George Alfred Townsend, writing under the pen name "Gath," visited the ruins. Charles Town was "four miles from the Shenandoah," he wrote, "and strange to say, is growing, and in the direction of the gallows of John Brown … four new houses now stand on part of the site of his suspension." "The gallows-spot is a corn-field, full of shocks of fine tall corn," he added, "and it has changed in few respects since the execution. The only ruined parts of Charles Town are the Courthouse and the jail. The former maintains its walls and outlines, and the four brick and plaster Doric Columns before it are still standing; but the roof is reduced to a few beams, the whole interior is torn out, and the edifice has now only one floor,—the cellar,—and is, to speak truthfully, the cess-pool for all the vagrants in the village." Opposite the courthouse was the jail, "also roofless and torn out." Both the courthouse and the jail "had been despoiled by soldiers to make

quarters and tens of thousands of men have marched through Charles Town, singing 'John Brown's Body lies mouldering in the grave, His soul's marching on!'"[6]

In March 1871, the West Virginia legislature reestablished Charles Town as the seat of Jefferson County, and its citizens raised $10,000 to restore the courthouse, which reopened for the November 1872 session. It appeared as though the area had returned to normal. Yet the memories of Brown lingered. In 1892–93, the scaffold boards and the old engine house, dubbed "John Brown's Fort," were shipped to Chicago and displayed at the World's Fair. They returned in 1895 and were rebuilt on the Alexander Murphy farm, later purchased by Storer College, and moved to that campus in 1909, the fiftieth anniversary of Brown's raid.[7]

If scholars have been reluctant to identify Brown's raid as the spark that ignited the Civil War, perhaps it is because the mission's violence clouds the morally admirable goal of wanting to purge slavery from American soil. Brown, whose legacy remains complicated, has been one of the most fiercely debated and enigmatic figures in American history. Historians have both venerated and vilified him as controversial, often concluding that he was a religious but flawed reformer deeply devoted to liberating American blacks held in bondage. Whether or not his actions brought on the war, his words certainly prophesied it—after all, it was Abraham Lincoln who ended up fulfilling Brown's hope, a fact noted disapprovingly by Charles C. Burr's New York magazine *The Old Guard*, a deeply conservative publication, which declared that the "administration of Abraham Lincoln was a John Brown raid on the grandest scale." For many at the other end of the political spectrum, Brown became, in the month between his conviction and execution, a Christlike martyr who welcomed his end for its enduring significance. "I am worth now infinitely more to die than to live," he asserted after his trial.[8]

Whether or not, in Ralph Waldo Emerson's words, Brown made the "gallows glorious like the cross," his fame came at significant cost to Americans. In an 1881 speech at Harpers Ferry commemorating the fourteenth anniversary of Storer College, Frederick Douglass observed that if Brown "did not end the war that ended slavery, he did at least begin the war that ended slavery." In an ironic twist that day, Andrew Hunter, who had prosecuted Brown and whose home was burned during the war by his cousin the Union general David Hunter, was seated on the speaker's platform directly behind Douglass. After the speech, Hunter congratulated Douglass, shook his hand, and remarked that if Robert E. Lee had been living he would have done the same.[9] Yet, who could have predicted that twenty-one men who sought to inspire a slave insurrection would have precipitated a war that cost more than 730,000 lives while liberating more than 4 million slaves.[10]

Today, people who travel to Harpers Ferry seeking an exploration in American and Civil War history can complete the journey Brown made in 1859. Under National Park Service guidance, they can venture six miles to Charles Town, pass through the old courthouse, and end in the courtyard behind my grandparents' old homestead. It is silent now, but visitors can conjure images of those breezy days in autumn when the gavel's stroke adjourned the famous case and Brown's body swayed slowly in the wind to the echoes of Julia Ward Howe's "Battle Hymn of the Republic," recalling the generational ties that bind them to the past.[11]

NOTES

I wish to acknowledge Jefferson County historian Doug Perks for his assistance with this essay.

1. Judge David Hartley Sanders, "The Story of the Jefferson County Courthouse," *Jefferson County Historical Society Magazine*, December 1996, 17–44.

2. Brian McGinty, *John Brown's Trial* (Cambridge, Mass.: Harvard University Press, 2009), 270–71; Stephen B. Oates, *To Purge This Land with Blood: A Biography of John Brown* (New York: Harper and Row, 1970), 307–52. See also Tony Horwitz, *Midnight Rising: John Brown and the Raid That Sparked the Civil War* (New York: Henry Holt, 2011).

3. Alexander R. Boteler, "Recollections of the John Brown Raid," *Century Illustrated Monthly Magazine, May 1883, to October 1883*, vol. 26, new series, vol. iv (1883), 412–16; W. E. Forster. "Harper's Ferry and 'Old Captain Brown,'" *Macmillan's Magazine* 1 (November 1859–April 1860): 306–17; Horwitz, *Midnight Rising*, 186; Oates, *To Purge This Land with Blood*, 304; *New York Times*, November 1, 1987.

4. Oates, *To Purge This Land with Blood*, 274–306; *Harper's Weekly*, November 12, 1859; Lou V. Chapin, "The Last Days of Old John Brown," *Overland Monthly and Out West Magazine*, April 1899, 322–32; *New York Times*, November 1, 1987.

5. David S. Reynolds, *John Brown, Abolitionist: The Man Who Killed Slavery, Sparked the Civil War, and Seeded Civil Rights* (New York: Alfred A. Knopf, 2005), 377–99; Glenn Tucker, "John Wilkes Booth at the John Brown Hanging," *Lincoln Herald* 78 (1976): 3–11; Terry Alford, *Fortune's Fool: The Life of John Wilkes Booth* (New York: Oxford University Press, 2015), 70–81; Oates, *To Purge This Land with Blood*, 351.

6. Cecil D. Eby, ed., "A Reconstruction Philippic: George Alfred Townsend's Visit to Jefferson County, 1869," *Magazine of the Jefferson County Historical Society* (December 1986): 15–32; Sanders, "The Story of the Jefferson County Courthouse," 17–44; Clarence S. Gee, "John Brown's Fort," *West Virginia History* 19 (January 1958): 93–100. Townsend's account of his visit to Harpers Ferry and Charles Town initially appeared in the *Chicago Tribune*, November 15, 16, 1869.

7. Sanders, "Story of the Jefferson County Courthouse," 17–44; Eby, "Reconstruction Philippic," 15–32; Robert Shackleton Jr., "John Brown's Raid and Its Localities," *The National Magazine: A Monthly Journal of American History* 17 (April 1893): 523–34; James C. Malin, *John Brown and the*

Legend of Fifty-Six (1942; repr., New York: Haskell House, 1971), 469–72; Vivian V. Gordon, "Section E: A History of Storer College, Harper's Ferry, West Virginia," *Journal of Negro Education* 30 (1961): 445–49.

8. President Johnson, "History of Old John Brown," *The Old Guard* (July 1865): 324–30; Reynolds, *John Brown*, 388; Paul Finkelman, ed., *His Soul Goes Marching On: Responses to John Brown and the Harpers Ferry Raid* (Charlottesville: University Press of Virginia, 1995), 41–115; Sean Wilentz, *The Rise of American Democracy* (New York: W. W. Norton, 2005), 747–753; *The Independent*, December 8, 1859.

9. Wilentz, *Rise of American Democracy*, 751–52 (Emerson quotation); Frederick Douglass, *John Brown: An Address by Frederick Douglass at the Fourteenth Anniversary of Storer College, Harper's Ferry, West Virginia, May 30, 1881* (Dover, N.H.: Morning Star Job Printing House, 1881), 1–2, http://www.wvculture.org/history/jbexhibit/bbspr05-0032.html (accessed October 31, 2017, via the West Virginia Division of Culture and History web page); Chester G. Hearn, *Six Years of Hell: Harpers Ferry during the Civil War* (Baton Rouge: Louisiana State University Press, 1996), 253–54.

10. Some scholars echoed Douglass's sentiment at Storer College, claiming that if slavery could not be ended but by force of arms, then Brown's raid on Harpers Ferry helped move the issue from the political to the military realm. See, for example, Arthur Meier Schelsinger Jr., *A Life in the Twentieth Century: Innocent Beginnings, 1917–1950* (Boston: Houghton Mifflin, 2000), 448–49; Paul Finkelman, "John Brown: America's First Terrorist?," *Prologue* 43 (Spring 2011): 1–8; Wilentz, *Rise of American Democracy*, 747–53; and Reynolds, *John Brown*, 395–99.

11. *Harper's Weekly*, January 31, 1885; John Stauffer and Benjamin Soskis, *The Battle Hymn of the Republic: A Biography of the Song That Marches On* (New York: Oxford University Press, 2013), 3–106; McGinty, *John Brown's Trial*, 269–87.

23 MY SOLDIERS' HOME

JAMES MARTEN

he far northwest corner of the grounds of the Soldiers' Home in Milwaukee is dominated by a stone monument built by the Grand Army of the Republic early in the twentieth century. The determined if generic soldier at its top is surrounded by the graves of over 30,000 soldiers, and some of their family members, from virtually all of America's wars.

The home itself—officially the Northwestern Branch of the National Home for Disabled Volunteer Soldiers (NHDVS)—was one of the three original soldiers' homes established by Congress in 1865 (there were eventually twelve). The branch was unique in that its funding came partly from the $100,000 raised at a Soldiers' Home Fair organized by the women of Milwaukee during the summer of 1865. After caring for hundreds of soldiers at a downtown building during the war, the women had intended to open a permanent facility. Following a vigorous and very public debate, they were finally convinced to donate their money by a group of local politicians angling to get a federal home at Milwaukee. The commitment of these funds to the project was crucial to Milwaukee's successful bid, and the Northwestern Branch opened in May 1867 on a 400-acre site west of town. By the 1890s, over 2,000 men lived at the home.[1]

A century and a half later, standing under the shadow of the GAR monument, you are about sixty yards from a freeway carrying commuters from Milwaukee to its western suburbs and even closer to the parking lots encircling the brick and steel pile of Miller Park, the home of baseball's Milwaukee Brewers. You can just see the stadium's retractable roof through the oak trees, and on a clear day you can even spot the highrises of downtown Milwaukee.

Soldiers' Home, Milwaukee, Wisconsin
(Photograph by Will Gallagher)

But relief from the humming traffic is available simply by turning south and walking through the rows upon rows of small stone markers. The first few honor veterans of the Second World War, but soon you reach a section for Civil War veterans. Some of the stones show their age, but you can make out a few names and units. The severe and ascetic orderliness of the markers is softened by the slightly rolling terrain. Cast-iron plates fastened to large boulders scattered throughout the cemetery feature verses from "The Bivouac of the Dead," the sentimental poem penned, ironically, by the Confederate veteran Theodore O'Hara.[2]

Your journey into the late nineteenth and early twentieth centuries continues as you work your way south and east toward a collection of white frame buildings: a short row of duplexes and several other houses built as homes for the administrators of the Soldiers' Home and their families; the nondenominational "Shingle"-style chapel, with its slender steeple, dormers, and gables; the brick hospital and long, two-story wooden barracks with deep verandas running their entire lengths. Looming over this part of the old home grounds is "Old Main"; the central section and tower was built in 1869, with northern and southern wings added later. Constructed of cream-colored brick, with dramatic green and red shingles and trim, it provides a dramatic backdrop over the right field stands for fans watching Brewers games from the left field seats. Until many of the other buildings were completed, Old Main housed all of the veterans, medical services, administrative offices, and a bowling alley. As the tallest building at the top of the tallest hill in the area, it dominates the skyline west of Milwaukee. Along a street south of Old Main are smaller brick and stone structures: the Headquarters Building, with its

low veranda and clock, the Wadsworth Library, and the Recreation Hall.[3]

Descending a short hill and crossing the right of way of the old Milwaukee Road, you come to the Queen Anne–style Ward Memorial Theater, built in 1882. Entertainers like Bob Hope, George Burns and Gracie Allen, Jack Benny, W. C. Fields, Will Rogers, Jimmy Durante, and Eddie Cantor performed at the 900-seat theater, along with countless traveling productions of plays, lectures, and other shows. Before he found fame and fortune in Las Vegas and television, a young local piano virtuoso named Wladziu Valentino Liberace got his start in show business entertaining veterans on the piano in this very building.

To the southeast, you can glimpse through the trees the wonderful 1867 residence where the branch governor lived. But directly south and west of the theater, you soon encounter evidence of the newer history of the Soldiers' Home: rather utilitarian brick and steel structures built in the 1930s and 1940s after the Veterans Administration took over the NHDVS. "Lake" Wheeler and its pavilion—which date back to the picturesque youth of the Soldiers' Home—are near the monument to Spanish-American War veterans and the behavioral health building. Labs and the Wood National Cemetery offices are also nearby, and a little farther on are buildings housing a modern domiciliary and facilities services and Fisher House, which offers lodging for families of hospitalized veterans. At the bottom of the hill, on National Avenue, is the huge Clement J. Zablocki VA Medical Center, named after the local congressman who got it funded in the 1960s.

Even as the twentieth and twenty-first centuries have encroached on the old Soldiers' Home grounds, a few things have remained the same. The head of the

Zablocki Center still lives in the governor's residence and VA employees live in the old duplexes, while current VA patients can still check out newspapers and magazines at the Wadsworth Library (although the stained-glass skylights are obscured by the inevitable drop-down ceilings) and bowl at the alley in the recreation building. The old entrances to the grounds have survived—the south gate on National Avenue (named after the home many years ago) no longer sports a vine-covered pergola, but it's in more or less the same place as the original south entrance. And the road to the old north entrance still skirts the edge of Calvary Cemetery and emerges onto Blue Mound Road, just as it did 140 years ago.

But much has changed. The original 400-acre campus was reduced by nearly two-thirds with the completion in the 1960s of the interstate highway and the building in the 1950s of County Stadium, the predecessor to Miller Park. Gone are the greenhouse and the manicured gardens and flower beds, the farm that grew much of the produce consumed by the old soldiers, the natural spring, three of the four man-made ponds, many of the hundreds of trees that lined the drives, and the cross-shaped hall where the veterans drank a low-alcohol version of Pabst beer. The old railway is now a bike trail named after Hank Aaron, who played for the Braves for the decade before the team moved to Atlanta in 1966. The long hospital and barracks appear worn and virtually unused, except for a few VA administrative offices. Veterans used to be able to watch Milwaukee Braves games from bleachers perched on the bluff overlooking right field (on top of a Silurian coral reef now on the National Register of Historic Places), but the bleachers were removed decades ago and the bluff is overgrown with trees and brush. And the many taverns that clustered near the south gate have been replaced by one or two tiny bars and a Dry Hootch coffee shop, which offers veterans a safe place to discuss their pasts and their problems, as well as to seek counseling and therapy.

But the present can illuminate the past in another way. The men served by the old NHDVS and the men and women served by the modern VA faced and continue to face the ambiguity encountered by veterans of America's wars throughout time, especially those marked by physical or psychological scars. That ambiguity was reflected in the very design and conception of the roughly three dozen federal and state soldiers' homes that opened between the 1860s and 1880s. The homes were an unprecedented effort to care for men who could not care for themselves—federal and state governments had never provided so many resources for the health care of any portion of the population—and this commitment, along with the sheer beauty of the spaces that were created, celebrated the heroes who lived in them. But they also led to an exaggerated isolation of this community of veterans from the rest of society. Part of this was physical; the homes were virtually always built in small towns or outside larger cities. The vast grounds were a kind of buffer between the civilians and the "old" soldiers (who in the 1890s were still largely in their fifties!). Even the fact that the grounds often served as community resources did not lessen the separation, as tourists and other visitors focused more on the buildings, ponds, and entertainment than on the men who lived there. One can almost literally imagine tourists stepping over and around the old soldiers who, according to a woman who had grown up at the Milwaukee branch of the NHDVS, often lay on the grass on nice days.[4]

The homes were clearly meant to be grand representations of the nation's gratitude, but they were also theatrical sets that put veterans on display. The dignified, elaborately designed buildings and grounds masked the crowded, barracks-style living arrangements and military discipline that shaped the veterans' every waking moment. They followed a strict schedule—from reveille to taps (each marked with a single cannon shot), although with few organized activities in between—and could be punished in various ways for violating regulations; they could even be put in the guardhouse for weeks at a time. The definition of "disability" was quite loose, meaning that while many would not have been able to support themselves through manual or any other kind of labor, they were relatively healthy. Some worked odd jobs for low wages, but most were grown men, often in their thirties and forties, who were completely dependent on the home.

Publicly honored and individually respected, veterans collectively often gained reputations as disreputable drunks and public nuisances. For various reasons, large and small, local governments and citizens came to resent their presence and often characterized all residents as undesirables. Much of this negativity originated in those bars and taverns that clustered at the northern and southern entrances, with many crowded into "The Line," a two-block stretch of National Avenue. Veterans crammed into these establishments every afternoon and evening; on pension day, they were easy pickings for con artists or thieves. Sometimes they were arrested for disturbing the peace or, on occasion, killed by trains while drunkenly walking the tracks back to the home.[5]

Most veterans were not alcoholics, but many were unhappy with their aimless, protected, isolated lives. One veteran at the Milwaukee home testified before a congressional committee that the men with whom he lived "are all dissatisfied, every one of them.... We are not comfortable. We are unhappy. I would venture to say—in fact, I know it to be the case—that this petty persecution has caused men to commit suicide. I know this to be a fact, because I know my own feelings, and I can judge others by those. Often I wish I was in the penitentiary; that I was hanged or dead, or in some other place." We have no idea how many veterans living in the Milwaukee home were actually suicidal, but other evidence suggests that there was a strong undercurrent of dissatisfaction and dismay.[6]

In a way, the old buildings are now stand-ins for the old soldiers. Treasured by those who admire their architecture and historical importance, the structures have twice been honored by preservationists: the state of Wisconsin created the National Soldiers' Home Historic District in 1994, and the federal government created the Milwaukee Soldiers Home National Historic Landmark District in 2011. Yet the historic district was also named to the National Trust for Historic Preservation's List of 11 Most Endangered Historic Places.[7] Although there are plans to restore a few into offices and veterans housing, some of the buildings are in appalling condition, with construction fences blocking entrances, roofs sagging raggedly, and paint faded and chipped. The clumsily executed stained-glass window of a mounted General Ulysses S. Grant, presented to the home by the GAR in the 1880s, has been removed from the old Ward Theater because the building is untenable.

The efforts to restore the buildings began as a grassroots movement called "Save the Soldiers' Home," led by a coalition between the National Trust for Historic Preservation and the Milwaukee Preservation Alliance. These groups have mounted an educational campaign that includes a Facebook page featuring videos by local residents and politicians (including Milwaukee mayor Tom Barrett and Congresswoman Gwen Moore). Called "My Soldiers' Home," the short videos focus on the beauty of the buildings, nostalgic childhood memories, and the opportunities offered by restoration. Two of the eight brief videos, featuring a VA therapist and a veteran, refer to the PTSD suffered by many current patients at the home and connect the "rehabilitation" of the Soldiers' Home with the rehabilitation of these scarred veterans.

"My" Soldiers' Home makes a similar connection. Despite the exciting plans to renew the home (unrealized as of the fall of 2017), the condition of the buildings reminds us of the ambiguities that veterans of all wars face. No group of soldiers has been more honored than the "Greatest Generation" who fought Hitler, but the struggles of the hundreds of thousands of maimed survivors are rarely mentioned, while the veterans of the Vietnam conflict are famously painted with a very broad brush of disaffection and dishonor. Even veterans of our current wars, despite the countless homecoming celebrations and the recognition of individual veterans at sporting events and other ceremonies, have often suffered from indifferent efforts to keep up VA hospitals and other aspects of veteran health care.[8]

These contradictory responses would have seemed very familiar to the men housed in this gilded, isolated Soldiers' Home. They represent the best intentions of Americans seeking to honor and protect the heroes of the Union at the same time that they reflect the inability of Americans to adequately understand those veterans. *My* Soldiers' Home reminds us of a time when the men who had fought and won the Civil War came to be seen as charity cases dependent on the public's goodwill rather than as heroes deserving of the country's gratitude.

NOTES

1. "Brief History," National Soldiers' Home District, Milwaukee, Wisconsin, http://historicmilwaukeeva.org/Brief_History.html (accessed May 1, 2017). The freeway built in the 1960s cut through the original cemetery. A number of graves were moved, and the oldest part of the cemetery is actually maintained separately, north of the freeway. The most useful history of the development of the NHDVS is Patrick J. Kelly, *Creating a National Home: Building the Veterans' Welfare State, 1860–1900* (Cambridge, Mass.: Harvard University Press, 1997).

2. For the full text of the poem, go to the website titled Great Books Online, http://www.bartleby.com/102/147.html.

3. The architectural details in this and subsequent paragraphs can be found in Patricia A. Lynch, *Milwaukee's Soldiers Home* (Charleston, S.C.: Arcadia, 2013).

4. Elizabeth Corbett, *Out at the Soldiers' Home: A Memory Book* (New York: Appleton-Century, 1941), 38.

5. James Marten, "Nomads in Blue: Disabled Veterans and Alcohol at the National Home," in *Disabled Veterans in History*, ed. David A. Gerber (Ann Arbor: University of Michigan Press, 2000), 275–94.

6. *Investigation of the National Home for Disabled Volunteer Soldiers*, H.R. Rep. No. 2676, 48th Cong., 2nd Sess., December 1, 1884–March 3, 1885, 134–35.

7. "America's Most Endangered Historic Places—Past Listings," National Trust for Historic Preservation website, https://savingplaces.org/11most-past-listings#.WZA7I2eWzVM (accessed August 13, 2017).

8. "Conversion of Historic Milwaukee Soldiers Home to Veteran Apartments Gets Tax Credits," *Milwaukee Journal Sentinel*, May 16, 2017.

24 THE GREEN-MELDRIM HOUSE

JACQUELINE JONES

Savannah's Green-Meldrim House is at 14 West Macon Street in Madison Square. The square, which is situated in Savannah's Historic District, is between Pulaski Square to the west and Lafayette Square to the east. Madison Square was named for James Madison, the fourth president of the United States, who died in 1836, the year before the square was laid out. Surrounding the square, which features a statue honoring Revolutionary War soldier Sergeant William Jasper, are fine examples of Gothic Revival, Greek Revival, and Romanesque architecture.

A distinctive feature of the magnificent Green-Meldrim residence is the gorgeous, sinuous free-standing staircase that leads from the first floor to the second. Embellished with an intricate ironwork railing, the staircase is illuminated by a skylight of glass flower petals set into an ornate dome.[1] At eight o'clock on the evening of January 12, 1865, twenty black preachers ascended these stairs to meet with President Lincoln's personal emissary, Secretary of War Edwin M. Stanton, and Major General William Tecumseh Sherman, the Union officer who had liberated the city from Confederate control three weeks earlier. Sherman's famous March to the Sea, which began in Atlanta on November 15, 1864, and ended on December 21, had thrown Savannah into an uproar, with an estimated 62,000 Union troops and nearly 20,000 black refugees taking up uneasy residence among each other in the river port town.

Wealthy British merchant Charles Green had offered Sherman the use of his spacious, well-equipped mansion as the officer's headquarters and personal residence. Green hoped that this magnanimous gesture on his part would prevent the general from destroying the house and Northern troops from seizing and selling

Green-Meldrim House, Savannah, Georgia
(Photograph by Will Gallagher)

his considerable stockpile of cotton hidden in the city. It was from the Green House that Sherman sent his famous telegram to Lincoln on December 22: "I beg to present you as a Christmas-gift the city of Savannah, with one hundred and fifty heavy guns and plenty of ammunition, also about twenty-five thousand bales of cotton." Four days after the January 12 meeting with the preachers, Sherman had issued his Special Field Orders No. 15, setting aside for black refugees a broad swath of coastal Georgia—an estimated 400,000 acres encompassing the Sea Islands and the area thirty miles inland, from Charleston, South Carolina, to the St. John's River in Florida. The orders gave rise to the fervent hope among blacks throughout the South that the federal government would guarantee each freed family a plot of land. In 1892, the Green family sold the house to Savannah jurist Peter E. Meldrim, and fifty-one years later his heirs sold the house to the church next door, St. John's Episcopal, which owns and operates the property today.[2]

In the course of doing research for my book on wartime Savannah, I often thought of that historic meeting on January 12—of the preachers who attended it, what the "colloquy" (as it was called) meant for the city's vibrant black community, and what its larger significance was for the fraught period of Reconstruction. Signing up for a tour in late February 2008, I was curious to see how this history would be rendered by a guide taking me and several others through the house for an hour or so. Bringing together such a luminous set of characters from the South and the North—the preachers, Sherman, Stanton, and Green (who continued to reside in the house, appropriating for himself and his family two rooms above the dining room)—the place would seem to represent a true gem in the history of Savannah, the

South, and the United States. As I entered the house that winter weekday, Madison Square was quiet; I tried to imagine the turmoil in the streets and in the slaveholders' mansions when Savannah fell, 143 years before.

In the twenty-first century, Savannah boasts a robust tourist economy, luring people from all over the world with its many charming parklike squares and historic buildings, tangible markers of a fascinating past peopled with blacks and whites, enslaved and free people, Christians and Jews, rich and poor, native-born and immigrant. Yet with the exception of the Ralph Mark Gilbert Civil Rights Museum and a statue memorializing slavery down by the riverfront, the city's significance as a site of African American history goes largely ignored among the monuments, statuary, plaques, and other forms of public remembrance scattered throughout the Historic District.

Our tour guide seemed resolutely and, I thought, much too narrowly focused on the house's historical significance in terms of its architecture and the decorative arts. Designed by the New York architect John S. Norris and built between 1853 and 1861 at a cost of $93,000—$2.7 million in today's money—it is one of the finest examples of Gothic Revival architecture in the South. It received National Historic Landmark designation in 1976.

A covered porch on three sides of the house features elaborate ironwork trim, and, as seen in the accompanying photograph, above the front door and first-floor windows are unusual crenellated parapets and an oriel (a bay window that projects from the wall). Even by Savannah's impressive standards for nineteenth-century residential luxury, the interior of the house is unique for its crown moldings, silver doorknobs, marble mantels, Austrian gold-leaf mirror frames, and American black walnut woodwork trim. A prominent part of the tour I took was the story of Charles Green, the cotton merchant and shipbuilder. Missing was mention of Green's enslaved labor force of eight men and women, ages sixteen to fifty, or the enslaved artisans who did the woodworking, molding, and bricklaying in the house.

Ascending the gorgeous staircase in 1865, the preachers might have marveled at the grandeur of Green's residence; but most, as workers, already had a firsthand familiarity with slaveholders' mansions and townhouses of brick and stucco filled with lavish imported furnishings. These black visitors were no doubt preoccupied with the prospect of meeting the famous general, who had, a few days before (as he recounted in his *Memoirs*), "sent out and invited the most intelligent of the negroes, mostly Baptist and Methodist preachers, to come to my rooms to meet the Secretary of War." Now that the end of the conflict seemed in sight, Lincoln had dispatched Stanton to Savannah to glean information about the means by which nearly four million black men and women might weather the transition from slavery to freedom, from dependence on their masters to independence for themselves and their families. Sherman received the group in his quarters located upstairs.[3]

To me, the January 12 meeting encapsulated all the drama and complexity of Civil War–era politics. Conventional wisdom promoted a triumphalist narrative: that Sherman was so impressed by the Reverend Garrison Frazier's bold statement—the best way for blacks to care for themselves, Frazier said, "is to have land, and turn it and till it by our own labor"—that he created what later came to be called the Sherman Reservation.[4] Many people since have assumed that this initiative represented an implicit promise on the part of the

federal government that it would allocate "forty acres and a mule" to freed families throughout the South. However, in reality the meeting revealed a much more complicated and much less uplifting chapter in the history of emancipation.

During the antebellum period Savannah possessed a number of independent black churches, including three Baptist congregations, one Methodist, and one Episcopalian. Despite denominational rivalries, the black clergy came together in ecumenical solidarity on a number of occasions during the war—for example, when they held a "watch-meeting" on New Year's Eve, 1862, in anticipation of the announcement of the Emancipation Proclamation the following day; and on January 1, 1865, when they banded together to create the Savannah Education Association, to provide schooling for hundreds of the city's black children. Likewise, during the meeting of January 12, these Baptist, Methodist, and Episcopal leaders put aside doctrinal and personal differences and called upon Garrison Frazier, age sixty-seven and a retired Baptist minister, to speak for the group.

Nevertheless, the twenty preachers were a diverse lot, representative of the substantially different ideologies, political inclinations, and temperaments characteristic of Savannah's black male leadership class. Their ages ranged from twenty-six to seventy-two, with most in their forties and fifties. With the exception of Adolphus Delmotte, who had come in from Milledgeville, and James Lynch, recently arrived from Baltimore, all hailed from Savannah. Five were freeborn, and three, by dint of long years of hard work, had purchased themselves before the war. Another three had been emancipated by their owners' wills. Nine had tasted freedom for only a matter of days; they were, they said, slaves "until Sherman freed [them]." Together the men represented a range of professions, including teamster and butcher as well as full-time preacher. James Porter, a music teacher who had operated a clandestine school before the war, served as choirmaster and warden of St. Stephen's Episcopal, a relatively small church.[5]

Despite the united front they presented at the meeting, the group was racked by internal tensions, reflective of their different origins and political priorities; these tensions would flare after the war. William J. Campbell was pastor of the largest black church, First African Baptist, with 1,800 members and a physical plant worth $18,000. He remained wary of other Baptists who aspired to citywide leadership within that denomination. James Lynch, a Baltimore missionary representing the Northern-based African Methodist Episcopal Church, did not let his newcomer status hinder him from aggressively seeking influence within established congregations, provoking the wrath of their leaders. Some of the ministers counseled their freed-people followers to be patient and accommodating to white demands, while others advocated a more militant approach to freedom.

A tanner and butcher by trade, the Reverend Ulysses L. Houston (of Third African, later First Bryan Baptist Church) would, soon after the January meeting, take a group of 362 congregants representing 99 households to Skidaway Island, near the mouth of the Savannah River. There he hoped to establish an independent black colony that would thrive apart from whites. Most other meeting participants disagreed with this strategy and cast their lot with what they hoped would be a new egalitarian regime in Savannah, one that would allow them to continue to live in the city, now at peace with and independent from their former owners.

Differences among the preachers became more

obvious as they followed divergent paths when the war ended and emancipation became the law of the land. Abraham Burke would play a major role in the city's many black mutual aid societies, small knots of people who banded together and paid modest monthly dues to ensure the welfare and proper burial of the group's members. Houston and James Porter would help found the Chatham County Republican Party and run for public office, political activities that aggravated some of their coreligionists. Porter would become a bold, outspoken proponent of black civil rights, disregarding the counsel of Frazier and others who believed he should moderate his rhetoric and scale back his aspirations for full and equal treatment under the law. "God deals justice to all, irrespective of race, color, or intelligence," Porter declared, at a time and in a place where such words could get a person hanged or shot.[6] And bitter interdenominational rivalries persisted, with Alexander Harris and Houston eventually organizing respective factions in First Bryan Baptist Church and seeking the ouster of each other. As the postwar years unfolded, additional issues split black clergy, who disagreed among themselves over the worth and efficacy of agencies and associations sponsored by Northern interlopers—the United States Bureau of Refugees, Freedmen, and Abandoned Lands; the Northern freedmen's aid societies, especially the powerful American Missionary Society; and the Republican Party.

Sherman and Stanton had their own differences. At one point in the discussion the secretary asked the general to leave the room and then proceeded to quiz the ministers about their faith that the man they hailed as liberator would protect them until they could protect themselves. Sherman later expressed his indignation that Stanton had called into question "the character of a general who had commanded a hundred thousand men in battle, had captured cities, conducted sixty-five thousand men successfully across four hundred miles of hostile territory, and had just brought tens of thousands of freedmen to a place of security."[7] The ministers seemed to be in agreement though that the general, in his limited dealings with them and other blacks over the last few weeks, had treated them with respect. Perhaps they knew little of his contemptuous treatment of refugees who attached themselves to his army on its march, and they probably could not foresee the abuse his men would mete out to able-bodied black men within the next few weeks.[8]

The January 12 meeting stretched into the early hours of the morning, and the future seemed full of promise and possibilities. Frazier impressed Sherman and Stanton with his eloquence, his deep knowledge of the war and its progress, and his insistence that black people wished to "reap the fruit of our own labor and take care of ourselves and assist the Government in maintaining our freedom"—priorities that would seem to dovetail exactly with those of the Northern Republican Party and Lincoln in particular.[9]

Observers at the time interpreted Sherman's Field Orders No. 15 as a direct, affirmative response to Frazier's plea and the Sherman Reservation as an audacious, if hopelessly idealistic, blueprint for a postwar society. In establishing policy for the new reservation, Sherman stipulated that black people should be able to seek work from Union gunboats and grow their own food, all without interference from their former masters and mistresses.

In reality, Sherman's intent was not nearly as altruistic as it seemed on the surface. In the course of his long slog from Atlanta to Savannah he had attracted an estimated 17,000 black refugees fleeing from vengeful masters and seeking safety behind Union lines. Sherman cared little about the great moral drama that was the war for freedom; he barred black soldiers from the ranks of his army and remained all too eager to exploit able-bodied men as fatigue workers. Entering Savannah in late December, he was vexed by the large numbers of refugees overwhelming the small city—desperate souls seeking food, shelter, and fuel. On January 4, he ordered his men to round up "all unemployed negroes" to cut wood, load ships, and otherwise provide muscle power to the occupying army. He also turned a blind eye to bounty hunters and "recruiters" who used deceptive practices and promised black men twelve dollars a month to enlist and thus help Northern states meet their quotas for soldiers.

Sherman's intent with the Special Field Orders was to settle black women, children, and the elderly and disabled on the nearby coast and islands and so rid the city of Savannah of nonproductive people, so many hungry mouths to feed. Meanwhile, he and his men would oversee the labor of their husbands, fathers, and brothers. He wrote, "The young and able-bodied negroes must be encouraged to enlist as soldiers in the service of the U. S., to contribute their share towards maintaining their own freedom, and securing their rights as citizens of the United States."[10]

In fact the orders amounted to only a temporary measure and failed to guarantee landownership to the freed people (such a bold gesture would have been outside the general's authority in any case). Sherman left Savannah on January 26 in a driving rain, taking his men north to Columbia, South Carolina. Soon after the troops left, the preachers came together again under the leadership of Frazier, this time to protest the brutality of the occupying army toward blacks, a form of neoslavery that mocked the promise of the January 12 meeting.

And in the fall of 1865 President Andrew Johnson rescinded Sherman's orders; eventually most of the land in the Sherman Reservation was returned to its original white owners.

My guide at the Green-Meldrim House said nothing about the historic meeting that was held there on January 12, 1865. After the tour, I asked her about the omission, which left me puzzled and greatly disappointed. She said that she was indeed aware of the meeting but that it was not included in the official script for tour guides, and so she could not really talk about it. Perhaps this should not have been surprising. Certainly the "official scripts" of many Southern historic sites pointedly omit mention of the African Americans who had labored to build and were in other ways associated with those sites.

Two historical markers now stand near the Green-Meldrim House. One, located on church property near the building, is titled "Sherman's Headquarters"; it focuses on the general and his brief time spent in Savannah. The other marker stands on city property, in Madison Square; dedicated in 2011 (when it generated some controversy), this one is titled "History of Emancipation" and identifies the house as the site of the historic meeting of January 12. This second marker departs from white Savannah's overarching, blinkered narrative of its own past and gives the black preachers a prominent place in the history of the city's last months of the Civil War.

For the sake of tourists and non-historians of all kinds at sites such as the Green-Meldrim House, gradually perhaps we shall meld an accurate rendering of Southern history with its material remnants to provide a more complete and compelling account of the past.

NOTES

1. For a history and description of the house, see the National Registry of Historic Places Inventory-Nomination Form, available online at https://npgallery.nps.gov/GetAsset/05a02be8 -9614-403e-aba2-a3629c3d036 f. For photos, including one of the staircase, see St. John's Church, Green-Meldrim House website, http://www.stjohnssav.org/green-meldrim-house/.

2. William Tecumseh Sherman, *Memoirs of General W. T. Sherman*, 2nd rev. ed. in 2 vols., 1886; 1-vol. repr., ed. Charles Royster (New York: Library of America, 1990), 711, 724–32; Jacqueline Jones, *Saving Savannah: The City and the Civil War* (New York: Alfred A. Knopf, 2008), 218–19.

3. Sherman, *Memoirs*, 725.

4. Quoted in Jones, *Saving Savannah*, 219.

5. U.S. War Department, *The War of the Rebellion: A Compilation of the Official Records of the Union and Confederate Armies*, 127 vols., index, and atlas (Washington, D.C.: Government Printing Office, 1880–1901), ser. 1, vol. 47, pt. 2, 37–43. See also clipping from the *New-York Daily Tribune*, February 13, 1865, "Negroes of Savannah," Consolidated Correspondence File, series 225, Central Records, Quartermaster General, Record Group 92, National Archives, Washington. For biographical sketches of the men, see Jones, *Saving Savannah*.

6. Quoted in Jones, *Saving Savannah*, 284.

7. Sherman, *Memoirs*, 727.

8. Bennett Parten, "'Somewhere toward Freedom': Sherman's March and Georgia's Refugee Slaves," *Georgia Historical Quarterly* 101 (2017): 115–46.

9. Sherman, *Memoirs*, 725–26.

10. Jones, *Saving Savannah*, 208–9; Sherman, *Memoirs*, 729–32 (text of Special Field Orders No. 15 on 730–32).

25 A ROOM OF HIS OWN

CATHERINE CLINTON

The Petersen House—the dwelling where Abraham Lincoln was pronounced dead—is a rather nondescript Federal-style row house, located at 516 10th Street NW in Washington, D.C. Visiting our nation's capital for the first time during my freshman year of college, I was there for the largest demonstration in American history—a rally against U.S. involvement in Vietnam held on November 15, 1969. I had no time for historical pilgrimages, and at that time, Lincoln was little more to me than the face on the five-dollar bill.

As a young girl, I had spent countless hours with parents who loved to drag their daughter to historical sites and Civil War commemorations. Those Civil War centennial years during my youth created good family memories. But by the time I was in high school—wearing a black armband to protest the war in Vietnam—my affection for the 1860s had faded. I could barely imagine a time when hundreds of thousands of young men might be cheered off to war by young women like me, when waves of the best and brightest of a nation were mowed down by fratricidal intensity. Until the Lincoln penny dropped, my mantra might have been "War, what is it good for?"

Civil War studies revived dramatically for me during the first year of my history PhD program when I arrived at Princeton to work with James M. McPherson. After a long fallow period, excavating the emancipationist roots of the Civil War seemed not only possible but a priority. Heated discussions in seminars rekindled youthful curiosity.[1]

I had not yet been inducted into the cult of Lincoln that would hold sway in my personal and professional life at the turn of the twenty-first century. Before long, I would speak at my first summer institute at Gettysburg

College thanks to Gabor S. Boritt, a kind invitation that would also be extended to me many years later by Peter S. Carmichael. I had not yet sat through the moving naturalization ceremony on the Gettysburg battlefield, following the annual Lincoln Forum championed by Harold Holzer and Frank J. Williams. And certainly, I was just getting to know David Herbert Donald, who would become a friend and colleague and who encouraged me to take on my own Lincoln project: *Mrs. Lincoln: A Life* (2009), the first new biography of Mary Lincoln in over twenty years. Thank goodness, I had a few years of seasoning before I encountered the gale-force winds expelled by Lincolnistas in attack mode. The field is littered with the remnants of gladiatorial combat over all things Lincoln.

So when I finally visited the Petersen House, I was deeply transfixed. Enamored by it. It gave off the vibe of fuzzy black-and-white photographs in the Lincoln books I had come to love. A patchwork of simplicity accidentally elevated.

Visitors will approach the building by mounting concrete steps with winding iron handrails—slipping into a perfectly perfunctory front hall. Parlors on the left and a nondescript stairway on the right; arrival without fanfare. During my first visit, I found myself pulled forward—drawn into the house as if by some magnetic force: a mystic chord, sense memory kicking in, gliding those last few steps into the small rear bedroom where Lincoln breathed his last.[2]

Stepping over the threshold into this chamber, the tourist is held back by a railing with a large plexiglass protector above it, with access to step only a few inches into the room. (And thank you, National Park Service guards, who allowed me beyond the barrier when I was researching my book.) Moving into this space, spending some time alone within these four walls, allowed me to conjure the transfiguration of Lincoln from a dying man into our immortal president. I spent meditative time within the room ... from the vantage point of the accompanying photograph.

Will Gallagher's evocative portrait of the room, taken from deep within this hallowed space, hints at its spare allure: a simple spindled bedframe, a trio of extremely plain chairs, and an old-fashioned dresser. These are in stark contrast to the ornate, striped Victorian wallpaper, the richly patterned floor coverings, and sentimental prints dotting the walls. A room so impersonal while sprinkled with mementos of the era—a half-empty, half-full scene. This image captures an insider's viewpoint—not the tourist looking in but a member of the inner circle. So we imagine ourselves, in this place, transported back in time, surrounding the frail and failing president as his labored breath rises and falls, rises and falls while all else falls away. Closing our eyes, we can almost taste the sour, metallic smell of drying blood and feel the stillness within.

German-born tailor William Petersen constructed his home in 1849 and supplemented his income with boarders, even after he became flush supplying Union army officers with uniforms. The flow of boarders moving in and out of what became Lincoln's deathbed chamber was constant. William Clarke was the tenant on the night Lincoln died, but the room had been occupied as recently as the month before by an actor friend of John Wilkes Booth. Perhaps Booth borrowed the conveniently located, discreet bedchamber for one of his assignations with Lucy Hale, daughter of the abolitionist senator from New Hampshire, whose clandestine relationship with Booth allowed him access to inaugural events; or with prostitute Ella Starr, who attempted suicide shortly after Lincoln's death, with a picture of Booth under her pillow; or perhaps with

Effie Germon, an actress and former lover who was performing in *Aladdin* at Grover's Theater for Lincoln's son Tad on the night his parents attended *My American Cousin* across town at Ford's Theatre? So many bodies flowing and souls mingling in this unprepossessing space.

With Booth's shooting of Lincoln on the evening of April 14, 1865, the Petersen House became a destination, as soldiers carried the wounded president across the street, up the stairs, and down the darkened hallway. All through the night nearly a hundred individuals paraded through as the president lay dying. Scholars have demonstrated that artistic representations of this long night stretch credulity concerning the room's capacity.[3] After Lincoln was pronounced dead at 7:22 A.M. on April 15, this chamber, less than 170 square feet, became a hallowed site overnight.

Later that morning, after the president's body was removed, two boarders, Henry and Julius Ulke, took a photograph to preserve the moment, the sense of historic loss. From this moment forward, the ordinary chamber seemed to now represent the extraordinary—a room transformed by love and loss, symbolic of the era. After he returned home, William Clarke felt his room was haunted—not by Lincoln but by souvenir seekers who pilfered mementos.

In 1878 German American William Schade, publisher of the *Washington Sentinel*, bought the structure for his home and business. After 1883 a tablet affixed to the house declared it the "House in which Abraham Lincoln died." The former theater across the street, Ford's, was turned into a government office space until the building collapsed in 1893. That same year Lincoln collector Osborn Oldroyd moved into the Petersen House and put his Lincoln collection on display. After his death in 1930, much of Oldroyd's collection moved back to

the first floor of the rebuilt Ford's Theatre building. It wasn't until the 1950s that Congress funded an authorized replication of the theater where Lincoln was assassinated. In 1968 the restored Ford's Theatre and the Petersen House together became an independent unit of the National Park Service, comanaged by the Ford's Theatre Society. It has become a working theater, offering daily tours at adjoining museums, supported by dynamic outreach programs in cultural and educational enrichment.[4]

We know Lincoln spent his presidency up against dramatic odds, steering the great ship of state into port. His sleep was often interrupted by bad dreams over the years, understandable with all the burdens weighing on him. He had a particularly bad bout of nightmares following the death of his beloved son Willie in February 1862. Later in the war, he might be awakened by images of storms, or battlefields, or other disasters. When he had a fearful dream about his son Tad, he wrote to ask his wife to locate and hide a pistol so that misadventure might be averted. His warning indicated that Lincoln experienced powerful visions in his sleep, and he feared such premonitions might be prescient. There's even an apocryphal tale of his dreaming that he awakened at night and wandered downstairs to discover people weeping at the body on display on a catafalque. When he asked a soldier who had died, the man replied that the president had been killed by an assassin. This story was reported much later, after Lincoln's death, as an example of his prophetic gifts.

Whether such tales were true or not, Lincoln clung to the vision of the nation reuniting and dreamed of a restored Union. After Robert E. Lee's surrender at Appomattox on April 9, 1865, he contemplated a new chapter, putting the war behind him with brighter days ahead.

So after stormy seasons of war, Lincoln reached landfall and welcomed peace. After enemies stacked arms and trudged home, perhaps other dreams might come true? He shared his hopes for a trip to the Holy Land. He was discussing these future possibilities while on a carriage ride with his wife, anticipating life beyond the cares of office, pledging to be happier … on what would become the last afternoon of his life.

Lincoln's cares came to an abrupt halt, felled by an assassin's bullet, with blood pouring from a head wound, his life's blood seeping out onto the pillow in a humble upstairs chamber. He would survive the long night encircled by a parade of friends and family in the darkened, claustrophobic bedroom. Hundreds milled outside the building, waiting to hear news. When Lincoln's death was finally announced early on Easter Saturday, a terrible hush crept across the city and onto the wires. Lincoln's lifeless body was escorted back to the White House.

He would lie on a catafalque under the Capitol Rotunda, as thousands filed past to pay their respects. The nation was bowed with grief, as the dead president's coffin was loaded onto a funeral train, making the long journey homeward—crossing seven states, through 180 towns and cities, bound for burial in Springfield, Illinois. Lincoln encouraged the better angels of our nature and demanded we confront the gaps between what we know to be true and what we wish to make true. That such magnificent dreams, such powerful accomplishments, might be reduced to mush by a bullet rattling round his brain is an inconceivable miscarriage, an incomprehensible dread, all playing out in the modest chamber on 10th Street.

Lincoln struggled to make good on the Revolutionary pledge of all men being equal while confronted with secession and the Confederacy's armed rebellion. He had reminded during his First Inaugural Address in March 1861 that "we were not enemies but friends." However, the horror of 1,458 days of bloodshed demanded explanation. Lincoln poetically justified such sacrifices in his Second Inaugural: "Every drop of blood drawn with the lash shall be paid by another drawn with the sword." As swords were laid down, a shot rang out, and he became the war's most famous fatality: Lincoln's enduring gift to Americans.

Looking for Lincoln is often triggered by a transformative visit to Washington's Lincoln Memorial or perhaps by thumbing through the pages of Maira Kalman's enchanting 2012 book, *Looking at Lincoln*.[5] Books and monuments inspire us to seek traces of the actual man, the life behind this American icon. I have sought out our sixteenth president with multiple visits to Hodgenville, Kentucky (the Lincoln Birthplace National Historic Park), and several pilgrimages to boyhood and adolescent homes, including the reconstructed village at New Salem, Illinois, where he sought a home after emancipation from his family. The magnificent preservations in Springfield beckon, particularly the National Park Service's Lincoln Home, which, not surprisingly, reflects Mary Lincoln as much if not more than her husband. There's a whole lot of Lincoln at the lovingly restored Lincoln Cottage, the sixteenth president's summer home, now a historic site in suburban D.C. Finding Lincoln is possible at each and every one of these historic places. But for me, he is *always* present in the back room on the second floor of the Petersen House.

Lincoln has a room of his own, a place for contemplative revival.

On a sunny day, the dancing dust motes floating round the chamber remind visitors that we shall all be gone one day. Shall we struggle, as he did, with depression and self-doubt, yet determine to make something of ourselves? And the silent room echoes back Lincoln's message for each of us, a message deeply buried within the place where he breathed his last.

NOTES

1. For examples of the lively scholarly issues of the time, see John S. Rosenberg, "Towards a New Civil War Revisionism," *American Scholar* 38 (Spring 1969): 250–72; and Philip S. Paludan, "The American Civil War: Triumph through Tragedy," *Civil War History* 20 (September 1974): 239–50.

2. James Swanson gives a very personal account of the Petersen House and his experience as a collector and writer in his Special Report for the Smithsonian website: http://www .smithsonianmag.com/history/the-blood-relics-from-the -lincoln-assassination-180954331/ (accessed September 4, 2017).

3. Harold Holzer and Frank J. Williams, "Lincoln's Deathbed in Art and Memory: The 'Rubber Room' Phenomenon," in *The Lincoln Assassination: Crime and Punishment, Myth and Memory*, ed. by Harold Holzer, Craig L. Symonds and Frank J. Williams (New York: Fordham University Press, 2010), 9–54.

4. Paul R. Tetreault, "Petersen House," Ford's Theatre, http:// www.fords.org/home/plan-your-visit/daytime-visits-fords -theatre/petersen-house (accessed September 4, 2017).

5. Maira Kalman, *Looking at Lincoln* (New York: Penguin Books, 2012).

Thoughts about Shooting the Images in *Civil War Places*

WILL GALLAGHER

Entrance to Union tunnel, Petersburg battlefield, Virginia (Photograph by Will Gallagher)

Places: 26

States: California, Colorado, District of Columbia,
Georgia, Maryland, Mississippi, New York,
Pennsylvania, Tennessee, Virginia, West Virginia,
Wisconsin

Lenses: Canon 24mm TS E Tilt-Shift, Canon
17–40mm f4.0L, Canon 70–200mm f2.8L, Canon
100mm f2.8L, DJI MFT 15mm f/1.7 ASPH

Cameras: Canon 5D Mark IV, DJI Inspire 1
Quadcopter

In many ways, this was the project of a lifetime for me.
I had wanted to work with my father on a project for
years, so when he called me in January 2016 with the
idea for this book, I was very excited. I loved *Lens of
War: Exploring Iconic Photographs of the Civil War*,
another work that he and Matt Gallman coedited. It is
a beautiful book with powerful and interesting images.
The idea of taking modern photographs of Civil War
places appealed to me.

While I was eager to get started on the project, I
was also a little nervous. The last thing I wanted was
to drag down the quality of the essays with average
or forgettable images. Knowing my father's place in
the Civil War community, I also worried about living
up to his name and reputation. But as with most of
my projects, once I started communicating with the
authors about their places and taking pictures, things
fell into place. I appreciated the variety of subjects—
buildings, monuments, interiors, exteriors—and the
fact that the book has many different types of images.
In most cases, I used the available ambient light, but a
few shots required some off-camera flash to help light
my subject. Although limitations of space prevent my
discussing all of the photographs, I am pleased to be

able to offer some thoughts regarding highlights of my
year crisscrossing the country.

Site: Emancipation Oak
Location: Hampton, Virginia
Author: Brenda E. Stevenson
Lens: Canon 17–40mm f4.0L
Camera: Canon 5D Mark IV

We have a very famous tree in Austin called
Treaty Oak. It is a live oak in what is now downtown
Austin and was inducted into the American Forestry
Association's Hall of Fame of Trees in 1927. As
impressive as I have always found Treaty Oak to be,
the Emancipation Oak on the campus of Hampton
University is bigger and more spectacular in every
way. A huge live oak with a beautiful and symmetrical
canopy, it is listed as one of the 10 Great Trees of the
World by the National Geographic Society. One of the
best parts of being a photographer is that assignments
afford access to some unique and special places. Anyone
traveling near Hampton should take a few minutes
to visit this tree for an experience they surely will not
forget.

Site: Petersen House
Location: Washington, D.C.
Author: Catherine Clinton
Lens: Canon 17–40mm f4.oL
Camera: Canon 5D Mark IV

If pressed to select my favorite place in this book, I would probably say the Petersen House. I shot the space early one morning before the house opened for visitors and was struck by the small, modest room where Lincoln died. All I could think of was the chaos and frantic nature of the night he was shot and the contrast between how he died and how a modern president would be treated with similar wounds. The most challenging part of this image came during editing. I had to remove, with some careful Photoshop work, the permanent plexiglass barrier the National Park Service has placed between the bed and the door. I understand why it is necessary to keep visitors from touching the bed, but the barrier—obviously not part of the room when Lincoln was brought here from Ford's Theatre across the street—is very distracting.

Site: Shiloh Church
Location: Shiloh, Tennessee
Author: Stephen Berry
Lens: Canon 24mm TS E Tilt-Shift
Camera: Canon 5D Mark IV

Of all the authors in the book, I think Stephen Berry had the clearest vision of the type of image he wanted for his essay. Every other author had at least a couple of options they were contemplating, but Stephen had a very specific description of the interior of the simple church at Shiloh with light coming in through a side window. When I arrived at the church it looked exactly as he described it to me: light streaming in through a small window and the doorway illuminated the pew at the front of the room. The ambient light in the room was very low, so I used off-camera flash to highlight the benches and back wall.

Site: Camp Allegheny
Location: Camp Allegheny, West Virginia
Author: A. Wilson Greene
Lens: DJI MFT 15mm f/1.7 ASPH
Camera: DJI Inspire 1 Quadcopter

Camp Allegheny and Sand Creek in Colorado are the two most remote places in the book. Will Greene provided very detailed directions on how to get to this spot, but my father and I still had a little trouble finding it. The camp's remains are on the top of a mountain in West Virginia, and even on a summer day it was windy and a little cool. It was not hard to imagine how bone-chillingly cold it would have been for the soldiers who spent a winter on this mountain. From ground level, it was impossible to tell how the camp was organized, so the best camera for this picture proved to be my Inspire 1 flying copter. The perspective from the air reveals the trenches and campsite mounds/remains and conveys a sense of the remote nature of this spot.

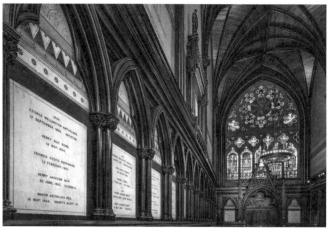

Site: Memorial Hall
Location: Cambridge, Massachusetts
Author: Drew Gilpin Faust
Lens: Canon 24mm TS E Tilt-Shift
Camera: Canon 5D Mark IV

This is a great space on the Harvard campus. On the day I showed up to shoot, most of the building was open, including a huge dining hall full of students—but not the area I was supposed to photograph. I made my way to the main office of the building, where I learned the transept was closed for repairs. President Faust did not know about this situation but quickly made some calls to get me access the next day. What initially seemed to be a problem worked out very well. Instead of having to photograph the space with all the people who would normally be in the transept, I was able to shoot it completely empty. It was a privilege to spend almost an hour photographing the space—one of my favorites in the book.

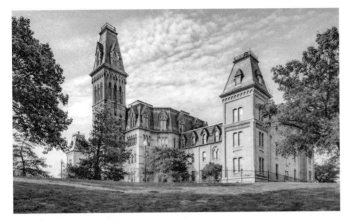

Site: Soldiers' Home
Location: Milwaukee, Wisconsin
Author: James Marten
Lens: Canon 24mm TS E Tilt-Shift
Camera: Canon 5D Mark IV

One of my favorite buildings from this project, the Soldiers' Home looks like it should have dragons flying around it or possibly be the setting for a horror movie. The day I shot it started out completely overcast, but as the morning clouds burned off I got some sunlight and a great sky to go with it. The home is part of the large Milwaukee VA Medical Center campus and is currently fenced off and empty, but there is a chance that it will be renovated and used again. The project has been approved and if funded will transform the building into living spaces for people at the medical center.

Site: Vicksburg cave
Location: Vicksburg, Mississippi
Author: Sarah E. Gardner
Lens: Canon 70–200mm f2.8L
Camera: Canon 5D Mark IV

I got very excited when Sarah Gardner told me she wanted to use a photograph of one of the caves in Vicksburg for her essay. Being from Texas, I am more familiar with caves situated in rock formations; the natural earth variety, like the one in this photo, is more subject to erosion and internal collapse. That has been the case with most of the Vicksburg caves from the Civil War era. Fortunately, Pat Strange from the National Park Service knows about one cave that remains intact and was very helpful in connecting me with the property owner.

When I went to shoot the cave, the entire hillside was smothered in kudzu. It took more than an hour of yanking out kudzu and digging to make the small hole revealing the cave's entrance. Unfortunately, the cave is extremely unstable and offers no way to photograph it from the inside. Unsuccessful efforts to do so left me soaked in sweat and covered in mud that took hours to get out of my camera, lens, and tripod. This picture was taken from the opposite hill. I wanted to document how the kudzu had swallowed everything and given the scene a very *Invasion of the Body Snatchers*–type of feeling. Although I was initially depressed about not getting the interior shot, Sarah ended up selecting this image to accompany her amazing essay.

Site: Petersburg tunnel
Location: Petersburg, Virginia
Lens: Canon 17–40mm f4.0L
Camera: Canon 5D Mark IV

My father and Matt Gallman agreed that I could choose one image that does not precede one of the contributors' essays. Early in the project, I photographed monuments and other places at the Petersburg battlefield for the essay my father initially considered writing. We ended up getting some very good shots, but my favorite is this one from the entrance to the famous Union tunnel from the battle of the Crater.

There is a gate in front of the entrance to prevent access to the inside of the tunnel, and the interior is very dark. But when I opened this image on my computer later and brightened it up, I saw the painting of a man making his way toward the entrance. I thought it was really interesting and liked it even more when my father said he had never noticed the painting—for perhaps the first time in my forty-nine years, he did not know about something on a Civil War battlefield.

Site: Soldiers and Sailors Memorial Hall
Location: Pittsburgh, Pennsylvania
Author: Carol Reardon
Lens: Canon 24mm TS E Tilt-Shift
Camera: Canon 5D Mark IV

This is a great building near the University of Pittsburgh campus. For Carol Reardon's essay, I needed to capture something with this statue of a Union soldier (there are other statues around the building honoring soldiers from other wars). I spent quite a bit of time taking pictures from numerous angles, but I like this one best. Not only is the Union soldier prominent, but the viewer also gets an appreciation for all the detail work in the architecture of the building. I think these kinds of structures should feel majestic and important, and this one has both of those qualities. I also believe the sky and clouds give the shot a sense of movement.

Site: Statue of William Tecumseh Sherman
Location: New York City
Author: Stephen Cushman
Lens: Canon 70–200mm f2.8L
Camera: Canon 5D Mark IV

I had a perfect summer afternoon for this picture of the William Tecumseh Sherman statue in New York City. Very impressive in person, thanks to being regilded and restored in 2013 and 2014, it sits in the southeast corner of Central Park and greets lots of visitors. To get my pictures, I had to wait patiently for moments when there were not people standing in front of the statue. I like it from this angle because the trees from Central Park in the left background suggest a calm and peaceful place. You would not necessarily know the landscape includes skyscrapers, city buses, honking horns, and all of the other sights and sounds of Manhattan.

Contributors

Edward L. Ayers is president emeritus of the University of Richmond and past president of the Organization of American Historians. His many books include *In the Presence of Mine Enemies: War in the Heart of America, 1859–1863* (2003) and *The Thin Light of Freedom: The Civil War and Emancipation in the Heart of America* (2017).

Stephen Berry is Gregory Professor of the Civil War Era at the University of Georgia. His books include *All That Makes a Man: Love and Ambition in the Civil War South* (2003) and *House of Abraham: Lincoln and the Todds, a Family Divided by War* (2007).

William A. Blair is a liberal arts research professor and director of the Richards Civil War Era Center at Pennsylvania State University. The founding editor of the *Journal of the Civil War Era*, he is the author of *Cities of the Dead: Contesting the Memory of the Civil War in the South, 1865–1914* (2004) and *With Malice toward Some: Treason and Loyalty in the Civil War Era* (2014), among other books.

David W. Blight is Class of 1954 Professor of History and director of the Gilder Lehrman Center for the Study of Slavery, Resistance, and Abolition at Yale University. His many books include *Race and Reunion: The Civil War in American Memory* (2001) and *Frederick Douglass: American Prophet* (2018).

Peter S. Carmichael is Robert C. Fluhrer Professor of Civil War Studies and director of the Civil War Institute at Gettysburg College. Among his books are *The Last Generation: Young Virginians in Peace, War, and Reunion* (2009) and *The War for the Common Soldier* (2018).

Frances M. Clarke is a senior lecturer in history at Sydney University, Australia. She is the author of *War Stories:*

Suffering and Sacrifice in the Civil War North (2011), which was the cowinner of the American Historical Association's biennial Hancock Prize for the best first book in any field.

Catherine Clinton is Denman Chair in American History at the University of Texas at San Antonio. She has written or edited more than twenty-five books, including *Harriet Tubman: The Road to Freedom* (2004) and *Stepdaughters of History: Southern Women and the American Civil War* (2016).

Stephen Cushman is Robert C. Taylor Professor of English at the University of Virginia. He has written several volumes of poetry and literary criticism, as well as *Bloody Promenade: Meditations on a Civil War Battle* (1999) and *Belligerent Muse: Five Northern Writers and How They Shaped Our Understanding of the Civil War* (2014).

Stephen D. Engle is professor of history at Florida Atlantic University. His books include *Don Carlos Buell: Most Promising of All* (1999) and *Gathering to Save a Nation: Lincoln and the Union's War Governors* (2016).

Drew Gilpin Faust is former president of Harvard University and of the Southern Historical Association. Her many books include *Mothers of Invention: Women of the Slaveholding South in the American Civil War* (1996) and *This Republic of Suffering: Death and the American Civil War* (2008).

Gary W. Gallagher is John L. Nau III Professor in the History of the American Civil War Emeritus at the University of Virginia and past president of the Society of Civil War Historians. His recent books include *Becoming Confederates: Paths to a New National Loyalty* (2013) and *The American War: A New History of the Civil War Era* (with Joan Waugh, 2015).

Will Gallagher is a photographer based in Austin, Texas. For a sampling of his photographs, see http://willgphoto.com/walldogs.html, https://gallagherstudios.smugmug.com/Other/Infrared-Images/, and www.gallagherstudios.com.

J. Matthew Gallman is professor of history at the University of Florida. His books include *America's Joan of Arc: The Life of Anna Elizabeth Dickinson* (2006) and *Defining Duty in the Civil War: Personal Choice, Popular Culture, and the Union Home Front* (2015). He is coeditor with Gary W. Gallagher of *Lens of War: Exploring Iconic Photographs of the Civil War* (2015).

Sarah E. Gardner is professor of history and director of southern studies at Mercer University. She is the author of *Blood and Irony: Southern White Women's Narratives of the Civil War, 1861–1937* (2004) and *Reviewing the South: The Literary Marketplace and the Southern Renaissance, 1920–1941* (2017).

Judith Giesberg is professor of history at Villanova University and editor of the *Journal of the Civil War Era*. Her books include *Army at Home: Women and the Civil War on the Northern Home Front* (2009) and *Sex and the Civil War: Soldiers, Pornography, and the Making of American Morality* (2017).

Lesley J. Gordon is Charles G. Summersell Chair of Southern History at the University of Alabama and past editor of *Civil War History*. Her books include *General George E. Pickett in Life and Legend* (1998) and *A Broken Regiment: The 16th Connecticut's Civil War* (2014).

A. Wilson Greene is executive director emeritus of Pamplin Historical Park and the National Museum of the Civil War Soldier. He is the author of, among other titles, *Civil War Petersburg: A Confederate City in the Crucible of War* (2007) and *A Campaign of Giants: The Battle of Petersburg* (2018).

Caroline E. Janney is John L. Nau III Professor in the History of the American Civil War at the University of Virginia and past president of the Society of Civil War Historians. She is the author of *Burying the Dead but Not the Past: Ladies' Memorial Associations and the Lost Cause* (2008) and *Remembering the Civil War: Reunion and the Limits of Reconciliation* (2013).

Jacqueline Jones is Ellen C. Temple Chair in Women's History and Mastin Gentry White Professor of Southern History at the University of Texas at Austin. Her many books include *Saving Savannah: The City and the Civil War, 1854–1872* (2008) and *Dreadful Deceit: The Myth of Race from the Colonial Era to Obama's America* (2013).

Ari Kelman is Chancellor's Leadership Professor of History at the University of California, Davis. His books include *A Misplaced Massacre: Struggling over the Memory of Sand Creek* (2013) and *Battle Lines: A Graphic History of the Civil War* (2015).

James Marten is professor of history at Marquette University and past president of the Society of Civil War Historians. Among his books are *The Children's Civil War* (1998) and *Sing Not War: The Lives of Union and Confederate Veterans in Gilded Age America* (2011).

Carol Reardon is George Winfree Professor of American History Emeritus at Pennsylvania State University and past president of the Society of Military History. She is the author of several books on Civil War and American military history, including *Pickett's Charge in History and Memory* (1997) and *With a Sword in One Hand and Jomini in the Other: The Problem of Military Thought in the Civil War North* (2012).

Aaron Sheehan-Dean is Fred C. Frey Professor of Southern Studies at Louisiana State University. His books include *Why Confederates Fought: Family and Nation in Civil War Virginia* (2007) and *Concise Historical Atlas of the U.S. Civil War* (2009).

Brenda E. Stevenson holds the Nickoll Family Endowed Chair in History at the University of California, Los Angeles. Among her books are *The Contested Murder of Latasha*

Harlins: Justice, Gender and the Origins of the L.A. Riots (2013) and *What Is Slavery?* (2015).

Elizabeth R. Varon is Langbourne M. Williams Professor of American History at the University of Virginia. Her books include, among other titles, *Disunion! The Coming of the American Civil War, 1789–1859* (2008) and *Appomattox: Victory, Defeat, and Freedom at the End of the Civil War* (2013).

Joan Waugh, professor in the Department of History at UCLA, researches and writes about the Civil War, Reconstruction, and Gilded Age eras. She has published many essays and books on Civil War topics, including *U. S. Grant: American Hero, American Myth* (2009) and *The American War: A New History of the Civil War Era* (with Gary W. Gallagher, 2015).

Index